SATHER CLASSICAL LECTURES

Volume Fifty Six

Dionysius and
The History of Archaic Rome

Dionysius and *The History of Archaic Rome,*

Emilio Gabba

University of California Press

BERKELEY · LOS ANGELES · OXFORD

University of California Press
Berkeley and Los Angeles, California

University of California Press, Ltd.
Oxford, England

Library of Congress Cataloging-in-Publication Data

Gabba, Emilio.
    Dionysius and The history of archaic Rome / Emilio Gabba.
       p.   cm. — (Sather classical lectures : v. 56)
    Includes bibliographical references and index.
    ISBN 0-520-07302-9
    1. Dionysius, of Halicarnassus.   Roman antiquities.
2. Rome—History—To 510 B.C.—Historiography.
3. Rome—History—Republic, 510-265 B.C.—
Historiography.   I. Title.   II. Series.
DG233.G33   1991
937—dc20   90-11138
                                     CIP

Printed in the United States of America
9 8 7 6 5 4 3 2 1

The paper used in this publication meets the minimum requirements
of American National Standard for Information Sciences—Permanence of Paper for Printed Library Materials, ANSI Z39.48-1984. ∞

Contents

           Structures of Early Rome   152

CHAPTER 6. The Political Meaning of Dionysius's
           History   190

           Bibliography   217
           General Index   239
           Index Locorum   247

Elias Bickerman
Arnaldo Momigliano
magistris et amicis

Preface

The six chapters that make up this book correspond in number and broad outline to the lectures of the same title that I had the honour to deliver as Sather Professor of Classical Philology at Berkeley in the autumn of 1980.

These lectures (including the second, which was previously published in *Classical Antiquity*) have been thoroughly reworked and amplified without, however, any modification of their overall thrust or the ideas central to their argument. In many cases I have made fresh additions to the text based on studies worked out independently. I have also taken the principal developments of modern criticism into account while preparing the footnotes, without intentionally pursuing any ideal of exhaustiveness.

All of this reelaboration required more time than I had foreseen. The duties of teaching ancient history at the University of Pavia (and indeed the many responsibilities of modern academic life) did not allow me a great deal of spare time for the pursuit of studies which require, above all else, freedom to concentrate. I was thus extremely fortunate to have been able to pass the autumn of 1985 as a Fellow of the Institute for Advanced Study at Princeton, where, in the serene tranquillity of those splendid surroundings and with the ample facilities for study there provided, I was also able to work on the preparation of this text. I am deeply obliged to the Institute for the opportunity thus provided.

My warmest gratitude is naturally reserved for my colleagues in the Department of Classics of the University of California at Berkeley, in acknowledgment of their courteous invitation to so prestigious a lectureship and their cordial collaboration during my stay in California.

The dedication of this volume is intended as testimony to a great debt of knowledge, humanity, and friendship toward two mentors by whose acquaintance I have been greatly honoured and from whom I have learned so much over the years.

I would like to focus briefly on the scope of the present work and of the original lectures. It is in no way intended as a complete analysis of the historical text of Dionysius; such a labour would in any case require a commentary, which is still lacking. As I indicate in Chapter 1, I have attempted to locate and understand Dionysius's work within the context of the atmosphere prevailing in the Augustan era and of course within the framework of Greek historiography concerning Rome. The analysis of particular aspects or problems in the historical narrative of Dionysius forms part and parcel of my work here; as such it is undertaken almost exclusively with the purpose of clarifying the historian's thought processes and methods of work and not as a specific enquiry into individual moments in the history of ancient Rome. It is obvious that other difficulties or facets of Dionysius's work could have been singled out for this purpose; I believe, however, that the particular examples chosen for examination may adequately serve to throw light upon a somewhat singular reflection on Roman history.

The book builds upon my previous studies of Dionysius, dating back almost forty years. They will be cited in the notes. I would also draw attention to the updated bibliography contained in my essay "La 'Storia di Roma arcaica' di Dionigi d'Alicarnasso" (*ANRW* II.30.1 [1982] 799–816), though at certain points the essay is not altogether in line with my present thinking.

It remains for me to thank my friend John Dowling for the kindness demonstrated in the preparation and revision of the English text of my work.

—Università di Pavia, summer 1987

Introductory Note
on the Text

Dionysius's work entitled Ῥωμαικὴ Ἀρχαιολογία, generally translated as *Roman Antiquities* but referred to by me as his *History of Archaic Rome,* originally consisted of twenty books (Photius *Bibliotheca,* cod. 83, I.190 Henry) and concluded with the war against Pyrrhus. This was done with the intention of having it form a natural precursor to the *Histories* of Polybius. The first eleven books of the work (bringing us down to the year 443 B.C.) survive in their entirety, while extracts from the remaining books are known from a variety of sources. As a rule I have used the edition of C. Jacoby (4 vols., Leipzig, 1885–1905; *Supplementum et Indices,* 1925), as well as the frequently republished edition of E. Cary, printed in the Loeb Classical Library with accompanying English translation (7 vols., Cambridge, Mass., 1937–50). The recent Italian translation of F. Cantarelli (Milan, 1984) contains a good bibliography.

It would appear that Dionysius himself may have written a more compact version of his work and, by omitting whatever appeared unnecessary, reduced the contents to five books (Photius *Bibliotheca,* cod. 84, II.8 Henry), though the work suffered stylistically as a consequence; perhaps the removal of some of the speeches may be imagined.

List of Abbreviations

A&A	*Antike und Abendland*
AAPal	*Atti della Reale Accademia di Scienze, Lettere e Arti di Palermo*
AAWG	*Abhandlungen der Akademie der Wissenschaften in Göttingen. Philologisch-historische Klasse*
AFC	*Anales de Filología clásica*
AHR	*American Historical Review*
AIIS	*Annali dell'Istituto italiano per gli studi storici*
AIPhO	*Annuaire de l'Institut de Philologie et d'Histoire Orientales et Slaves de l'Université Libre de Bruxelles*
AJPh	*American Journal of Philology*
AncSoc	*Ancient Society*
ANRW	*Aufstieg und Niedergang der römischen Welt.* Berlin, 1972–
A&R	*Atene e Roma*
ArchClass	*Archeologia Classica*
ARW	*Archiv für Religionswissenschaft*

ASNP   *Annali della Scuola Normale Superiore di Pisa.*
            Classe di Lettere e Filosofia

BASP   *Bulletin of the American Society of Papyrologists*

BCH   *Bulletin de Correspondance Hellénique*

BFI   *Bollettino di Filologia Classica*

BICS   *Bulletin of the Institute of Classical Studies of the*
            University of London

BIDR   *Bollettino dell'Istituto di Diritto romano*

CB   *Classical Bulletin*

CIG   *Corpus inscriptionum graecarum.* 4 vols. Berlin,
            1828–77

ClAnt   *Classical Antiquity*

CPh   *Classical Philology*

CQ   *Classical Quarterly*

CR   *Classical Review*

CS   *Critica storica*

DArch   *Dialoghi di Archeologia*

FGrHist   Jacoby, F. *Die Fragmente der griechischen*
            Historiker. Berlin, 1923–58

HSPh   *Harvard Studies in Classical Philology*

H&T   *History and Theory*

HZ   *Historische Zeitschrift*

IBM   *The Collection of Ancient Greek Inscriptions in*
            the British Museum. 4 vols. Oxford, 1874–1916

IGRR   *Inscriptiones graecae ad res romanas pertinentes.*
            4 vols. Paris, 1911–27

ILLRP   Degrassi, A. *Inscriptiones latinae liberae rei*
            publicae. Vol. 1, 1957. Vol. 2, 1963. Florence

ILS	Dessau, H. *Inscriptiones latinae selectae.* 3 vols. Berlin, 1892–1916
IOS	*Israel Oriental Studies*
JCP	*Jahrbücher für Classische Philologie (Neue Jahrbücher für Philologie und Paedagogik)*
JRS	*Journal of Roman Studies*
MAAR	*Memoirs of the American Academy in Rome*
MAL	*Memorie della Classe di Scienze morali, storiche e filologiche dell'Accademia dei Lincei*
MAWA	*Mededelingen der Koninklijke Nederlandse Akademie van Wetenschappen te Amsterdam, Afdeling Letterkunde*
MEFRA	*Mélanges d'Archéologie et d'Histoire de l'Ecole Française de Rome*
MH	*Museum Helveticum*
NAWG	*Nachrichten der Akademie der Wissenschaften in Göttingen. Philologisch-historische Klasse*
PG	Migne, J.-P. *Patrologiae cursus completus. Series graeca.* 161 vols. in 166. Paris, 1857–
PIR	*Prosopographia imperii romani saeculi I, II, III.* 2d ed. Berlin, 1933–78
PP	*La Parola del Passato*
P&P	*Past and Present*
PW	Pauly-Wissowa, *Real Encyclopädie der classischen Altertumswissenschaft*
RAAN	*Rendiconti dell'Accademia di Archeologia, Lettere e Belle Arti di Napoli*
RAL	*Rendiconti della Classe di Scienze morali, storiche e filologiche dell'Accademia dei Lincei*

RBi	*Revue Biblique*
REA	*Revue des Etudes Anciennes*
REL	*Revue des Etudes Latines*
RFIC	*Rivista di Filologia e di Istruzione Classica*
RhM	*Rheinisches Museum*
RIL	*Rendiconti dell'Istituto Lombardo, Classe di Lettere, Scienze morali e storiche*
RPh	*Revue de Philologie*
RSA	*Rivista storica dell'Antichità*
RSF	*Rivista critica di Storia della Filosofia*
RSI	*Rivista Storica Italiana*
SAWW	*Sitzungsberichte der Österreichischen Akademie der Wissenschaft in Wien, Philosophisch-Historische Klasse*
SCO	*Studi Classici e Orientali*
SIFC	*Studi Italiani di Filologia Classica*
SIG	Dittenberger, W. *Sylloge inscriptionum graecarum.* 3d ed. Leipzig, 1920. Reprint. Hildesheim, 1982
SS	*Storia della Storiografia*
TAPhA	*Transactions and Proceedings of the American Philological Association*

CHAPTER ONE

Greek Historiography and Rome before Dionysius

I

When Dionysius of Halicarnassus chose to journey to Rome in the aftermath of Octavian's victory over Anthony and the East in 30 B.C., his decision was charged with emblematic value. As with other members of the contemporary Greek intellectual world whose presence would lend so distinctive a character to the culture of Augustan Rome, his choice had both cultural and political implications.[1] Of his previous life nothing is known, but we are probably correct in assuming that he belonged to the patriciate of Halicarnassus. After a few short years he would come to be numbered among the glories of that town, along with Herodotus, the father of history, and the poet Heraclitus.[2] Only a generation earlier the city, which seems by tradition to

---

1. Dionys. I.7.2 (in the middle of the 187th Olympiad = late 30 B.C.). Strabo came to Rome, which he had visited already before, soon after: X.5.3. G. W. Bowersock, *Augustus and the Greek World* (Oxford, 1965), 122 ff.; G. Aujac, *Strabon, Géographie* (Paris, 1966–), vol. 1, pt. 1, xxxv.

2. Strabo XIV.2.16; on Heraclitus, the friend of Callimachus: W. Swinnen, "Herakleitos of Halikarnassos, an Alexandrian Poet and Diplomat?" *AncSoc* 1 (1970) 39–52. Dionysius, son of Alexander, must have been born toward the beginning of the sixties. Nothing is known of his death; the date 7 B.C. found in the preface to his work (I.7.2) is of little help to us, particularly as Book I was indeed published separately (VII.70.2).

have been pro-Roman, had suffered, however indirectly, the terrible experience of Mithridates' ravages. The Civil War between Caesar and Pompey and, to an even greater extent, the conflict between Caesar's assassins and the Triumvirs had serious repercussions, particularly in Asia Minor; Halicarnassus, situated as it was, did not escape these disturbances unscathed.[3] The freshness of such memories within city and family as well as personal experience could only serve to underline the decision to move closer to the centre of power following the victory at Actium and the fall of Egypt.

3. On the history of Halicarnassus, see L. Bürchner, *PW* s.v. "Halikarnassos," 7 (1912) 2253–64. The city was at its most spectacular around 370 B.C. following its re-establishment during the synoecism put in train by the Persian satrap, Mausolus of Caria. His rule saw renewed impetus given to the processes of hellenization and the integration of Greek and Carian elements: S. Hornblower, *Mausolus* (Oxford, 1982), 78 ff., 332; D. Asheri, *Fra ellenismo e iranismo. Studi sulla società e cultura di Xanthos in età achemenide* (Bologna, 1983), 42–44; A. Laumonier, *Les cultes indigènes en Carie* (Paris, 1958), 621–42. After its conquest and destruction by Alexander the Great it was embroiled for a long period in the conflicts between the Hellenistic monarchies: A. Mastrocinque, *La Caria e la Ionia meridionale in epoca ellenistica (323–188 B.C.)* (Rome, 1979), passim. It sided with Rome during the Syrian War (190 B.C., Livy XXXVII.16.2) and thenceforth remained independent while the greater part of Caria and Lycia was granted to Rhodes: D. Magie, *Roman Rule in Asia Minor* (Princeton, 1950), 1:107. Having become part of the province of Asia in 129 B.C. it had to undergo occupation by Mithridates in 88 B.C., though Appian does not specifically name it in this context (App. *Mith.* 80–82; Magie, 1:213–18). The statue erected to Sulla for benefits received (*ILS* 8771) may indicate that Cicero's testimony (II *Verr.* 1.49) that Verres, legate in Cilicia of the propraetor Cn. Cornelius Dolabella, had exported statues from Halicarnassus must be related to what we know of other Asian cities that had been forced to sell their votive offerings, pictures, and statues of divinities to meet the savage taxes levied by Sulla (Plut. *Luc.* XX.1–4). Having suffered attacks from pirates for some time it was given a new lease on life under the proconsulate of Q. Tullius Cicero (61–58 B.C.), who succeeded in quelling attempted revolts in the city, smoothed over internal disagreements, and imposed a reasonable system of oligarchic government (Cic. *QFr.* 1.25; Magie, 1:381–82, 2:1244 n.13). The predominance of the upper classes in the Augustan era seems to be confirmed by *IBM* 892, which may allude (in line 17) to an opposing faction as well as containing a possible reference to benefits received from Caesar. There is no doubt that *SIG* 1065 = *IGRR* IV.1064 refers to games in honour of Caesar (Καισάρηα) in 1 B.C. The

There is an immediate and precise programme underlying Dionysius's choice of Rome. In coming to the city he was attempting a positive approach to Roman culture in an effort to come to terms with it and thus understand every facet of a city whose leadership was now without rival. Such an experience differed vastly from that of Polybius, who, a century and more earlier, had meditated on the causes of Rome's irresistible political and military dominion. Polybius had lived as a hostage, exiled among his enemies, though these would soon become his friends and disciples. Dionysius's approach, however, is distinguished by its voluntary nature. His knowledge of the Latin language allowed him direct access to Roman literature, in particular to its historiography, and he was thus enabled to perceive its validity and motivations. This further enrichment of his already excellent theoretical and practical background allowed Dionysius to articulate a literary and historiographical programme that aimed at embracing both the Greek and Roman worlds,

---

Halicarnassian decree in favour of the local Jews found in Josephus *A.I.* XIV.256–58 may date from Caesar's reign *or* that of Augustus. (On the authenticity of this material: E. Bickerman, "Une question d'authenticité: Les privilèges juifs," *AIPhO* 13 [1953] 11–34, now in E. Bickerman, *Studies in Jewish and Christian History* [Leiden, 1980], 2:24–43.)

It is also probable that Halicarnassus was involved, at least indirectly, in the campaign waged by Cassius against Rhodes in 43 B.C. (App. *BCiv.* IV.279 ff.) and similarly in the Parthian expedition of Labienus in Caria (Cass. Dio XLVIII 26.3–4; Magie, 1:430–31), though the city is not referred to for these events in the sources quoted. The city must, however, have enjoyed the patronage of Augustus since it became the seat of a small *conventus* in his era (C. Habicht, "New Evidence on the Province of Asia," *JRS* 65 [1975] 70 and 80). This may explain the presence in the city of the decree for the κοινόν of Asia (*IBM* 894, perhaps for 15 A.D.), in which Augustus appears (line 6) deified and identified with Zeus Patroos: W. H. Buckler, "Augustus, Zeus Patroos," *RPh* 9 (1935) 182–86; C. Habicht, "Die augusteische Zeit und das Erste Jahrhundert nach Christi Geburt," in *Le culte des souverains dans l'empire romain* (Geneva, 1973), 87; and in general S. R. F. Price, *Rituals and Power. The Roman Imperial Cult in Asia Minor* (Cambridge, 1984), on the presence of these decrees in cities that acted as *conventus* centres and line 43 of *IBM* 894. Cf. also lines 28 ff. of *IBM* 892. On statues to Tiberius and Drusus: *CIG* 2657.

showing their substantial historical and cultural unity, while taking Rome as the contemporary centre. Well received by the Roman ruling class and soon intimate with several of its leading figures,[4] Dionysius showed that he was fully aware of the precise political value and significance of his activity. He was also conscious of the fact that his stance did not merely derive from the traditional self-interested conformity of the greater part of the Greek intelligentsia to their Roman masters, but had roots of a much greater complexity. This is particularly evidenced by his exceptional awareness of various aspects of the empire and its development toward a unity of cultural and political life.

From this standpoint Dionysius's literary activity and his teaching in Rome must be seen as a unified whole. Not only is *The History of Archaic Rome* contemporary with the treatises on literary criticism, but in fact the two projects are inseparable aspects of the same approach and comprise a single cultural undertaking. This oft-repeated statement is true, for his writing of history reflects and in effect carries through the critical and theoretical principles elaborated in his rhetorical pamphlets. In the chapters that follow I, too, shall attempt a closer examination of the theoretical aspects discussed by Dionysius in his literary essays in terms of their practical historiographical application. However, the single most important observation is the political and cultural unity of the two facets of Dionysius's literary activity, which at first sight seem so distinct. The reasons for this underlying unity are not to be found in the often problematic rhetorical character of the historical writings. An appreciation

4. G. W. Bowersock, "Historical Problems in Late Republican and Augustan Classicism," in *Le classicisme à Rome aux I^{ers} siècles avant et après J.-C.* (Geneva, 1979), 65–72. Cf. W. Rhys Roberts, "The Literary Circle of Dionysius of Halicarnassus," *CR* 14 (1900) 439–42; G. P. Goold, "A Greek Professional Circle at Rome," *TAPhA* 92 (1961) 168–92; A. Hurst, "Un critique grec dans la Rome d'Auguste: Denys d'Halicarnasse," *ANRW* II.30.1 (1982) 839–65.

of Dionysius's rhetoric places a critical and literary emphasis on his activity, and discerning critics and admirers have always been attracted to this aspect of his work, if only because this part of his output represents the most important body of work of its kind to survive from antiquity. The *History,* however, suffers somewhat under these auspices when compared with other, quite different historical works that, for a variety of reasons, are assumed to be unsurpassable models.

Dionysius's *History* has for some time past been judged negatively, and this fact must be seen in relation to the great critical enquiry into Rome's origins and early history undertaken during the last century. Already in the eighteenth century the approaches of Pyrrhonian criticism had begun to cast doubt on the reliability of Dionysius's reconstruction of the first five centuries of Roman history.[5] It is quite apparent that Dionysius's ways of examining and writing history were far removed from the kind of critical history that, in the form of a great scientific advance, has come to dominate the field of earlier Roman history. It may be said that the final and most damaging blow to Dionysius's *History* was inflicted by Ed. Schwartz's contribution to the great *Encyclopädie der Classischen Altertumswissenschaft.*[6] The cultural and ideological background of Schwartz's assessment is complex, conditioning not only his judgment of Dionysius but also his general understanding of Greek historiography and his overall vision of ancient history. At this point it is worth pausing for a moment to consider Schwartz's perspective so that our own point of view will be all the clearer in the chapters that follow.[7]

5. Louis de Beaufort, *Dissertation sur l'incertitude des cinqs premiers siècles de l'histoire romaine* (1738), ed. A. Blot (Paris, 1866), 122–41.

6. "Dionysios von Halikarnassos," *PW* 5 (1905) 934–61, reprinted in E. Schwartz, *Griechische Geschichtschreiber* (Leipzig, 1957), 319–60.

7. The following section is based on my article "Eduard Schwartz e la storiografia greca," *ASNP*, 3d ser., 9 (1979) 1033–49; some phrases are reproduced verbatim.

II

Schwartz continually insists on the close relationship between history and the writing of history: really significant historiography is found only in moments of great moral and political tension. Thus the peak attained by Greek historiography with Thucydides' work on the Peloponnesian War has never been equalled. Hence a kind of law is implied for Greek and classical historiography by virtue of which history, to be true, must fundamentally be concerned with the contemporary. Such critical rethinking of the present provides a framework allowing reflection on the past. The absence or slackening of political and moral tension in periods of peace brings about cultural involution, imitation, "classicism." In such circumstances authentic historians are not to be found, and in their stead "narrators" of historical events abound; historiography, it is asserted, becomes overladen with a rhetoric that has become an end rather than a means.

Derived as they are from the presupposition of a rigid connection between a particular historical climate and the writing of history, such considerations lead, of necessity, to a negative appreciation of the historiography of the fourth century B.C. and indeed of the greater part of Greek historiography during the Roman imperial period. Schwartz's judgment of Ephorus, for instance, is coloured by his distaste for universalistic tendencies that, bound up with the "King's Peace," meant a levelling of the greater and lesser. The "enlightened" rationalism of Ephorus, he would hold, disperses the vital energy of the Greek *polis* and of its politically active classes. Rationalism of this type did not derive from any spiritual exigency but was, rather, the outcome of a cultural levelling. The universal history written by Ephorus is regarded as a compilation that cannot be compared with the type of historiographic reflection that could come into being from the exemplary political experience of a power like Athens.

Conversely, the first phase of the Hellenistic period is assessed positively by the German historian. The interpretation is typical of the last century's positivist mentality, which considered the Hellenistic period primarily an era of scientific and technical progress. But the Hellenistic period also represented something new in the field of political relationships, culture in general, and the refinement of critical procedures in particular. There was an opening onto wider horizons, new experiences, and previously unknown exigencies in which the new social classes were also politically and culturally involved. The theory dating the fall of ancient civilization to the victory of Rome, just at the end of the Hellenistic era, is well known.[8] This question gains in relevance in the light of Schwartz's negative attitude vis-à-vis Rome and its position of dominance.

In the field of Greek historiography Schwartz also passes positive judgment on the trends reflected in the work done by diplomats and generals who were ruled by a sense of the concrete. This work, he holds, corresponded to the new social and political realities. Caesar is the last name in a line that stretches from Nearchus and Ptolemy by way of Polybius and Posidonius. Both these latter historians, whatever their individual differences, bear witness to the conflict between Greece and Rome. Rome's imperialistic power is now the central and most relevant problem as it crushes Greek civilization in the Hellenistic monarchies. Polybius, deeply involved in the drama, saw the emergence of Rome and the decline of the Greek world as the beginning of a new universal history. He was, however, conditioned by Roman power. Posidonius is seen to have had more freedom, as the last great Greek historian, the only one capable of uniting history and philosophy, combining a strong religious feeling with an independent rethinking of contemporary reality in all its

8. For instance J. Beloch, "Der Verfall der antiken Kultur," *HZ* 48 (1900) 1–38.

historical and geographical complexity. We shall return to these two historians further on. According to Schwartz, Greco-Roman culture after Posidonius remained a lifeless imitation of outworn models in the realms of politics and literature down to the fourth century A.D. The dominant classicism of imperial culture in the Augustan age, Schwartz's bête noire, is regarded as the consequence of a type of cultural sclerosis that had already begun in the last phase of the republic: the political activity of subjects lacking a sense of liberty was sapped, while domestic peace destroyed vitality and favoured conformity and repetition.

In judgments of this kind we can discern a recurrence of motifs already present in ancient historical and literary thought, as, for example, when the decay of outstanding eloquence and great historical writing is attributed to the absence of liberty. Schwartz's reasoning forms part of a discussion that was particularly lively in the final decades of the last century, especially in Germany. The arguments involved political and literary historians of antiquity and took "classicism" in literature of the Roman empire as their theme or polemical target. The political and ideological presumptions underlying the cultural climate of that period in the nineteenth century were fraught with grave consequences, but it is sufficient here to note that such a critical approach entailed a negative judgment of the political reality and culture of the Roman empire, whose vitality was apparently renewed only by the advent of Christianity. Naturally enough, the idealization of the Antonine empire, so typical of eighteenth-century rationalism, is played down by Schwartz, who singles out Edward Gibbon and slightingly casts him as the English Voltaire. Even Mommsen, who, in the fifth volume of his *Römische Geschichte,* exalted the reign of Severus Alexander, is rejected by implication.

Pride of place in this negative assessment is given to Dionysius of Halicarnassus, who is represented as a typical example of rhetorical historiography, characterized by the worst kind of classicism and displaying no feeling at all for the dramatic problem of a Greek world faced with Roman domination. He is seen as a small soul before a vast theme that had furnished inspiration of a vastly different kind to the histories of Polybius and Posidonius. In addition, Dionysius's attempted application of the principles of historical writing expounded in his *Letter to Pompey* has no importance for Schwartz, since such principles were derived from the worst rhetorical traditions of the fourth century B.C.

Schwartz's point of departure entails a complete misunderstanding of Dionysius, which, given the prestige of the German historian, has been imposed in turn on a lengthy period of subsequent research. I have no intention of defending Dionysius from the charges laid at his door by Schwartz, nor do I mean to revalue or exalt him as a model of historiography. My aim is simply to understand him. Indispensable to such an understanding is a comprehension of Dionysius's position within the cultural and political context of his own time, faced as he was with the reality of Augustan Rome. He undoubtedly has a place in the centuries-long development of Greek historiography, but there is no question here of a unified or uniform process. Thus, for example, any contrast of Dionysius with Thucydides makes sense only because Dionysius wrote an important, partly critical, treatise on that author. It is quite impossible to make a comparison between the two historians in terms of ideals or political content, and the same may be said of their thought processes and the methods they used in writing history.

III

It must be admitted, however, that in recent times a more balanced judgment of Dionysius's work has been taking shape. The grounds for this lie not so much in an overall reexamination of his approach to writing as in a growing awareness of his worth in the light of his knowledge and reconstruction of the Roman sources available at that time. In fact, for reasons we shall later have occasion to define, Dionysius is more faithful to his sources than, for example, Livy. An accurate and, let us say, stratigraphic examination of his text frequently allows an identification of the original material he adapted. Its political bias may then be determined and the personal contribution made by Dionysius himself defined. In pursuing this approach, modern research sets its sights primarily on Roman historiography of the second and first centuries B.C. This approach consequently overlooks the reasons for the choices made by Dionysius and in doing so obscures the way he employs the historiographical and antiquarian material of his studies as well as the motivations and goals of his revision.

Nor can it be said that the political problems that inspired Roman annalistic writing have in every case simply been taken over as they stand by Dionysius; in fact the opposite is true. The problems and themes of the annalists have been sifted, selected, and inserted into a culturally and methodologically distinct context with historiographic ends that are totally new. Our investigation, in other words, needs to advance beyond the study and reconstruction of Dionysius's sources in order to arrive at an analysis of his historiographical method, taking into account the cultural milieu of the Greek world within the framework of Roman imperial history.

The original Greek character of the Roman people is one of the basic tenets of Dionysius's work. Insofar as it underpins his argument rejecting those anti-Roman tendencies referred to in the programmatic preface to his *History*, it assumes a primary function in his historical and political vision. Such a thesis obviously lends itself to the sense of irony prevalent among modern historians, but our own approach should be tempered with greater caution for a number of reasons, not the least of which is the fact that in Dionysius, perhaps for the first time, materials and topics normally confined to the antiquarian and ethnographic fields are employed outside their usual orbit for the purposes of a complex historical reconstruction.

We do not intend to defend the factual validity of Dionysius's assertion. Nonetheless, given what we now know of the inroads made by Greek culture first in archaic Rome[9] and later in the Rome of the middle republican period, Dionysius's intuitive premise of Greek participation in the formation of the Roman ethnos merits respect. Not only do his arguments serve to answer the accusations of barbarity made against the Romans, but they also give consideration (here in full accord with reality) to the first step in the hellenization of Rome, projecting it all the way back to a prehistoric stage antedating the more recent cultural influences of the Hellenistic period. This primitive Greek component is all the more important for Dionysius because it ties in with the very origins of the Greek national character, long before the degeneration of Hellenistic culture. The fact that his proposal was made in the Augustan period cannot be construed as a mark of conformity or flattery, for the ideology of that era laid stress, as far as Italy was concerned, on the peninsula's own ethnography. Indeed the literature of the period abounds in such overtones and, carrying forward and developing the earlier theme of *laudes Italiae,* emphasizes regional traditions (ethnic, historical, and cultural) that had, in turn, been incorporated into the amalgam of a greater Roman reality. With the confrontations of the Social War still fresh in mind, the aim was to stress, once again, joint Italian participation in the history of Rome and its undertakings. Italian ethnography, though always

9. G. Maddoli, "Contatti antichi del mondo latino col mondo greco," in *Alle origini del latino,* ed. E. Vineis (Pisa, 1981), 43–64.

related back to Rome, is reworked by Dionysius in a different manner. Where his goals do not coincide with those of Augustan propaganda, however, it cannot be assumed that Dionysius was aligning himself with the "opposition."[10] In fact, with more complicated intentions, he was reviving a theme that had been fully present to both Roman and Greek historians from the fourth to the second century B.C., and whose origins were of even greater antiquity.[11]

Toward the end of the fifth century B.C. the historian Hellanicus of Lesbos had already referred to a Greek participation, in the person of Odysseus, in the foundation of Rome by the Trojan Aeneas.[12] In all probability he was making use of the Hesiodic reference to Odysseus on the coasts of Latium,[13] and he thus stressed the excellent knowledge of Rome that must have existed in southern Italian circles at least from the sixth century, when Rome's fortunes flourished under the Etruscan kings. Hellanicus's reference must, however, be placed in context, that is, as part of western Greek history, along with the *nostoi* of the heroes of the Trojan War: Rome, in other words, merited no more

10. E. Gabba, "Il problema dell' 'unita' dell'Italia Romana," in *La cultura italica,* ed. E. Campanile (Pisa, 1978), 11–27, esp. 22–23.

11. My interpretation is the result of a series of studies to which I refer the reader: "Il latino come dialetto greco," in *Miscellanea di studi alessandrini in memoria di A. Rostagni* (Torino, 1963), 188–94; "Considerazioni sulla tradizione letteraria sulle origini della repubblica," in *Les origines de la république romaine* (Geneva, 1967), 135–69; "Storiografia greca e imperialismo romano (III–I sec. a.C.)," *RSI* 86 (1974) 625–42; "Sulla valorizzazione politica della leggenda delle origini troiane di Roma fra III e II secolo a.C.," in *I canali della propaganda nel mondo antico,* ed. M. Sordi (Milan, 1976), 84–101. This approach is in sharp contrast to that of Erich S. Gruen, who minimizes the problem in *The Hellenistic World and the Coming of Rome* (Berkeley, 1984), 1:316 ff. I need not go into the pros and cons of the matter here since I have dealt at length with this important work in my review in *Athenaeum* n.s. 65 (1987) 205–10. In addition cf. B. Forte, *Rome and the Romans as the Greeks Saw Them* (Rome, 1972).

12. *FGrHist* 4 F 84 = Dionys. I.72.2; D. Ambaglio, *L'opera storiografica di Ellanico di Lesbo* (Pisa, 1980), 150–51.

13. Hes. *Theog.* 1011–16.

than a passing interest. We are at any event within an ethno-graphic framework that is typically Greek and whose aim was to gather centripetally into the Hellenic world whatever new peoples the Greeks encountered.[14] Again, if we look to the fourth century B.C., Rome is somewhat vaguely known to Aristotle and Heracleides Ponticus as a Greek foundation.[15]

From the second half of the fourth century B.C. onward, the problems of Rome's origins assumed a new importance as the Romans ever more decisively affirmed their power in Campania and southern Italy. Knowledge of Rome then became a political fact of life for the world of Magna Graecia, and the theory of a Greek or Trojan origin of Rome, no longer confined to the ru-minations of ethnography, became charged with fresh signifi-cance. A complex political and cultural process was elaborated in Magna Graecia, particularly in Tarentum, which aimed at drawing Rome into the framework of Greek history not only by means of prehistoric or protohistoric ethnography but also by means of history itself. It is almost as if the intention were to assuage existing doubts and preoccupations regarding the status of the new and powerful neighbour. The asserted apprenticeship to Pythagoras of the Roman king and lawgiver Numa Pom-pilius,[16] probably first put forward by Aristoxenus, clearly be-trays a desire to include the Romans within the cultural orbit of one of Magna Graecia's most striking contributions to civiliza-tion. While the underlying anachronism would be pointed out soon enough (probably by Timaeus), nonetheless the theory had a long life, persisting in Rome during the third and again during the second and first centuries B.C. It owed its popularity to the

14. E. Bickerman, "Origines Gentium," *CPh* 47 (1952) 65–81, now re-printed in E. Bickerman, *Religions and Politics in the Hellenistic and Roman Periods* (Como, 1985), 399–417.

15. Arist. fr. 568 Rose = Plut. *Cam.* 22.3; Heraclid. Pont. fr. 102 Wehrli = Plut. *Camil.* 22.3; *FGrHist* 840 F 13 a-b-c.

16. Gabba, "Considerazioni sulla tradizione letteraria," 157 ff.

general influence of Pythagorean culture among the Romans; in addition it appealed to the vanity of a number of noble families in the city.

Already in the fourth century B.C. the favourable hearing given to the theory of a Greek or Trojan origin of the city indicates a markedly pro-Greek spirit among a Roman ruling class receptive to the world of Magna Graecia. A variety of complex factors contributed to this trend, including ancient family traditions as well as independent Etruscan traditions concerning the arrival of Aeneas in Italy, and a number of legends in Latium. In all probability these same motifs also led to the rejection, during the third century, of the thesis of a *purely* Greek origin of the city. Following upon the references to Rome by the poet Lycophron and the historian Xenagoras,[17] the Latin translation of the *Odyssey* by Livius Andronicus (ca. 240 B.C.) is in fact an attempt to present the Greek poem as a Roman national epic. The reader of the poem is assumed to be familiar with the tradition making Odysseus founder or cofounder of Rome. This was a final effort to promote this version of the story and it had no successors. From this point on, the Aeneas theory holds the field. It is quite apparent, however, that the Trojans, while not Greeks themselves (though one tradition held otherwise), were looked upon as being very close to the Greeks or, better still, actually assimilated to them. Hence there was no veiled hostility whatsoever in attributing the foundation of Rome to the Trojans: instead it constituted another argument bringing Rome closer to the Greek world.

The idea of a Greek origin of Rome was readily adopted by the earliest Roman historiography toward the end of the third century B.C. Greek was the language chosen for this purpose, and the projected audience was, initially, located among Greek circles in Sicily and Magna Graecia. Traditions concerning the

17. Lycoph. *Alex.* 1242–45; Xenagoras *FGrHist* 240 F 29 = 840 F 17.

origin of Rome were borrowed from contemporary Greek local historiography (Diocles of Peparethus [18] or slightly earlier sources such as Timaeus [19]). These provided a strong argument to explain, support, and justify Rome's predominant presence in southern Italy and its anti-Carthaginian policies. These same traditions would later serve to legitimize Roman incursions both into Greece itself and into Asia Minor. Indeed, the Roman setting of the Aeneas myth and, more generally, the presence of Greek elements in archaic Roman history (for example, Evander and the Arcadians) gained an ever greater politico-diplomatic significance in the course of the second century B.C. They were given historical validity in the light of problems contingent upon particular phases of Roman expansion. In addition, a number of strictly cultural considerations (for instance, the derivation of Latin from Greek dialects) would independently assume an all the more significant value because they emerged at the same time as the Hellenic penetration of Roman culture during the second century B.C.

IV

In closing, for the moment, our examination of the first phase of Greek historiography concerning Rome, it must be emphasized that this early research on the origins of Rome preceded any process of blatant political exploitation. For the Greek world the problem was of an exclusively historical-ethnographic nature, devoid of political implications and judged in largely historical terms. A Pythagorean attempt to claim credit for the origin of Rome had come to nothing.

18. *FGrHist* 820 T 2 a-b; Plut. *Rom.* 3.1, 8.9.
19. A. Momigliano, "Atene nel III secolo A.C. e la scoperta di Roma nelle Storie di Timeo di Tauromenio," *RSI* 71 (1959) 529–56, reprinted as "Athens in the Third Century B.C. and the Discovery of Rome in the Histories of Timaeus of Tauromenium," in A. Momigliano, *Essays in Ancient and Modern Historiography* (Middletown, Conn., 1977), 37–66.

Greek and Latin documentation of the origins of the Roman ethnos, heavily weighted toward a predominance of the Greek elements, was known, investigated, and quoted by Dionysius. His approach, however, differed substantially; for him it was not limited to the period of the city's origins. Instead, the Greek character of the Romans takes the form of a lengthy process, a structure underlying the city's history and culture, which survived not only in the external aspects of the civilization (writing, language, and artistic production), but also in the nature and customs of the people, its religious and political institutions, and the high ideals that presided over the life of the city. He had a special view of the development of Roman history: hellenization, or rather the original Hellenic character, predating the phase of post-Alexandrian corruption, is seen not as surviving in fossil form but as continuing to be a vital and operative force throughout the course of Roman history. It is the primary historical and moral justification for a Roman hegemony that was superior to all previous hegemonies. It is also a preliminary and indispensable element in the groundwork for Dionysius's political viewpoint and the future it prefigured.

With an historical outlook of this type, Dionysius is quite clearly far removed from the interpretations of Polybius, who had no interest in the problem of origins or in interracial relationships. Dionysius thus also distances himself from the anti-Roman historians of the second and first centuries B.C., with whom, directly or indirectly, he comes into conflict. The most dramatic moment in Polybius's reflections on Roman world hegemony is contained in the additions to the preface to the third book of his *Histories*. These explain the reasons behind his extension of the work beyond the intended limit of 167 B.C. down to 145–144 B.C.[20] These extra years covered a period in which

20. Polyb. III.4.1–5.9; F. W. Walbank, *Polybius* (Berkeley, 1972), 27 ff., 173 ff.; E. Gabba, "Aspetti culturali dell'imperialismo romano," *Athenaeum* n.s. 55 (1977) 68–73.

the defence of previous conquests compelled those in power to use terror and repression for the maintenance of their dominant position. The historical necessity for such draconian measures was recognized by Polybius, who had reconstructed the political, military, and economic reasons leading to Roman superiority. His observations do not imply acceptance or approval, merely understanding, and he was well aware of the dangers inherent in political measures of this type. It will become clear, he says, from the analysis of such policies whether "for contemporaries, Roman leadership is to be rejected or, on the contrary, accepted, and whether for future generations their hegemony is to be judged worthy of approval and admiration, or of blame." A little further on he states that political leadership must find its justification and hence its validity in high-minded and noble aims. He stands aloof, however, from moral assessments of any kind. For him the goals of leadership are to be looked for in the political sphere, in the exercise of power itself. Perhaps in response to the doubts of Polybius, Panaetius, at the end of the second century B.C., elaborated a series of political justifications for Roman imperialism, and these in turn found an echo in Cicero's *De re publica* and *De officiis*.[21]

It is obvious that this type of problem, dramatically relevant in the mid second century B.C., was irrelevant in Dionysius's lifetime. Any comparison between Dionysius and Polybius on this terrain is therefore otiose. The work of Posidonius, however, does invite contrast with that of Dionysius. Writing a century after Polybius and fifty years before Dionysius, Posidonius no longer sees the acceptance of Roman domination as a political problem worthy of consideration. What now comes to the fore in his interpretation is the social impact of Rome's predominance in the light of the agreement gradually arrived at be-

---

21. K. H. Abel, "Die kulturelle Mission des Panaitios," *A&A* 17 (1971) 119–43; E. Gabba, "Per un'interpretazione politica del de officiis di Cicerone," *RAL*, 8th ser., 34 (1979) 120–22.

tween Rome and the wealthier, more conservative classes among her subjects. The social problem is centred, according to Posidonius, on the relationship between those exercising power and those submitting to it. He recognizes the inevitability of a Roman supremacy that derived its authority from pacifying the local aristocracies and guaranteeing their interests. The internal divisions within the Roman ruling class, on the other hand, entailed grave repercussions for the exercise of imperial power as well as for Rome's attitude and behaviour toward her allies and subject peoples. He maintains, however, that the senatorial class has sufficient moral resources, in addition to the traditional examples of its culture, to enable it to restore a balanced administration and its own credibility. Posidonius is clearly a long way from the political problems of a doubt-ridden Polybius and significantly closer to Dionysius, for whom, as we shall later see, Rome was the social and cultural guarantor of the empire's well-being and stability.

For the Greek who came to Rome after the Battle of Actium there could be no substitute for the historical role of Rome and its empire. There is no question here of self-interested gratitude or of a rancorous acceptance of the inevitable, as was the case with his contemporary, the historian Timagenes. Dionysius's adherence is the result of a conscious political and cultural choice. He is thus distinguished from that segment of Greek intellectuals who, in the course of the last century of the republic, had played a part, along with various members of the Roman ruling class, in promoting their own cultural interests. They had profited from the Roman desire to win acceptance in a Greek cultural world whose superiority was an acknowledged fact. These Greek intellectuals were in turn different from those philosophers and literary men who, with Polybius and Panaetius, had attempted to prepare the Roman elite of the previous century for their duties in government by arousing or affirming in them a strong imperial consciousness. In the first century B.C.,

Greek intellectuals subordinated their own beliefs to the aim of obtaining favours and benefits for themselves and their cities from their Roman patrons. Theirs was an attitude of flattery, which humoured men like Lucullus and Pompey by entertaining their aspirations to Greek culture. Undoubtedly in such cases the survival of the Roman regime also guaranteed the survival of the society from which these intellectuals sprang. But Dionysius is clearly distinguished by his perception (shared with the geographer Strabo) of a cultural and political function that could be linked to the great models and ideals of the classical period and to the cultured upper classes of the Greek cities. It is an awareness that supplies a premise for the admission of the latter into the empire's ruling class.[22]

It is no accident that Dionysius sees as the greatest achievement of Roman statesmanship the capacity for assimilation that the city had displayed throughout the course of its history. Rome is distinguished by this characteristic from the narrow-minded exclusivity of the traditional Greek *polis.*

Dionysius's opposition to the anti-Roman tendencies of that section of Greek society whose efforts culminated in the support given to the political programmes of Mithridates also has a social aspect (as is also the case with Posidonius), grounded in the fact that this movement had found its widest support among the masses.[23] The need to counter these tendencies was at least par-

22. E. Gabba, "The Historians and Augustus," in *Caesar Augustus. Seven Aspects,* ed. F. Millar and E. Segal (Oxford, 1984), 61–67.

23. As M. Hengel (*Jews, Greeks and the Barbarians* [Philadelphia, 1980], 73) remarked, "from the end of the second century B.C. onwards support for 'Hellenistic Civilisation' became more and more identical with loyalty to Rome, which was the sole means of protecting the petty Hellenistic states from barbarian alienation." In the famous speech of Sulla reported in App. *Mith.* 236–37 (from Posidonius?) Rome is represented as the symbol and bulwark of public and private morality, the guarantor of order in social relationships and hence fully deserving preeminence in the world. The opposite naturally applies in the case of Mithridates, and here the social aspects have been studied in P. Desideri, "Posidonio e la Guerra Mitridatica," *Athenaeum* n.s. 51

tially responsible for Dionysius's undertaking, for, even in the age of Augustus, such sentiments were still far from dormant.

V

In this sense the historiographical activities of Dionysius are of significant value and really do provide a new opening for the cultural and political integration of the Greek upper classes into imperial life. At this juncture one is inevitably led to a comparison with a Latin historian who, like Dionysius, was working in Rome at that time on a history of its archaic period with a view to that period's position in the more general unfolding of Roman history.[24] Both Livy and Dionysius rework the same materials for the archaic period that were furnished to them by the earlier annalists, and, as far as subject matter is concerned, there are many points of coincidence between their works that transcend the differences in narrative technique. Naturally, the problem of the original formation of the Roman ethnos does not have the same importance for Livy as for Dionysius, and yet it is not on this matter that the greatest divergence will be found between the two contemporaries.

As the *praefatio* of his work indicates, Livy shared Sallust's pessimistic vision of history and regarded the present with distrust and disillusionment. This attitude is markedly at variance with the prevailing atmosphere of Augustan Rome. Sallust, however, had aimed at a political examination of those events in recent Roman history that most clearly displayed the corruption of the oligarchic ruling class, a corruption symptomatic of an

---

(1973) 26–27 (the whole article is required reading for our subject, since the reconstruction of Posidonius's thinking on the Roman empire provides a natural premise to the understanding of Dionysius).

24. I reproduce here, sometimes verbatim, several reasonings proposed in my chapter "Literature," in *Sources for Ancient History*, ed. M. H. Crawford (Cambridge, 1983), 17–18.

even greater contagion that had invaded the whole social body. He strove to analyse the social, economic, and political grounds for the decline of Rome, while also relating them to a wider anthropological framework. Writing in the midst of civil wars and the rule of the Triumvirs, Sallust was unable to propose any future resolution of the problems. Nor was Livy able to suggest any concrete remedy for the crisis, although he was quite capable of measuring its extent and gravity even under the new conditions prevailing in the Augustan restoration. In a certain sense his pessimism was even greater than that of Sallust, for Rome had now come through the civil wars, and their seemingly happy outcome apparently did not redeem a decadence that Livy observed with moralistic longing for a past that could know no repetition. The narration of Roman history thus provided Livy with the best method of showing how the city's spectacular rise to power had always been shored up by the presence of certain sterling values, while the present crisis had been determined by the weakening of those same values to the point of disappearance. The facts of history, in the rise and fall of Rome, are seen by Livy as a moral problem. It is fairly obvious that this type of idolatry of Roman history prior to its moral and political corruption could only have been pursued from the perspective of a conservative ethic. Stress was laid upon those high-minded, civic, individual and collective virtues that had, in the first instance, been the heritage of an oligarchical class and that had later been inculcated, by example, in the citizenry as a whole. Thus Livy subscribed to the senatorial ideology even if he did not follow the path of political involvement that can be discerned in the annals written by the senatorial historians. Indeed, confined as he was by the limitations of his moral problems, it was only at the most superficial level that he entered on the question of the relations between the new regime and the traditional ruling class, to which he did not belong. Futhermore, the wider imperial perspective so clearly evident in the ideological premises of his contemporary Dionysius is completely alien to Livy.

It may well seem a paradox, yet Dionysius, and not Livy, is in reality the authentic historian of the Augustan age. Accepting the traditional Roman outlook, Livy had every reason in the world to be preoccupied and uncertain, while the Greek from Halicarnassus prefigured and foretold the rise of new ruling classes within a universal empire.

CHAPTER TWO

Political and Cultural Aspects of the Classicistic Revival in the Augustan Age

In this chapter I intend to clarify the explicitly political foundation and significance of the literary classicistic revival as it was proposed and argued by several Greek intellectuals during the Augustan age. This revival was intended as a return to the glorious literary models of the fourth century B.C., and in particular to the orators and the ideals that they represented. I do not wish to negate or minimize the literary value of this cultural tendency, a favourite theme of modern criticism, but I believe a better understanding of it can be arrived at by stressing its wide political implications, especially in relation to the then inescapable reality of Roman dominion. It is clear, moreover, that the proponents of classicism were well aware of these implications.

The fundamental text that will be discussed here is the initial section of the treatise *De antiquis oratoribus* by Dionysius of Halicarnassus, which presents, in a sense, a genuine political and cultural program. The interpretation of this text that I propose may be confirmed by several famous passages of the treatise *On the Sublime,* which, I maintain, dates to the beginning of the imperial age. Several passages of the historical text known as the *Ineditum Vaticanum* are also, in my opinion, relevant in supporting my interpretation; and Strabo, too, a contemporary

of Dionysius, expresses concepts and ideas of cultural politics
rather similar to those described by Dionysius.

Examination of these texts involves the important issue of the
relationships prevailing, during the first century of the Roman
empire, between the empire itself and, on the one hand, its own
upper classes and, on the other, the Greek intellectuals. In order
to completely clarify Dionysius's position and the significance of
his cultural proposal, I believe it will be useful to conclude this
chapter by comparing him with another Greek intellectual,
Plutarch of Chaeronea, who lived slightly more than a century
after Dionysius. Plutarch consciously supported a position different from that upheld by Dionysius in the Augustan age; he
thus attests to the variety and complexity of the attitudes of the
Greek cultural world toward Rome.

I

The concepts expressed by Dionysius in the preface of his *De
antiquis oratoribus* are fundamental for the delineation of the
cultural-historical phenomenon that characterizes the Augustan
age—the flowering of classicism.[1] His few chapters describe, in
the beginning, the havoc wreaked by the fashion of Asian eloquence, and, subsequently, the classicistic revival, a complex
phenomenon that was just beginning to unfold and whose first
important achievements had already been witnessed. In chap-

1. The preface was written after the draft of the first part of the treatise,
which was devoted to the most ancient orators: Lysias, Isocrates, and Isaeus.
It is generally maintained that this treatise belongs to Dionysius's first phase as
a literary critic, even though the chronology of his rhetorical works is not at all
certain (G. Pavano, "Sulla cronologia degli scritti retorici di Dionisio d'Alicarnasso," *AAPal,* 4th ser., vol. 3, pt. 2 [1942] 211–363; S. Usher, *Dionysius
of Halicarnassus, the Critical Essays* [Cambridge, Mass., 1974], 1:xxii–
xxvi; G. Aujac, *Denys d'Halicarnasse, Opuscules rhétoriques* [Paris, 1978],
1:22–28). In any case, the composition of the "rhetorical" writings is parallel
to the draft of the *History of Archaic Rome.*

In the introductions to the two volumes cited by Usher and Aujac, there is
useful information regarding Dionysius's rhetorical ideas and his position in

ter 3 the principal cause of the resurgence is cited, and finally Dionysius introduces his own work and his own precepts of literary criticism into this new cultural development, interpreting its function and goals. It is imperative to study these chapters in detail in order to gain insight into their vital importance.

Dionysius considers the historical development of Greek civil eloquence.[2] The basic categories of oratory—judicial, deliberative, and epideictic, together constituting οἱ πολιτικοὶ λόγοι— are all referred to the πολιτικὴ τέχνη because they all involve discussion within the circle of political life.[3] Ancient eloquence, once nourished by philosophy, had suffered a serious decline dating from the Alexandrian age and culminating in its near disappearance in the author's day. It had been replaced by a theatrical, irreverent eloquence, far removed from philosophy and every tenet of liberal education, that took advantage of the ignorance of the masses. This degraded form of eloquence, inflated by rich pomposity, had not only supplanted the other forms but had also become the means of attaining positions of power and leadership in the cities. Dionysius holds that access to these positions should be reserved for those whose eloquence is based upon philosophy. In contrast to philosophical oratory, this vul-

---

the Atticism-Asianism controversy. The well-known books by G. Kennedy, *The Art of Persuasion in Greece* (Princeton, 1963), *The Art of Rhetoric in the Roman World, 300 B.C.–A.D. 300* (Princeton, 1972), and *Classical Rhetoric and Its Christian and Secular Tradition from Ancient to Modern Times* (Chapel Hill, 1980), also provide the best historical background for understanding the reception in pre-Augustan Rome of the Greek rhetorical theories and for understanding the contemporary intellectual atmosphere. Cf. C. Schultze, "Dionysius of Halicarnassus and His Audience," in *Past Perspective. Studies in Greek and Roman Historical Writing*, ed. I. S. Noxon, J. D. S. Smart, and A. J. Woodman (Cambridge, 1986), 121–41.

2. *De antiq. orat.* I.1.1–2 (I refer to this work according to the Aujac edition).

3. The significance of the expression πολιτικοὶ λόγοι of I.1.1 (distinct from the historiography and the philosophical treatments: I.3.2) is clarified, in my opinion, by III (*Isocrates*) 1.4 and by II (*Lysias*) 16.1–3; cf. Aujac, *Opuscules*, 175–76.

gar eloquence is likened to a courtesan who, vying with the virtuous and prudent wife, has destroyed a family and its riches.[4]

This degenerate trend, according to Dionysius, had invaded
every city, without exception, including those boasting the highest cultural attainments (perhaps an allusion to the fact that
even Athens was not exempt); immediately thereafter Dionysius
says that the ancient and native Attic Muse had been divested of
her possessions. Her adversary, hailing from farthest Asia (who
might have been Mysian, Phrygian, or Carian), had seized rule
over the Greek cities, expelling culture and wisdom.[5] Fortu-
nately the author's period was witnessing a return to the sage
eloquence of former times, either as the result of divine intervention, or as a natural, cyclical return, or perhaps as a response to
that inherent tendency that compels the destiny of most men in
one direction. The new brand of irresponsible eloquence was
decaying. And significantly this change, this resurgence, had
been rapid and its success great: with the exception of some culturally backward cities in Asia and apart from the utterances of
a few incurable individuals, this vulgar and crude eloquence was
everywhere on the wane.[6]

In the above, Dionysius alludes to a threefold reason, either
divine, human, or natural, for this return to prudence. Now he
specifies Rome as the cause and origin of this great metamor-
phosis. It was Rome's conquest of the world that constrained the
cities to turn to Rome and its ruling class (οἱ δυναστεύοντες),
which governed the state with virtue and wisdom. The Roman
leaders, Dionysius holds, were men of high culture and noble
adherents of justice; the wiser elements within the cities had
once again advanced under their guidance, while the irrational
had been forced to give way to the rational.[7]

4. *De antiq. orat.* I.1.2–5.   5. *De antiq. orat.* I.1.6–7.
6. *De antiq. orat.* I.2.1–5.
7. *De antiq. orat.* I.3.1. I also intend οἱ δυναστεύοντες in the sense of
"Roman ruling class" without a specific reference to Caesar or Augustus, as

The results, Dionysius claims, were already evident in the area of Greek and Latin literature. Important works in historiography, political eloquence, philosophy, and every other field were being published or prepared for publication. The infatuation, the passing fancy for coarse eloquence, was rapidly losing sway and would disappear in the course of a single generation.[8]

Dionysius is not content to resign himself to passive approval of this cultural renaissance. He wishes to promote its progress through the study of the most famous orators and ancient historians (those who lived before the age of Alexander). These would provide valuable models for those interested in political philosophy: scholars who envisaged a culture formed by and strictly connected to political action, as exemplified by the pattern found in the orations of Isocrates. Dionysius is keenly aware that, in pursuing these goals, he is laying new groundwork in the field.[9]

This text of Dionysius, which I have paraphrased without neglecting anything of importance, has of course been studied at great length and has recently been the object of some pertinent analysis.[10] In the following I shall point out several of the more worthwhile findings, while including a few of my own observations.

In the first place, the preface presents problems of literary his-

has often been supposed, lately by S. Cagnazzi, "Politica e retorica nel preambolo del Περὶ τῶν ἀρχαίων ῥητόρων di Dionigi di Alicarnasso," *RFIC* 109 (1981) 52–59; see also in this sense Pavano, 234–35.

    8. *De antiq. orat.* I.3.2–3. As Usher rightly notes (1:10 n.2), the stress on Latin literature is purely instrumental.

    9. *De antiq. orat.* I.4.1–3.

    10. *Le classicisme à Rome aux I^{ers} siècles avant et après J.-C.*, Fondation Hardt, Entretiens 25 (Geneva, 1979); especially important for us, T. Gelzer, "Klassizismus, Attizismus und Asianismus" (1–41), and G. W. Bowersock, "Historical Problems in Late Republican and Augustan Classicism" (57–75), with the relative discussions. See also P. Desideri, *Dione di Prusa, un intellettuale greco nell'impero romano* (Messina, 1978), 78–80; Hurst, 839–65. Dionysius's text occupies a central position in the discussion of the characteristics of culture in the Hellenistic and Roman ages that was carried out in Germany during the last quarter of the nineteenth century and involved among

tory and dating.[11] Dionysius offers a double chronological framework that is not without a certain ambiguity. The decline of ancient eloquence began with the age after Alexander, but the
period of the most intense domination of Asian eloquence would
seem to have been short-lived and to have surfaced only latterly,
in Dionysius's time. This would correspond to the middle of the
first century B.C. The possible relationship of this particular period to the post-Alexandrian age in general is not, at first glance,
either clear or explicable. It would seem that Dionysius takes
the post-Alexandrian age (which, as one finds by analogous reasoning in Cicero,[12] must traditionally have been held responsible
for the growth of Asianism) and juxtaposes it to the most recent
Asian period.[13] Underlying such an idea must be the consideration that the expansion of Greek culture beyond the confines of
Hellas to barbarian countries represented a decline of the culture itself. In any case, Dionysius distinguishes three phases in
the historical development of eloquence and, as we shall see, of
culture in general: the Classical age until Alexander; the post-
Alexandrian age, which concludes with a brief, intense period of
Asian supremacy; and the age, underway in Dionysius's time, of
the classicistic revival.

It is important to emphasize that Dionysius considers this cul-

others Rohde, Wilamowitz, Kaibel, and Schwartz; recent, and well worth examining, is Desideri, *Dione di Prusa*, 524–36.

11. Analogous to that on art, certified by Pliny *NH* XXXIV.51–52
(T. Gelzer, 32 n. 2); recently in this regard see P. Gros, "Vie et mort de l'art hellénistique selon Vitruve et Pline," *REL* 56 (1978) 289–313, and A. Stewart,
Attika: Studies in Athenian Sculpture of the Hellenistic Age (London, 1979),
38 ff.

12. Cic. *De or.* II.95; *Brut.* 36–37; T. Gelzer, 29–30. The passage of Cic.
Orat. 25 ("Itaque Caria et Phrygia et Mysia, quod minime politae minimeque
elegantes sunt") has naturally been compared to *De antiq. orat.* I.1.7 (Bowersock, "Historical Problems," 65–66), but it seems that Dionysius was thinking of concrete examples.

13. In the *De comp. verb.* IV.29 (II.20.15 Usener-Radermacher), Dionysius condemns the Asianism of Duris and Polybius: T. Gelzer, 29; Usher,
1:7 n. 1.

tural development from within the Greek world, within Greek cities. The reference to the Attic Muse confirms that the ancient age as well as the contemporary, classicistic resurgence has, for the most part, been understood in terms of Atticism. The theory of imitation sought to analyze and define the stylistic characteristics of an author so that he could be proposed as a model worthy of imitation; at the same time it sought the recovery and better understanding of the noble teaching contained in his moral, philosophical, and political ideas. Thus in his works of literary criticism and stylistics Dionysius demonstrates clearly that this theory of imitation is valid for a wide range of classical writers, including non-Attic authors.[14] Even the political and practical reverberations created by the irruption of Asian eloquence during the final period of the age after Alexander are regarded as a function of political life within the Greek cities, including the possibility of winning magistracies with the aid of that very eloquence.

A connection with the internal social structure of the Greek cities is also clearly indicated: Asian eloquence conquers and gains support among the untutored masses; prudent, classical oratory belongs to the upper classes.[15] Cultural phenomena and their social aspects are viewed as closely related.

Dionysius's representation of cultural and literary phenomena has engendered confusion and objections.[16] It has been pointed out that Dionysius's Atticist programme (and that of his colleague Caecilius of Kale Akte) had been anticipated approximately fifty years earlier in Rome by Latin orators and theorists of Atticism, particularly those in the grammatical field. What, it may be asked, is the relationship, if indeed there is one, between

14. T. Gelzer, 24 ff.
15. *De antiq. orat.* I.1.4, 7; 3.1.
16. Fundamental is A. Dihle, "Der Beginn des Attizismus," *A&A* 23 (1977) 162–77, esp. 164 ff. Cf. T. Gelzer, 17 ff.; Bowersock, "Historical Problems," 59 ff.

them and Dionysius? The Roman inclination to Atticism, in
turn, had its antecedents in a similar Greek predilection dating
from the third century B.C. precisely in the grammatical field. In
much the same way the predominant influence of fourth-century
Attic Greek prose style is evident in the Hellenistic age. The second century B.C. rhetorician Diogenes of Babylon has been mentioned in this context.[17] Although Dionysius does not appear to
deal with these Greek predecessors, they are perhaps tacitly
referred to. As has been said, the terminus a quo, the death of
Alexander, probably has political significance for Dionysius,
according to whom Asianism reached its climax and its most
visible manifestations more than 250 years after that date (and
was to continue still longer).

Apparently there is also some ambiguity in outlining the
causes of the sudden change ($\mu\varepsilon\tau\alpha\beta o\lambda\dot{\eta}$) by which the rational
Attic eloquence of a former age regained predominance. In sug-
gesting divine or natural reasons, Dionysius refuses to specify
times and persons. Instead, he confidently connects that change
with the foundation of Rome's universal empire; he believes that
the new social and political context has allowed the change and,
in a certain sense, has been its cause and origin. In my opinion
this interpretation of I.3.1 emerges clearly from Dionysius's
text. It is not, however, generally accepted.

It is widely held that the Greek Atticists of the Augustan age
(namely Dionysius and Caecilius) were the heirs of a small group
of Roman Atticists who were contemporaries of Cicero.[18] The
Greek intellectuals would have come in contact with them in
Rome after 30 B.C. The important role of cultural mediator
attributed to Dionysius's patron Q. Aelius Tubero should be
stressed: in fact, Dionysius dedicated his essay *De Thucydide* to
him as an historian of Thucydidean spirit. Tubero had been in

17. F. Lasserre, "Prose grecque classicisante," in *Le classicisme à Rome
aux I^{ers} siècles avant et après J.-C.* (Geneva, 1979), 52–53.
18. In this sense, Bowersock, "Historical Problems," 65 ff.

touch with the Ciceronian circle. Thus Dionysius appears to repeat, though on a much vaster scale, a polemic derived from the formulations used by Roman Atticists. Dionysius, however, like Cicero before him, is able to manoeuvre with greater liberty than his predecessors. Other points of similarity to Cicero have also been traced.[19]

Frankly, this interpretation, limited as it is to literary-historical facts, is unacceptable.[20] Dionysius insists that the cultural problem rests within the Greek cities. Latin literature is mentioned only as a fortuitous consequence of the classicistic revival. The idea that Dionysius may link the foundation of the cultural and literary movement of the classicistic revival to Rome is not at all consistent with Dionysius's text, though he was acquainted with Cicero and with the Roman political eloquence of the first century B.C., as he was, indeed, versed in historiography. The movement is described as spontaneous and generated within the Greek world. The relationship with Rome derives from the fact that the revival was rendered possible, encouraged, and propelled by the new reality of Roman dominion, by this time an uncontested power—an indication that the Asian tendency had been possible only because of a belief that Roman control was not yet fully established. Undoubtedly, the Roman leaders (οἱ δυναστεύοντες) were themselves responsible for this state of things, owing to their cultural training and judicial capacity, and this was evident from the just and excellent administration of the empire, which safeguarded the welfare of everyone. Because they were good administrators, and not because they were intellectuals, they served as models for the right-minded upper classes of the Greek cities (πόλις in I.3.1. has a

19. Supra n. 12.
20. The politico-cultural significance of the Atticistic movement is finally noted by Dihle and also by T. Gelzer, and is clearly emphasized by Desideri. The aims of Dionysius's program, also outside the literary ambience, are clarified by S. F. Bonner, *The Literary Treatises of Dionysius of Halicarnassus: A Study in the Development of Critical Method* (Cambridge, 1939), 11 ff.

collective value), which accordingly acquired power, while the uneducated part (the masses who had been easily swayed by the Asian eloquence) was constrained to submit. Such were the political consequences for the Greek cities resulting from Roman supremacy. This development accompanied the political dominance of right-minded oligarchic factions and was to follow on the defeat of vulgar eloquence and the resumed predominance of ancient, rational oratory nourished by philosophy.

Dionysius's reasoning develops within a well-defined political framework, the antecedents of which lie in the idealization by Greek historians and intellectuals in the second century B.C. of illustrious Roman personalities (Marcellus, Flamininus, Scipio Africanus, Aemilius Paulus, Scipio Aemilianus) as models of civic and human virtue.[21] Moreover, the goal of Panaetius's mission had been exactly that of forming a Roman political class prepared to uphold its imperial duties.[22] Toward the middle of the first century B.C. Posidonius gratefully embraced Roman imperial rule, which in a sense represented the natural authority of the most worthy; notwithstanding, he had criticized bitterly the methods and means of the Roman administration in the provinces, for he attributed primary responsibility for the misgovernment in the provinces and the serious social disorders that derived from it to vicious exploitation by the equestrian order. He did, however, continue to defend the Roman Senate as a repository of ancient virtues and high ideals that made it potentially capable of effecting a profound renovation.

Posidonius's faith in the ability of the Roman senatorial class to promote such a regeneration[23] becomes transformed in Dionysius into a paradigmatical representation of an educated and

---

21. Gabba, "Storiografia greca e imperialismo romano," 640.
22. Abel, "Die kulturelle Mission des Panaitios."
23. P. Desideri, "L'interpretazione dell'impero romano in Posidonio," *RIL* 106 (1972) 481–93.

just Roman governing class. Certainly in his *History of Archaic Rome* Dionysius is unable to conceal the serious process of decay and corruption, underway since the second century B.C., that had led to civil wars and had involved a large proportion of the Roman upper classes.[24] The fine example of the Greek classical ideals is also valuable for the Romans, as a reminder of their highest traditions.

It is equally clear that in Dionysius's reasoning, the new culture, the classicistic revival, corresponds to the principle of elite order, as opposed to the disorder supported by the masses. It is an order that is guaranteed by Rome. As Strabo, too, says (II.5.26), the Romans, as once the Greeks, are responsible for the civil and cultural advancement of the world, with the strength of their empire, which favors exchange and knowledge, enforcing this goal.

On the other hand, according to Dionysius's concept, the ancient civic eloquence (of the fourth century B.C.) is exalted for its extremely lofty political and moral value, for the ideals it maintains, and for the cultural model it offers. The critics who judged the quality of earlier writers by the principle of *imitatio* (Dionysius was one of them)[25] sought to identify, by means of a thorough stylistic and literary analysis, precisely that excellence of idealistic and moral content. Isocrates is offered as a prime model for the typical virtues he extolled: patriotism, justice, *eusebeia,* and moderation.

In the essay Dionysius devotes to the great orators, he returns to the theme of the practical, political value of instruction and

24. The most important passages are I.6.4, II.11.3, II.74.5, V.60.2, X.17.6, X.35.3.
25. H. Flashar, *Die klassizistische Theorie der Mimesis,* in *Le classicisme à Rome aux I^ers siècles avant et après J.-C.,* 79–97; G. M. A. Grube, *The Greek and Roman Critics* (Toronto, 1968) 207–30. In general, B. P. Reardon, *Courants littéraires grecs des IIe et IIIe siècles après J.-C.* (Paris, 1971), passim; Kennedy, *Classical Rhetoric,* 116–19.

thus of the imitation of Isocrates.[26] The selection of Isocrates' orations is consistent with the aims Dionysius proposes, which coincide only indirectly with those of Augustan propaganda.[27] The fact is that the high civic and political eloquence of the fourth century had, within the Greek world, a much greater significance than any propagandistic purpose of contemporary authority might suggest. The common possession of a rich literary tradition was perhaps the strongest factor behind Greek unity. This unity continued under the Roman empire much as it had within the ambit of the Hellenistic world, although the Greeks now lived under very different social, political, and economic conditions.[28] Dionysius interprets classicism as the best example afforded to the Greek upper classes for the preservation of unity and identity.

II

Classical Greek culture had always signified Athens. And Isocrates was not alone in proposing the idealization of Athens as a cultural model. Even in the second century B.C., the civic eloquence of Athens was remembered by Diogenes of Babylon as "an ethical model of oratorical art."[29] To recall an example from another sphere, in the well-known inscription of ca. 117 B.C. by the Amphictyons of Delphi honoring the *technitai* of Athens, the lavish praise bestowed on the city for the service it rendered to humanity in terms of civilization and culture is a significant echo of a familiar leitmotif.[30] Even in Rome this primacy of Athens was willingly acknowledged.[31]

26. *De antiq. orat.* III (*Isocrates*) 1.5, 4.3, 10.1; M. I. Finley, "L'héritage d'Isocrate," in *Mythe, mémoire, histoire* (Paris, 1981), 175–207.

27. In this sense see, for example, Bonner, 11.

28. Dihle, 169.

29. T. Gelzer, 26 ff.; Lasserre, 52, with the passages by Diogenes.

30. *SIG* 704E, lines 11–12; M. Rostovtzeff, *The Social and Economic History of the Hellenistic World* (Oxford, 1941), 2:755, 3:1507 n.22.

31. The most famous passages are Lucr. VI.1–5 and Cic. *Flac.* 62; reservations in Sall. *Cat.* 8; cf. Livy XXXI.44.9.

Dionysius's text transfers its attention from the model of Athens to the cultural mission of Rome, which guarantees, as Posidonius had already noted, the social order within the empire that was an indispensable condition for a cultural flourishing of classicism. The classical *paideia,* recovered from the Greek models of oratory and historiography in the fourth century, is now offered as a fundamental instrument for the formation of a unified consciousness among the upper classes in the Greek cities under the new order safeguarded by Rome. The cultural standard is thus understood in terms of the social interpretation of the relationship between the Greek world and Rome. In the same manner, the preface to *The History of Archaic Rome* clearly suggests that Rome has succeeded to the supremacy formerly belonging to Athens.[32]

Tradition had already established that Asia symbolized the antithesis of the Attic model. Isocrates points to the obvious geographic differences between Europe and Asia, but places his emphasis on their even more irreconcilable ethnic and cultural conflicts.[33] To Isocrates, "Europe" signifies Greece and the regions influenced by Greek culture. The cultural character of this contrast was increasingly emphasized, especially by Theopompus, who conceived of Europe as constantly expanding its limits. For Dionysius, the center of Europe was now, naturally, Italy;[34] but to him, as we know, the Romans were actually Greeks.

The beginning of the decline of classical Greek culture, heralded by Alexander's death and the waxing power of Asia, had an enduring political and cultural impact; we shall find it mentioned once again, for example, in Strabo. The significance of practically the entire culture that we today call Hellenistic was

32. I.3.1–2.
33. A. Momigliano, "L'Europa come concetto politico presso Isocrate e gli isocratei," *RFIC* n.s. 11 (1933) 477–87, now in A. Momigliano, *Terzo contributo alla storia degli studi classici e del mondo antico* (Rome, 1966), 1:489–97; T. Gelzer, 30 ff.
34. *History* I.35–36.

minimized by Dionysius: he labels as Asian even historians such as Duris, Phylarchus, and Polybius. Perhaps the Oriental influence upon the Greek world destroyed classical, traditional liberty and culture. The Hellenistic age, to which Timagenes, a contemporary of Dionysius who was hostile to Rome, had dedicated his historical work, is subjected by Dionysius to the scourge of disapproval.[35]

One wonders just what Asia, that uncouth, barbaric wilderness where a vulgar eloquence enjoying the favour and support of the masses continued to flourish, signified to Dionysius, who was himself a native of Halicarnassus and thus well acquainted with Asia. It has been observed that in Dionysius's period-system "the end of the Mithridatic war does not appear to have any significant impact on Greek literary activity. It is, rather, the Roman civil war and the ensuing age of Augustus that caused a change."[36] In general terms this is a valid observation, but it seems that in the cities of Asia Minor (those with which Dionysius concerns himself) the Mithridatic episode favoured the development and flowering of Asian culture up to Dionysius's own time and beyond. It is noteworthy that in the preface to his *History* Dionysius heatedly disputes the Mithridatic historiography (with greater ferocity perhaps than his refutation of the version of history that, in the Augustan age, exalted the empire of the Parthians)[37] and thereby attests the validity of the Mithri-

35. A. Momigliano, "Livio, Plutarco e Giustino su virtù e fortuna dei Romani," *Athenaeum* n.s. 12 (1934) 45–56, now in A. Momigliano, *Terzo contributo alla storia degli studi classici e del mondo antico* (Rome 1966), 1:499–511, esp. 505. In the Judaic tradition the centuries between Alexander and Augustus were also neglected; for an explanation see E. Bickerman, "La chaîne de la tradition pharisienne," in E. Bickerman, *Studies in Jewish and Christian History* (Leiden, 1980), 2:256–59.

36. Bowersock, "Historical Problems," 42.

37. H. Fuchs, *Der geistige Widerstand gegen Rom in der antiken Welt* (Berlin, 1938), 14–15, notes to 40–43. Diversely, Momigliano, "Livio, Plutarco e Giustino," 506–7.

datic historiography's themes.[38] The Mithridatic historiography had continued to diffuse anti-Roman propaganda, frequently of a populist nature,[39] which was accepted even by men of culture. This propaganda revived and recirculated still-vibrant coarse anti-Roman themes from the Seleucid age, which stressed the contrast between Asia and Europe (the latter identified as Italy and Rome). An emphasis on such themes may, for example, be seen in the prophecies of the third book of the Sibylline Oracles.

These ideas had won attention and were still given credence—and not only among the popular classes. It is significant that the well-known passage by Appian regarding philosophers, who even in his time were violently attacking the rich and the power-ful,[40] is a result of his reflections upon the Mithridatic tyranny in Athens, led by the pro-populist and anti-Roman philosophers Athenion and Aristion.[41]

It is highly probable that Dionysius's experiences in his native land and in the ambience of the Greek cities of Asia influenced his reasoning. He was well aware that in many of the Asian cities from the Mithridatic age to the Triumvirate, rhetoricians had enjoyed a political preeminence that was often populist, in spite of their origin among the upper classes.[42] The political atti-tude of these intellectuals was not, however, unanimous: while the majority sided with Rome, supporters of Mithridates were yet to be found. The case of Metrodorus of Scepsis is not en-

38. I.4.3; F. P. Rizzo, "Mitridate contro Roma tra messianesimo e messag-gio di liberazione," in *Tra Grecia e Roma: Temi antichi e metodologie mod-erne* (Rome, 1980), 185–88.

39. For the abolition of debts in Ephesus and the liberation of the slaves in 86 B.C.: App. *Mith.* 189–90, 251, 257.

40. *Mith.* 110–11.

41. J. Deininger, *Der politische Widerstand gegen Rom in Griechenland 217–86 v. Chr.* (Berlin, 1971), 245 ff.

42. The most significant examples are listed in Bowersock, *Augustus and the Greek World*, 5–6; C. P. Jones, "Diotrephes of Antioch," *Chiron* 13 (1983) 369–80.

tirely clear, because this famous philo-Mithridatic historian was probably the son of the academic philosopher, who later became a rhetorician of Asian stamp whose instruction was followed by many Romans.[43]

At the time of the Triumviral civil wars, occasional bitter disputes within the cities of Asia Minor directly involved elements of the intellectual order: the case of Tralles is noteworthy.[44] The external tensions and the Parthian invasions also favoured internal disturbances: in Patara, around 42 B.C., debts were abolished and slaves were freed.[45] It is very likely that when Dionysius refers to the political preeminence and to the honours reaped by Asian rhetoricians in the cities, he alludes to the well-known cases of Euthydemus and Hybreas of Mylasa[46] and of Dionysocles of Tralles.[47] The rhetoricians encouraging the Asian tendency may have enjoyed the support of M. Antonius, a disciple of the Asian style and, as such, reproached by Octavius.[48]

This crude, pro-populist eloquence, which had reigned for some time and was not yet entirely smothered,[49] was eliminated

43. Jacoby, *FGrHist* II B.608–9; Bowersock, *Augustus and the Greek World*, 6; Theophanes of Mytilene is the best example in the first century B.C. of a philo-Roman intellectual hostile to Mithridates. By his intervention with Pompey in 62 B.C. he saved his native city (Plut. *Pomp.* 42.8; Vell. Pat. II.18.3; Strabo XIII.2.3; *FGrHist* 188 T 4a–b, 1). His historical work exalts Pompey, who was a friend of his, and was thus hostile to the king of Pontus (Plut. *Pomp.* 38.4 = *FGrHist* 188 F 1); Jacoby *FGrHist* II B.614; W. S. Anderson, *Pompey, His Friends, and the Literature of the First Century B.C.* (Berkeley, 1963), 34–41.

44. Strabo XIV.1.42: F. Münzer, *PW* s.v. "Domitius (23)," col. 1330.

45. Cass. Dio XLVII.34.4: T. R. S. Broughton, "Roman Asia," in *An Economic Survey of Ancient Rome,* ed. Tenney Frank (Baltimore, 1938), 4:584 n.33.

46. Strabo XIV.2.24; cf. Plut. *Ant.* 24.5–6: E. Rohde, "Die Asianische Rhetorik und die zweite Sophistic," *RhM* 41 (1886) 175; L. Radermacher, *PW* s.v. "Hybreas (1)"; C. Habicht, "Zur Personenkunde des Griechisch-Römische Altertums," *BASP* 21 (1984) 69–72 (on Euthydemos of Mylasa).

47. L. Radermacher, *PW* s.v. "Dionysokles."

48. Plut. *Ant.* 2.8; Suet. *Aug.* 85.2.

49. In Rome itself, where Dionysius was writing, the Asian rhetoricians Damas Skombros (often recalled by Seneca the Elder: Brzoska, *PW* s.v. "Damas

by the rebirth of classicism, which found its surest guarantee and stimulus in the undisputed dominion of Rome and in the certain confirmation of Greek cultural supremacy.

If we accept this interpretation of the *De antiquis oratoribus*, we may now clarify even further the significance of Dionysius's historiographical work. *The History of Archaic Rome* is connected with the present, as is outlined in the preface. This means that the history of Rome is the premise for the realization of the classicistic political and cultural ideal in the present. Roman history is interpreted accordingly and integrated within this perspective. The Greek historian strives to demonstrate that Roman history develops, expands, and concretely realizes the ideals of military and civic value—justice, *pietas,* and moderation—that Isocrates had lauded in the history of Athens. These virtues were naturally present in the original Greek formation of the Roman ethnos, a formation Dionysius was to reconstruct in his prehistorical and protohistorical phases. In other words, the Greek influence absorbed by the Romans was not at all something acquired in the course of their history; Hellenism was far removed from Asianism, because it was an original element. Upon these solid bases, Rome had consequently been able to assimilate the best. Augustan Rome is the celebration of Greek classicism now integrated within the new imperial context. It is the conclusive achievement of an historical process that has been unfolding steadily by dint of the merits and virtues of the Romans. It is almost a fatal development, but it is a necessary one.

III

But the classicism that was founded with the omnipotence of imperial Rome is above all the premise for a new historical de-

---

[4]") and L. Cestius Pius of Smyrna (*PIR* C 694 Stein) were operating with success. Rome was full of men of letters from Tarsus and Alexandria: Strabo XIV.5.15.

velopment that Dionysius wishes to promote on a cultural level
by means of his teaching. The revived classical ideals represent,
even more than they had before, the basis for moral, cultural,
and political unity among the ruling class, and no longer was
this to be confined to the Greek cities. These ideals, shared by
Rome, pave the way to an ever-deepening acceptance of the new
imperial society. The increased adherence to these ideals obviously results in open and diligent collaboration with authority. It is no coincidence that Dionysius also wrote a lost essay
directed, it would appear, at the Epicureans, proponents of political apathy, which attacked those who denigrated political
philosophy.[50]

From this perspective the philo-Roman position, as mere clients, common to the majority of the Greek intellectuals of the
first century B.C.[51] is now superseded. The Posidonian type of
political-classicistic justification for Roman dominion is also
supplanted, since the spontaneous emergence of a superior and
united classical culture coincides with universal Roman rule. In
this sense, then, Dionysius's historiography goes beyond the direct political tension underlying the most valid Greek and Roman historiography, which was a literary extension of the political struggle. Politics is transformed into a cultural statement by
Dionysius, who experienced the age of peace that appeared to
achieve unification under Augustus. It is no casual coincidence
that we find the *De pace* singled out from the orations of Isocrates for examination and praise.[52] The grave problems that be-
set the internal structure and imperial security are still rather remote: these difficulties will characterize the works of Tacitus
and Cassius Dio.

50. Dionys. *Thuc.* 2; W. K. Pritchett, *Dionysius of Halicarnassus On
Thucydides* (Berkeley, 1975), 49 n. 8.
    51. M. H. Crawford, "Greek Intellectuals and the Roman Aristocracy in
the First Century B.C.," in *Imperialism in the Ancient World*, ed. P. D. A.
Garnsey and C. R. Whittaker (Cambridge, 1978), 193–207.
    52. *De antiq. orat.* III (*Isocrates*) 7.1–5.

The problem that now must be confronted is how the current revival of ideals upheld by Greek orators and historians of the fourth century B.C. can survive in such a vastly different historical context as the Augustan age. Or, more precisely, how the authentic ancient eloquence, given the cultural world, rich with the spirit of liberty, that it presupposed, will be allowed full expression within the reality of imperial Rome. That culture certainly represented eternal values, which, however, had to be applied to a far different political structure than the *polis* of Athens in the fourth century. It differed also from the archaic Roman state, whose internal political life, dynamic and varied, was described by Dionysius in his historical writing according to the ideal of the Greek model.

This problem is not only posed by modern historians: it was already considered by Dionysius—who is aware, moreover, that his is not a universally held position.[53] The ancient discussion in a certain sense confirms the validity of my interpretation. Naturally, by this I do not mean that the texts to which I shall now refer were intended to reply directly to Dionysius. But Dionysius was certainly not alone in his critical analysis, which was both literary and political. He took his place in a diffuse line of thought interpreting the realities of his era. These opposing positions were evidently debated. One explanation, rather than solution, of the problem formulated above holds that the generation to which Dionysius belonged had just emerged from a long and tragic civil war that had involved the entire Roman state. This dramatic experience, which even spread within the Greek cities, will have to be taken into consideration in interpreting our author's *History* (a similar consideration is demanded when dealing with Livy's work). The age demanded order and peace; the Augustan empire was forming this new political and, above all, social order. The regime was not motivated solely by propagan-

53. I.4.2, 5.2–3.

distic considerations. Harmony with the aspirations of the majority was secured. Roman supremacy defended the interests of everyone. In all probability Dionysius noticed the existing tension between the traditional Roman ruling class and the *princeps,* but his view was concentrated on the Roman empire, not the emperor. The governing class, with which he was well acquainted, seemed to him to be composed of persons well prepared for administration of the empire. He was perhaps indulging here a notable degree of optimism or exaggeration.

There were those, however, who believed that the "world peace" (ἡ τῆς οἰκουμένης εἰρήνη) and the concomitant privation of liberty would lead to intellectual confusion and a consequent decline. Others stressed the moral aspects of the corruption of eloquence and literature. It is not known who was the author of the treatise *On the Sublime,* which was written in response to a brief treatise by Caecilius of Kale Akte[54] and which probably may be traced to the beginning of the imperial age or at least to the first century A.D.[55] A recent hypothesis connects

54. *On the Sublime* 1.1.
55. This determination of date, fairly widely accepted, is based on the reasonings found in Chapter 44, which makes a dating toward the middle of the third century A.D. difficult to accept, if the authorship of the rhetorician Cassius Longinus is maintained. The later date is defended by G. Luck, "Die Schrift vom Erhabenen und ihr Verfasser," *Arctos* 5 (1968) 97–113, and also by G. Williams, *Change and Decline: Roman Literature in the Early Empire* (Berkeley, 1978) 17 ff. Grube, *The Greek and Roman Critics,* 340–42, leaves the solution uncertain, but he does give credence to the dating in the first century. It should be emphasized that a precise chronological determination on the basis of a lexical, syntactical, and stylistic analysis seems impossible: differing conclusions are reached by M. Ferrario, "Ricerche intorno al Trattato del sublime," *RIL* 106 (1972) 765–843, and by M. Pinto, "Aspetti dell'atticismo nell'autore del Sublime," *A&R* 20 (1975) 60–71. A dating in the age of Nero is maintained by J. M. Crossett and J. A. Arieti, *The Dating of Longinus* (University Park, 1975). Also to be kept in mind are the editions by A. Rostagni (Milan, 1947) and by D. A. Russell (Oxford, 1964). On Chapter 44: C. P. Segal, "Ὕψος and the Problem of Cultural Decline in the *De Sublimitate,*" *HSPh* 64 (1959) 121–46; J. Bause, "Περὶ ὕψους Kapitel 44," *RhM* n.s. 123 (1980) 258–66.

the treatise to the family of the Aelii Tuberones, Dionysius's patrons.[56] Let us consider the final chapter of the essay, number 44, which may in some fashion represent an appendix to the work. Here reference is made to the opinion of a philosopher—who remains anonymous, nor is there any reason to identify him with Philo—who ponders the current want of truly sublime geniuses and the general sterility in the field of eloquence (44.1). The problem in question is a typical one regarding the culture of the first century A.D. The philosopher's explanation is clearly a political one: perhaps democratic freedom is the true sustainer of eloquence and greatness. Liberty fosters ideas, controversies, the quest for excellence. Democracy refines the elevated nature of rhetoricians. He adds: We today seem to be enrolled in an unfortunately legitimate (or deserved) servitude that impedes, blocks, and inhibits our enjoyment of liberty; we are mere adulators of the upper ranks. The slave cannot be an orator, because he cannot develop the habit of free thinking. Slavery, even in its most legitimate form, entraps the soul (44.2–6).

The explanation proposed by the philosopher—that the principal cause of the decline of eloquence is the disappearance of free political competition—will be proposed again by Tacitus.[57] A somewhat analogous explanation will be furnished for the lack of a well-informed historiography, since in the monarchic regime the historian, though politically aware, is no longer an actor on the stage of history, as he had been in the republican era.

The reply to the philosopher's considerations clarifies even further the deepest significance of the proposed explanation. Great minds, replies the anonymous author of the treatise, are ruined not by "world peace," but rather by the war that dominates spirits and passions: love of riches and pleasure, the lux-

56. Bowersock, "Historical Problems," 71.
57. *Dial.* 36–40; *Hist.* I.1; Desideri, *Dione di Prusa*, 84–88.

ury that derives from it, and all associated vices have the effect
of corrupting every spiritual activity. A purely political explanation of the intellectual decline cannot suffice; a moral decline,
which was also widespread in the course of the first century
A.D.,[58] must be considered as well. The conclusion is equally
striking: "For men like us, it is better to be commanded than to
be free" (44.10).

This conclusion enhances the validity of the initial consideration of the philosopher. To acknowledge one's own inability to
be free is a bitter realization that does not hide behind any justification of some vitalizing or positive function of the man who
holds power.[59] The claim that "world peace" (44.6) is not responsible for moral and intellectual decline is more subtle. The
expression "world peace" refers to the elimination of political
disputes at all levels with the establishment of the imperial peace
brought about by the uniform Roman dominion and by the governing of one man alone. This observation implies a different social and historical explanation of the cultural decline: for example, that formulated in the well-known passage in Pliny *NH*
XIV.1 – 6. Pliny sets forth the theory that the qualities of the in-
tellect had once been stimulated and favoured by the limited nature of states and by the shortage of means, and he notes that
political powers had even taken upon themselves wholehearted
support of the development of the sciences. The decline of this
intellectual fervor, which had led to important human discov-
eries, was caused by the expansion of the world (*laxitas mundi*)
due to the onset of Roman dominion and by the increasing
availability of means (*rerum amplitudo*). The desire for power
and for material possessions, with a consequent upsurge in de-
plorable vice, had cut off the development of the liberal arts.

58. Sen. *Controv.* I *praef.* 6 ff.
59. As occurred, for example, in the theories defended by Cicero, *Rep.*
III.36, "quod talis hominibus sit utilis servitus," which must be traced to the
justification elaborated in the second century B.C. for Roman domination.

The philosopher of the treatise makes no explicit mention of this theory, but it is implicit in his argument. The theory is clearly well known; it will be taken up again in Germany in the late nineteenth century, in the context of evaluating Greek culture in the first centuries of the Roman empire and of classicism in the Imperial age;[60] and even in the ancient world this theory already had a long history.[61]

Certainly the anonymous philosopher completely overturned the optimistic perspective of Dionysius. But even his interlocutor finally accepts the validity and the truth of the initial datum, that is, the decline of the highest eloquence. In both cases, an opposition to Dionysius's view is clearly present.

IV

The so-called *Ineditum Vaticanum*, published in 1892 by von Arnim,[62] is a collection of historical excerpta relating to Roman history. Because of the obscure heading of the text in the codices, it has recently been supposed that Caecilius might be the author from whom the excerpta are drawn.[63] Chapter 3 is particularly interesting. There, a Roman ambassador in the age of the First Punic War expounds the well-known theory regarding

60. Gabba, "Eduard Schwartz e la storiografia greca," 1039–42.

61. H. Fuchs, "Der Friede als Gefahr," *HSPh* 63 (1958) 363–85, esp. 384 n.61; Gabba, "Scienza e potere nel mondo ellenistico," in *La Scienza Ellenistica*, ed. G. Giannantoni and M. Vegetti (Naples, 1984), 16–18.

62. H. von Arnim, "*Ineditum Vaticanum*," *Hermes* 27 (1892) 118–30. The text has been republished in A. B. Drachmann, *Diodors Römische Annalen bis 302 a. Chr. samt dem Ineditum Vaticanum* (Bonn, 1912), and in Jacoby, *FGrHist* 839, which tentatively proposes a date in the first century B.C. S. Mazzarino, *Il pensiero storico classico* (Bari, 1966), vol. 2, pt. 2, 148–49, suggested a date *ca.* 100 B.C. He has since, however, modified his opinion: M. A. Cavallaro, "Dicearco, l'*Ineditum Vaticanum* e la crisi della cultura siceliota," *Helikon* 11–12 (1971–1972) 220 n.40. The first editor supposed that, on the basis of paragraphs 3 and 5, it could be traced to the tradition of Fabius Pictor, but that the text originated in the first or second century A.D.

63. M. A. Cavallaro, "Dionisio, Cecilio di Kalē Aktē e l'*Ineditum Vaticanum*," *Helikon* 13–14 (1973–1974) 118–40.

the ability of the Romans to appropriate and improve on the useful inventions of their adversaries. This almost amounts to a theory of *imitatio* applied to the history of a nation. Chapter 1 is even more significant. This chapter permits, in my opinion, a post-Augustan dating of the text, inasmuch as the polemic on the preeminence of eloquence and of theorists in ancient political life appears to be directed against the reconstruction of ancient Roman history that had been offered in Dionysius's historical work. More generally, the conception of political life from a cultural standpoint is attacked in the text. Such a conception had formed the basis for the teachings of Dionysius himself.

The sense of Chapter 1 is that the ancient Romans, unlike the Greeks, had no interest in appearing wise and never sought glory through well-constructed speeches or refined maxims that might become well known for their incisive brevity. Furthermore, according to Dicaearchus such maxims were not even the work of wise men, because in ancient times philosophy was not carried on with speeches; rather, wisdom had then been the pursuit of good actions, and only later had it become the art of composing speeches to move the people. Contrary to the present situation, in which the great philosopher is the man who is able to speak persuasively, in ancient times the philosopher was simply the man who behaved well, regardless of whether he prepared marvellous speeches. There was no theorizing as to how one ought to behave in politics: one simply behaved well. Similarly, there was no discussion of whether one ought to get married, but, once united in matrimony in the proper fashion, men lived together with their wives. These were, Dicaearchus always stated, the actions of men and practices of the wise. Aphorisms were in themselves unrefined. And so, adds our evidently non-Roman author, "your" ancestors (that is, of the Romans) too wished to be good citizens, and they reached that goal with actions. They did not seek or know refined and elegant aphorisms.

They carried out every action according to appropriate reasoning, and they made use of appropriate speeches for this purpose. Their speeches were not concise, but they do have considerable appeal if one relates them to their purpose rather than considering them from an epideictic standpoint.

Dicaearchus's arguments, perhaps related to the Βίος Ἑλλάδος,[64] can be understood in the context of his polemic with Theophrastus over the preeminence of practical political life over contemplative political life. The influence of this theory, apart from the significance of Dicaearchus and of his work in Roman antiquarian research in the first century B.C., can be discerned in the political thought of Cicero and also in Sallust (for example, the preface to his *Bellum Catilinae,* 8.5).[65] In the text of the *Ineditum Vaticanum,* the application of Dicaearchus's theory and his arguments to Roman history involves a precise comparison with the Greek world. Our text recognizes and attributes to the politics of Rome a system of priorities that valued action above the refined oratorical theory of the Greeks and even over the highly praised maxims of their Seven Wise Men. This priority of practice corresponds, furthermore, to the ancient phase of wisdom Dicaearchus postulated in his anthropological picture of life in Greece.

The value of this first reflection is ambiguous. On the one hand, the sober concreteness of ancient Roman political life is praised; from this point of view Roman *praxis* outdoes Greek cultural and theoretical preeminence as argued, for example, by

64. Rather than to the Περὶ βίων, F. Wehrli, *Die Schule des Aristoteles: Texte und Kommentar,* 2d ed. (Basel, 1967), Dikaiarchos fr. 31 (to p. 19), comments to 51–52; Cavallaro, "Dicearco," 217–18.

65. F. Egermann, "Die Proömien zu den Werken des Sallust," *SAWW* 214 (1932), 3d abh., 49–57. Cf. A. Grilli, "La posizione di Aristotele Epicuro e Posidonio nei confronti della storia della civiltà," *RIL* 86 (1953) 31 ff.; W. Richter, "Einige Rekonstruktions- und Quellenprobleme in Cicero *De Re Publica,*" *RFIC* 97 (1969) 70–76; F. Della Corte, "L'idea della preistoria in Varrone," *Atti del congresso internazionale di studi varroniani* (Rieti, 1976), 1:137 n.37.

Dionysius. On the other hand, archaic Rome is viewed as culturally backward. However one looks at it, actions, not theories, prevail. True wisdom or political philosophy does not consist of oratory. It seems that this concept should be seen as a reply to the theory, maintained by Dionysius and applied historiographically, that political life is carried out primarily with speeches and therefore requires considerable oratorical and cultural preparation. This is the view Dionysius defended and sought to teach practically. Naturally, action, which is considered to be more important, is not impulsive behaviour but, rather, reasonable behaviour accompanied by speeches that are appropriate insofar as they are suited to the purpose of that very action.

Thus it may be suggested that the argument of the anonymous author has historiographical significance and may be seen as opposing the introduction of elaborate political speeches into the most ancient historical contexts and, in general, opposing the anachronistic reconstruction of the remotest historical periods. This was indeed the case in Dionysius's *History of Archaic Rome,* particularly regarding the age of kings, to many of whom long programmatic discourses are attributed: Romulus, for instance, in the framing of his constitution, establishes precise and complex norms for marriage.[66] It should be stressed that even Plutarch, in the preface to his biographies of Theseus and Romulus, denied that those ancient times had historical credibility; yet he relied on his reader's forebearance when reading those legends.[67]

V

If the anonymous authors of *On the Sublime* and the *Ineditum Vaticanum* appear to be in conflict with the cultural and political outlook of Dionysius, a third author, Strabo, who also

66. *History* II.24–25. Cavallaro, "Dionisio," 125–30, associates with Dionysius, paragraph 5 of *Ineditum Vaticanum.*
67. Plut. *Thes.* I.1–5.

came from Asia to Rome after Octavian's victory,[68] holds roughly the same outlook as Dionysius. He demonstrates how the position of the historian was supported.

Strabo was aware of the close connections between exploration, geographical knowledge, and political power (I.2.1). First Alexander and then the Roman and Parthian empires had promoted a widening of geographical knowledge (II.5.12). This knowledge obviously had great practical political value (II.5.13). Geographical science was developing, therefore, with continual enrichment. It might, then, seem surprising that Strabo's criticism is directed against the great scientist Eratosthenes (I.2.1ff.) Eratosthenes opposed the utilization of ancient poetical texts, especially Homer, for geographical purposes (I.2.3). He chose to base his work on the great advances in scientific knowledge in his own age. Strabo, on the other hand, exalts Homer at length as a source of knowledge and historical and geographical notions of scientific value. The reason for this is twofold. First, since Strabo fervently upheld classical ideals, he could not reject the global history lesson that Homer had always provided for the Greeks. Second, he reasserts the historical priority and the fundamental value of poetry in education (I.2.6). Poetry, characterized by myth, the marvellous, and the fantastic, could furnish fundamental historical, moral, and religious truths to children and to the less learned, who were incapable of comprehending philosophical reasoning. History represents a later stage; philosophy, having come last, is for the few. Poetry, most of all Homer, fills the theatres and is useful to the people (I.2.8). In Strabo, an openly declared social and political intention directed toward the masses is grafted onto the classicistic root.

Strabo's merit lies in his explicitly confronting the problem of the practical utility of his research (Book I of his *Geography*) and its relation to the public at whom it was aimed. He claimed

68. Strabo X.5.3; Bowersock, *Augustus and the Greek World*, 123, 126 ff.

that geography responds to the needs of the man who holds political power. This geography is not different from moral and
political philosophy, but is superior to them on the level of
praxis. This involves a noteworthy theoretical reflection: geography presupposes a distinct and different technical knowledge
on the part of the person whose task is to discover the causes of
phenomena. The *user* of this knowledge is placed in a separate
category. To the politicians, fundamental notions suffice and
are, in fact, indispensable (I.1.16, 18−21). In other words,
Strabo distinguishes between the specialized scientist and the in-
telligent political user of geographical doctrine.

It is clear that Strabo intends his *Geography,* like his now lost
Histories, to be both useful to the public and political in nature.
His work was not produced exclusively for specialist consump-
tion. He clarifies what he means by "political" man: he does not
at all have in mind the uneducated person but, rather, one who
has completed the full course of studies normal for a man who is
free and interested in philosophy. Any other reader would be incapable of judging actions and the speeches that relate to them
and would not be in a position to blame or praise with awareness (I.1.22). Strabo's historical works were also useful in the
area of ethical and political philosophy and were directed toward the same readers, especially those in positions of responsibility (I.1.23).[69]

The cultural horizon of Strabo is the same as that of Dionysius; the two agree on many issues. They presuppose the same
class of Greek and Roman readers who have the cultural training necessary for receiving historical, geographical, and literary
teaching.[70] Dionysius even endeavours to furnish this type of
training, offering the critical instruments for an analysis of clas-

69. Ἐν ταῖς ὑπεροχαῖς: the same expression is found in Nicolaus of Damascus (*FGrHist* 90 F 135), with reference to Herod.

70. The readers to whom Dionysius addresses himself are defined in *History* I.8.3, V.75.1, XI.1.2−6, and *Thuc.* 50−51.

sical texts. Strabo, in the area of his own science, also knows the practical value and the possibility, beyond the purpose of general cultural training, of practical utilization of the knowledge he provides. He thus, more than Dionysius, relates himself to those who have the responsibility of government, that is, to the actual rulers.

Strabo's high opinion of Homer, on the other hand, corresponds to the exaltation of classical models proposed by Dionysius. In addition, the profound ideological value for the Greek and Roman world of a reinstatement of Homer at all levels is extremely clear. Strabo's criticisms of Eratosthenes presuppose an attitude similar to that of Dionysius regarding the literature of the age after Alexander, as his polemic on the attitude assumed by Eratosthenes toward Alexander demonstrates.[71] Eratosthenes criticized the advice Aristotle had given to the king, to treat Greeks as friends and barbarians as enemies. He held that the criterion that distinguished between *aretē* and *kakia* was far superior to the purely ethnic criterion, inasmuch as many Greeks were evil and many barbarians, on the contrary, were well-mannered—for example, the Indians and the Aryans—and were endowed with excellent political constitutions—for example, the Romans and the Carthaginians. Eratosthenes had therefore praised Alexander for disregarding that advice and for having accepted and welcomed all men of merit.

Strabo's position is both ambiguous and uneven in its criticism. He attempts to reconcile the opinion of Aristotle with the contrary behaviour of Alexander: the counsel of the philosopher, which opposed Greeks to barbarians, should not have been taken in the purely ethnic sense but, rather, as alluding to a distinction based on political qualities and on education and eloquence. Alexander, according to Strabo, had understood the deeper sense of the suggestion. The argument of Strabo is cap-

71. Strabo I.4.9; cf. Plut. *De Alex. fort.* I.6 (329b–d).

tious and equivocal and is fundamentally tied to a classical ethnic interpretation of the distinction between Greeks and barbarians. Plutarch, on the other hand, saw Alexander's action in its
true sense, as an historical break with the past.[72]

VI

The political-cultural proposal advanced by Dionysius could
be understood and evaluated in various ways. These ancient
positions are repeated by modern criticism: the many discussions of the classicism of the Augustan age are clear proof of
this. We are particularly interested here in the political aspect of
the problem. Even without wishing to pass judgment based on
knowledge of what happened afterward, it is impossible to evaluate such an important situation without considering its consequences. Dionysius has often been accused of proposing a solution that represents the typical compromise with those in power
arrived at by intellectuals originating from the ranks of the
upper classes. These, so the theory goes, were always ready not
only to accept in conformist fashion directives emanating from
on high but even to furnish theoretical support for these directives, thus providing ideological cover for those in power in exchange for a guarantee of social well-being for members of their
class.[73] This line of reasoning clearly aims at attacking the upper
classes of the Greek and western cities, since the problem in Italy
was obviously quite different.

For almost two centuries those classes had, to a greater or

---

72. W. Peremans, "Egyptiens et étrangers dans l'Egypte ptolémaique," in
Grecs et Barbares (Geneva, 1962), 131, and H. C. Baldry, "The Idea of the
Unity of Mankind," ibid., 191–92; H. Dörrie, "Die Wertung der Barbaren im
Urteil der Griechen," in *Antike und Universalgeschichte. Festschrift Hans
Erich Stier* (Münster, 1972), 154–59; Hengel, 68; E. C. L. Van Der Vliet,
"L'ethnographie de Strabon: idéologie et tradition," in *Strabone. Contributi
allo studio della personalità e dell'opera*, ed. F. Prontera (Perugia, 1984),
1:27–86.

73. Desideri, *Dione di Prusa*, 76 ff.

lesser extent, recognized Roman hegemony. Their acceptance, first forced and later increasingly spontaneous, derived from the realization, already explicit in Polybius, that the dominion of Rome was inevitable and ineluctable. With the advent of the empire that acceptance became even more spontaneous and, as such, had the effect of conditioning the imperial regime itself. The theorization and the justification of this acceptance of Rome, undoubtedly a not entirely unselfish acceptance, had non-Roman cultural bases: Greek political ideals, especially Attic ideals from the Classical age. In actuality, it was the revenge of the vanquished side.

Acceptance of Rome also meant, or was to mean soon afterward, willingness to participate directly in the imperial regime. The regime and the upper classes of the Greek world, with their cultural heritage, came more and more to represent two complementary and mutually indispensable entities. Without the support of the Greek upper classes Rome would not have been able to adopt a new approach to government in relation to the republican system, and without Rome the Greek upper classes would not have been able to remain on their feet.

It is also important to examine the possibilities offered by other stances on this issue. A decidedly antithetical choice, for Mithridates first and later for the Parthians, would have meant nothing more than a change of dominating rulers. Internal opposing groups were well intentioned but fanciful and, on the whole, sterile. These groups had, in a certain sense, to accept even more backward positions: an example of this is the opposition of the senatorial nobility of the first century of the empire. Agnostic or recalcitrant groups can also be imagined—and they did exist, but they sometimes decided, as in Mithridatic Athens, to cast their lot with the masses, who were naturally hostile to Rome. In this way, these opposition groups lost everything.

I have mentioned these complex historical questions in a quite simplified fashion in order to introduce one last text, which ap-

peared slightly more than a century after Dionysius but which
seems to me useful for a clear perspective on Dionysius's political proposal. The text is the *Political Advice* of Plutarch.[74] Plutarch writes for the young descendants of noble families of the
Greek cities, but he is aware that he also has a considerable
number of Roman readers. He gives realistic advice to young
people regarding the way to understand the internal local administration of their cities. These suggestions can be grouped
according to two fundamental points: the mode of exercising
local power, especially in its effect on the masses; and the behaviour and relations to be maintained toward the superior Roman
authorities. Even though friendly personal relations must be established with the Romans, the reality is that the provincial governor oversees the actions of the local Greek magistrates.[75] Therefore, the exercise of local power is decidedly subordinated to the
relationship with Roman dominion.

What emerges from Plutarch's brief treatise is that the Greek
cities are disturbed by discord within the upper classes and by
tensions between these upper classes and the masses. It is absolutely necessary to avoid discord of the first type; and in order to
cope with the second type of discord, financial regularity, non-
violence, and philanthropy must be combined with the maintenance of due respect for authority. Certain demagogical forms,
for example, are to be avoided.[76] It is above all necessary to
avoid overly frequent recourse to the Roman authority, which,
in fact, prefers not to be obliged to intervene. Furthermore, it is
dangerous in the present situation, and entirely out of place, to

74. *Moralia* 798–825. T. Renoirte, *Les "Conseils politiques" de Plutarque: Une lettre ouverte aux grecs a l'époque de Trajan* (Louvain, 1951);
J. Bleicken, "Der Preis des Aelius Aristides auf das römische Weltreich,"
NAWG (1966) no. 7, 231 ff.; C. P. Jones, *Plutarch and Rome* (Oxford, 1971),
110 ff.; interesting reading is the essay by E. A. Freeman in *The Chief Periods
of European History* (London, 1886), 211–40.
75. 813e; C. P. Jones, *Plutarch and Rome*, 133.
76. P. Veyne, *Le pain et le cirque* (Paris, 1976), 296 ff.

mention the former glories of Greek history, which contrast too strongly with the petty realities of contemporary life. Such references are dangerous because they stir the spirits of the masses in vain and thus create illusions.[77] Plutarch's historical examples are drawn from the heroic times of Hellenism, from the age prior to Alexander,[78] but they are directed at the upper classes.

Furthermore, the limited nature of the powers of the local magistrate in relation to the Roman governor need not be considered such a great evil: after all, there is sufficient liberty, and peace reigns among the *poleis,* a peace, moreover, whose only guarantee is the imperial regime. The exercise of politics therefore seems superfluous.[79]

Plutarch recognizes the common interests of the Greek and Roman peoples, but he certainly does not imagine a political integration of the Greek upper classes into the empire and its ruling class; on the contrary, Plutarch rejects and condemns such an integration.[80] From this standpoint, the lesson of Dionysius, implicit in his *History,* has not been accepted and its logical consequences have not been developed; on the contrary, his lesson has been totally rejected. The friendly contrast between Rome and Greece remains; we must stop at a stage of subordinated cooperation, even if, as the *Parallel Lives* teach us, the history of Rome and the history of Greece are on a level of parity. The limitations of action of the magistrate are rigid; "free" po-

77. 814 a–c.
78. C. P. Jones, *Plutarch and Rome,* 120–21; for the hostility in the *Lives* toward the Hellenistic kings, the enemies of Rome, see 124 n. 17. Seven Hellenistic kings are included in the *Lives:* J. Geiger, "Plutarch's Parallel Lives: The Choice of Heroes," *Hermes* 109 (1981) 85–104.
79. 824 c.
80. In *De ex.* 605 b–c, and in *De tranq. anim.* 470 c: C. P. Jones, *Plutarch and Rome,* 116. In Plutarch's age, Arrian is the best example of the successful social integration of the Greek upper classes: P. A. Stadter, *Arrian of Nicomedia* (Chapel Hill, 1980). Pausanias was patriotically attached to the great past of Greece but he was also of necessity interested in the Hellenistic period and had certain reservations toward Rome: C. Habicht, *Pausanias' Guide to Ancient Greece* (Berkeley, 1985), 95 ff.

litical life in the city is contained within confines that, in the
final analysis, are useful, because they distinguish the life of the
cities of the empire and because Plutarch, like Dionysius, sees
the empire as a guarantee and defence against a potential upris-
ing of the lower classes.

Disagreement with Dionysius's formulation may also be observed in the passages in which Plutarch proclaims the danger of
openly reminding the Greek citizens of his day of the illustrious
models of the past. Obviously, and this comes across in all his
works, Plutarch does not question the cultural value of education according to the classical model. What he means is that the
everyday use in city politics of examples furnished by great
events and personages from the glorious past of Greece should
be avoided. His acknowledgment of the hold that classical Greek
history, with its associated ideals of liberty, independence, and
value, still had on the masses is indeed noteworthy; but, implicitly, Plutarch does not view the Greek past as having the political validity attributed to it by Dionysius. This is true precisely
because of Plutarch's view of the empire as an entity created by
the Roman conquerors and having no wider significance. Thus
Greek history continues to be seen as an alternative to Rome,
not as a common patrimony within the empire.

Plutarch states that Greece's momentous past ought to be left
to the sophists for use in their schools.[81] In fact, as has been
pointed out, the most heavily emphasized classical themes of the
Second Sophistic are the glories of Athens and of Alexander the
Great: in Philostratus none of the examples cited is later than
326 B.C.[82] Something analogous takes place in Greek historiography of the first and second centuries A.D. According to E. L.

81. 814 c.
82. E. L. Bowie, "Greeks and Their Past in the Second Sophistic," *P&P* 46
(1970) 3–41; reprinted with several additions and corrections in *Studies in
Ancient Society,* ed. M. I. Finley (London, 1974), 166–209.

Bowie, the educated Greek classes in the first two centuries of the empire took refuge in the glories of the fifth and fourth centuries B.C. because they were dissatisfied with their own lack of autonomy and independence; their position therefore can be characterized as anti-Roman.[83] Despite the fact that it may not apply universally, this explanation cannot be entirely ruled out. It is noteworthy that the history of the post-Alexandrian period was set aside, even though it would have permitted a more decidedly anti-Roman stance based on the example of Timagenes, the historian who had in Augustan times written history in tones hostile to Rome.

Arrian's position as a Roman magistrate and a Greek historian is unusual. He personified the value of classical Greek culture and in particular the influence of Alexander's personality as a pattern for the contemporary world. He constantly modelled himself on Xenophon, even to the extent of echoing certain phases in the life of the fourth century B.C. historian in his own biography. It is possible that after Trajan's unfortunate Parthian campaign he put Alexander forward once again as an exceptional military commander. It is not, however, an easy matter to understand the why and wherefore of his treatment of the Diadochian story, even allowing for its value as military history. Perhaps his allegiance to the imperial regime was not as complete during the second part of his life as it had previously been.

At any rate, at the midpoint of the second century A.D. Appian of Alexandria, in his *Syrian Book,* treated at considerable length the history of the kings of Syria. Appian had also certainly devoted even more attention to the Ptolemies in his four *Egyptian Books* (now lost). It may be readily understood that it seemed preferable to treat of Cyrus and Alcibiades; it was

83. In the same vein see R. MacMullen, *Enemies of the Roman Order* (Cambridge, Mass., 1966), 189 and passim; as opposed to C. P. Jones, *Plutarch and Rome,* 126 ff.

scarcely considered respectable to speak of Nero or contemporary figures in general.[84]

Naturally, it is difficult to distinguish the different intentions
with which Greek classical history was brought back into cir-
culation. Dionysius's motivations for his classicistic position
were the contrary of those posited by Bowie, but Dionysius himself provides clear evidence of the strong diffidence and hostility
felt toward Rome. Yet, after the Augustan age, the general attitude of the Greek upper classes had been progressively evolving
toward acceptance of Rome and participation in its imperial
dominion.

The heavy stress laid on the classical age of Greece can be
better explained, even in the case of the Second Sophists, precisely in the sense suggested by Dionysius: as an exaltation of
Greek glory within the framework of an acceptance of Rome's
empire. In those events and in the literature that recorded them
the true ideals were to be found, ideals valid even in a different
historical context. On the other hand, Plutarch's refusal to glo-
rify the Greek past was based on his utilitarian analysis of the
requirements of city politics.

To conclude: the vision and the program of classical restoration championed by Dionysius had intentions and goals that we
can clearly discern in his *History of Archaic Rome.* His goals
were readily comprehensible and indeed topical within the context of the Augustan climate. They constituted the premises for
adherence to the empire, integration into its political life, and
the creation of an imperial ruling class. But I must stress that
this aspect of the classical rebirth was not the only one, even if it
must clearly be viewed as the dominant one. Setting aside the
openly anti-Roman opposition, we must not ignore the fact that
certain members of the Greek upper classes emphasized their

84. Dio Chrys. *Or.* XXI.11.

glorious past in defiance of Roman domination. And there were, finally, those who, like Plutarch, were able to imagine life in the Greek cities among the local aristocracies being carried on in apparent detachment from the menacing Roman reality, while they endeavoured to safeguard the spirit and the memory of ancient independence.

CHAPTER THREE

Dionysius's Historical Tenets and Methods

I

The development of Greek historiography, despite the connections linking its various strands, was neither linear nor homogeneous.[1] One of its more fundamental and distinct elements may be seen in the type of audience for whom the individual historians chose to write. The narration of history was organized, in both style and content, according to the category and interests of prospective readers. The aim of Herodotus was to present great and memorable events, the glorious deeds of man, and the vicissitudes of cities so that their memory would not be lost. He supplied important and often curious information on many peoples and countries, recounting their religious and civic customs. There is a continuity with the cultural world of the epic, which had seen a constant honing of the concepts of truth and falsehood along with an affirmation of the author's personality and capacity for judgment and criticism. But Herodotus was equally concerned with affairs of practical and geographical interest, as well as ethnography, all of which were linked to the phenomena of colonization that dominated, to a great extent,

1. These early pages adopt and develop ideas found in my chapter "Literature," in *Sources for Ancient History*, 3 ff.

the earliest reflections and enquiries of Greek criticism. In all probability the Herodotean opus was intended for public reading. At any event it presupposed an interested and curious audience, one not necessarily specialist or politically committed in any particular way. It is we moderns who read Herodotus as a cultural historian, projecting back onto him an all-seeing historiographical approach that developed, through Herodotean influence, only late in the fourth century B.C. with Ephorus and Theopompus.

Thucydides had other ends in view when he wrote his history. His work shows the political reflections of a statesman upon events of the greatest moment, events that, for many reasons, could be considered more important than anything that had gone before. His thought develops within a narrative that constantly holds its final aim in view, choosing and arranging the historical material to follow a constant line of interpretation. The reader is seen as a politician who might profit from the accounts and thoughts of the historian because of the similarities and analogies that future events may have, on account of the immutability of human nature, with those of the past (I.22.4). Man is at the centre of history. There is a continuity of content between Herodotus and Thucydides, but the two authors intend and narrate their histories in different ways. With little doubt they stand at the bases of two distinct lines of development in historiography.

With Thucydides, contemporary history is central to political historiography. Such writing requires its exponent to be himself a politician, expounding his own reflections on history to other politically involved men of his own and future generations. As can be seen in the work of Thucydides and his imitator Polybius, the historical content is of necessity limited to political and military events and the political wranglings of a given city or state. Such an approach depends for its validity upon the historian's belonging to the ruling class of his state. Only in this way can his knowledge and competence in political and military matters be guaranteed. The required competence cannot rest on the theories and works of one's predecessors as in the case of bookish historians. The function of Thucydides' particular way of recounting history is to facilitate political and historical forecasting. Adherence to the truth is one of its indispensable elements, along with research into basic causes and the sure checking of sources. Such exigencies may be of less importance to other forms of historiography that hold truth in no less high a regard. The class of politicians for whom Thucydides destined his work was, naturally enough, quite limited, and not everybody would be able to understand and follow political reflections of such complexity and depth. It was no easy task to maintain the high levels that Thucydides laid down: Polybius, for one, comes nowhere close to the set standard.

On the other hand, the example of Herodotus had already indicated the possibilities of a less politically oriented historiography, one not limited to wars and the internal strife of cities but more varied and open to cultural events. Along with its appreciation for the history of customs and institutions and an awareness of wider human and geographical horizons went a widening of the circle of potential listeners for a history that did not exclude moral instruction. Studies leading to classification and sociological synthesis by Aristotle and his school, as well as by Dicaearchus, were facilitated in the fourth century by the history of institutions, based on a rich documentation, often of local provenance. Ephorus and Theopompus, using a strict methodology, addressed a circle of cultivated readers and consciously proposed a model history of civilization, or global history, reaching beyond the frontiers of Greece to a universal vision. The decline of the *polis* and its particular politics favoured this widening of perspectives. The Sicilian Timaeus, following the example set by Ephorus and Theopompus, shifted the epicentre of Greek historiography westward. The Theopompan model would be adopted by Dionysius in opposition to the historical vision of Polybius.

The discussion of whether historiography or epideictic oratory is superior, as presented in Ephorus and later taken up by Timaeus, was the target of Polybian sarcasm (XX.28)[2] and bears witness to an awareness of the differences that existed between the two approaches. But it also demonstrates the common aims of the two literary genres, which consisted in the formation and instruction of a motivated public opinion. In other words they exemplified a broad pedagogical and moral—and hence political—purpose, in the Isocratean sense, which Dionysius would later make his own.

II

Before examining the personal vision that Dionysius had of history[3] and its purpose, and his criticisms of Thucydides and Polybius, we should focus our attention on certain passages in Polybius relevant to methodology. These are of help in understanding his concept of history and also serve by contrast to clarify the position of Dionysius and his opposition to Polybius.

At the beginning of Book IX Polybius distinguishes his own pragmatic historiography from works whose main concern lay in genealogy, the foundation of cities, and the origins of colonies. The preoccupation of the latter with gods and heroes and the roots of nations is contrasted with his own more contemporary political and military history, whose interests lay in the affairs of peoples and cities and rulers.[4] Polybius recognizes the single-mindedness of his own historiography, directed as it was

2. Diod. XX.1–2.2: of importance on the necessity of using speeches with discretion: argues that they are often out of place, prolix, and examples of epideictic oratory.

3. H. Verdin, "La fonction de l'histoire selon Denys d'Halicarnasse," *AncSoc* 5 (1974) 289–307.

4. G. Schepens, "The Bipartite and Tripartite Divisions of History in Polybius (XII 25e & 27)," *AncSoc* 5 (1974) 277–87.

at a single category of readers, the political class. Other histories, which he disdains and excludes, addressed a wider public, some being purely interested in presenting a good read, others directed to doctrinal or educational needs. While fully conscious of the necessity for some element of pleasure in an historical work, Polybius nevertheless intentionally offers to his specialized audience a text that will stand by the yardstick of utility. Like Thucydides before him, Polybius boasted of the great scientific and cultural progress attained in his epoch. The usefulness of history is, therefore, all the more enhanced by its being contemporary. In this sphere the historian may have something new to say, while historians of genealogy and bookish lore must of necessity repeat, if not regurgitate, things already said and well said by their predecessors; it goes without saying that nothing further could be added to such work. Elsewhere (XII.25h) Polybius asserts that the liveliness and sense of reality in an historical treatise stems from the personal experience of the historian, an experience derived in turn from being at the heart, as a political actor, of the events recounted.

This is undeniably a key point in Polybius's thought, bound up as it is with the historical period he lived through and his own awareness of it. There were, however, serious limitations to such thought. Contemporaneity was another matter; it is the experience of the present that makes a history even of the remote past and all its problems contemporary. In our case the history of archaic Rome was just as vital and contemporary for Dionysius as the hegemony achieved by Rome in the Mediterranean was for Polybius. Admittedly, for Dionysius, as for Livy, there is no unity of history and the actors who participate in that history. But for Dionysius such a unity is approached through his own activity as a teacher and his awareness of the high pedagogical and political purpose of history. He is not himself part of the ruling class; he is not even an exile. But he knows the political and cultural value that the teaching of history and literary criticism may have for the upper classes of the empire.

At no point in his work does Dionysius write solely for erudition or diversion. He knows how to write to a political end, and that his work has a political and cultural aim. He belongs to a different school from Thucydides and Polybius. His approach undoubtedly bears a closer correspondence to modern historiography, and this makes our own task in interpreting and evaluating his conception of history all the more difficult. We are greatly aided, however, by our ability to combine the direct examination of his historical opus with an analysis of certain very important passages in his critical and theoretical essays. Let us now look briefly at his *De Thucydide.*[5]

III

For various reasons of content and style Thucydides is considered by Dionysius as inferior to Herodotus. The value of the work as a sort of autopsy and direct experience of the events described is, however, fully appreciated, and in Chapters 5–7 Thucydides is placed in chronology and content within the framework of previous Greek historiography. In addition to Herodotus, such a framework also contained the local historians, to whom we shall return later. Dionysius's criticism attacks key points in the work of Thucydides. One notoriously difficult point was the historian's choice of an appropriate "point de départ" for his opus. Polybius springs to mind as a similar case. According to Dionysius (Chapter 10) the problem of composition and organization was complicated by hesitation before the difficulty of indicating briefly and in order the causes of the war. Moreover, the significance of the early chapters,

5. W. K. Pritchett, *Dionysius of Halicarnassus On Thucydides* (Berkeley, 1975); G. M. A. Grube, "Dionysius of Halicarnassus on Thucydides," *Phoenix* 4 (1950) 95–110.

where Thucydides seeks to explain the complex growth of human civilization with the intention of highlighting the Peloponnesian war as one of the greatest human events, does not escape Dionysius, who holds (Chapter 19) that Thucydides deviated here from the scope of his programme and produced a work that stands by itself.

Dionysius's criticism (Chapter 9) of the chronological disposition of the material emphasizes the loss of narrative continuity and hence of expositional clarity. The subdivision by seasons and the constant interruptions do not allow for a continuous recounting of events. By adopting this method Thucydides intended to take account of the contemporaneity of developing facts in order to understand their interrelationships. What is important to Dionysius, on the other hand, is a complete and circumstantial account of each separate event. His stylistic criticism of Thucydides brings him to the point of daring to rewrite the text of Thucydides in a fuller and more normal style, specifically to avoid brevity and obscurity, which he saw as leading to an inappropriately expressed logic and a lack of clarity in the work. This view may now seem stupid and banal, but it must be realized that Dionysius intended his stylistic comments for those who wished and needed to imitate Thucydides. All his criticisms must be understood in relation to those who made use of the history. Hence the importance of Chapters 50–51, which touch on the usefulness of Thucydides. According to some (perhaps Caecilius of Kale Akte) the style of Thucydides was suitable for neither political oratory nor private conversation; nor was it fit for debates before a crowd or in the courts. It was, they held, of use for writers of history, who might be well served in their search for solemnity by an archaic expression, an elaborate, obscure, or strange turn of phrase.[6] In fact the use of this style is

6. Same remark in Cicero *Orat.* 30 ff.; *De opt. gen. orat.* 15 ff.; *Brut.* 287 ff.

explained by the category of its users, who were neither ordinary people nor artisans nor poorly educated, but rather readers who had followed a regular course of rhetorical and philosophical studies, to whom this manner of writing was by no means unfamiliar. On the other hand, some contended that the historian wrote for his contemporaries, to whom such language was customary, and not for the readers of another era.

This line of argument does not take into account the precise audience that Thucydides intended to address, namely the political class. On the contrary the critical discussion here referred to looks toward a different use of the historical text, that of imitation. Even the response of Dionysius in Chapter 51 shares the same ground: to restrict the enjoyment of an historical work to a small and learned circle means depriving a wider category of people of a useful and necessary tool of awareness, much as political participation was restricted under the systems of oligarchy and tyranny. Those capable of understanding Thucydides are few and far between, and even they require a grammatical commentary. Dionysius, comparing Thucydides' writings with the writings of his contemporaries, also denied that Thucydides used the normal language of his day. He held instead that Thucydides' was a conscious deviation, a means of distinguishing his writing from common language. His efforts were self-defeating.[7]

It is important to realize that Dionysius intended his own historical work to be necessary and useful and above all accessible to a wide circle of educated and politically interested people. The work should, both in its content and in its exposition, correspond to their needs and cultural level. For Dionysius the type of person who would make use of his work is a central and fun-

7. A. M. H. Jones, *Athenian Democracy* (Oxford, 1957) 66–67 notes that the speeches in Thucydides have little to do with political oratory of the fourth century but have a greater similarity to those later used by Aristotle as rhetorical models.

damental problem. His preoccupation with this problem dominates even those criticisms that he levels at Thucydides' use of
speeches in his work. These criticisms extend over several chapters (14–18), using a wide range of examples, among which the
analysis of the revolt in Corcyra is particularly relevant. These
examples allow us to understand the part that speeches played
in the work of Dionysius himself, where from Book III onward
they occupy a third of the text.

Dionysius's criticism concerns the absence of speeches and
debate on important historical occasions that would seem to de-
mand them, while speeches are inappropriately inserted at other
points for the author's own ends. Thus the Funeral Speech in
II.35–46 is inserted for the sole purpose of having Pericles de-
claim it (Chapter 18). The fact that no speeches appear in Book
VIII is taken as a mark of carelessness. Dionysius's analysis
(Chapters 37–41) of the Melian dialogue is astute and merits
greater attention: his attitude is one of complete disapproval.
The author, he says, was not present at the event and, as he
makes no claim to work from eyewitness reports, he must pre-
sumably have invented it. Well and good; but the upholding and
arguing of the rule of violence is not fitting for Athenian generals. There is an inherent contradiction between such a portrayal
and the ideal image of Athens as a civilizing agent of humanity
and liberator of Greece in the war against the Persians. Nor does
such conduct conform with Athenian behaviour beyond her
borders. To place such theories in the mouths of Athenians is, in
Dionysius's view, baldly offensive. The sharp contrast between
the traditional wisdom of Athens and the line of reasoning followed in the Melian dialogue reveals the hostility of the historian to the fatherland that sent him into exile and the deliberate
and negative distortion of Athenian representatives in order to
diminish the stature of Athens.

This analysis is important for an understanding of how Dionysius wrote history and especially speeches. He leaves aside the given fact of the destruction of Melos. The historian should, with speeches, concern himself with portraying a coherent image, an image that matches not only the particular occasion described but also the overall ideal handed down by tradition. We are face to face with a use and assessment of history whose end is not simply practical and political. That is not to say that such a method of representing the facts is in any way less true than any political interpretation of the same facts. It is presupposed, unless proof to the contrary is forthcoming, that everybody plays their appropriate role in history. More to the point, the historian is expected to conform to these traditional and ideal roles in his reconstruction of events. One should bear this conclusion in mind when reading the work of Dionysius and particularly when examining the policy speeches attributed to major historical personalities.

Let us attempt to get a more precise idea of the position of speeches in relation to attitudes on historiography and hence a clearer idea of their value in the work of Dionysius.[8]

IV

Speeches had always been seen in Greek historiography as "historical facts" having full parity with any of the other events involved in the narrative. This was not simply a legacy from the traditions of epic poetry. The status given to speeches derived its legitimacy from the very reality of history itself. Such validity was based on the practice of politics, the democratic forms of Greek political life, the search for truth through discussion, and

8. F. W. Walbank, *Speeches in Greek Historians* (Oxford, 1965), now reprinted in F. W. Walbank, *Select Papers* (Cambridge, 1985), 242–61; cf. K. Sacks, *Polybius on the Writing of History* (Berkeley, 1981), 79 ff., and "Rhetoric and Speeches in Hellenistic Historiography," *Athenaeum* n.s. 64 (1986) 383–95.

the arrival at political decisions after free and open debate between contrasting opinions.[9] The fact that historian and politician were often the same person (in Greece and frequently in
Rome) reinforced the significance and value of an inherent
parity between word and deed, both being fundamental con-
stituents of history.[10] Cato had so far understood this politico-
historiographical reality as to include certain of his political
speeches in the body of his *Origines*.[11] For Dionysius, "what
had been said" had precisely this value within the framework
that enclosed his overall treatment of historiography. Moreover,
he made a point of the fact that in his histories the speeches included belonged to the ἀληϑινοὶ ἀγῶνες.[12] Hence only those
speeches are included that were "real," that is, made in political
and judicial debates. On the other hand, speeches of an epideictic nature (like those of Isocrates), because they were never made
in the heat of reality, were excluded, though they could serve as
exemplars to the historian for the development of his style.

The credit for this attitude in the sphere of historiography
does not belong to Dionysius. The difference was already implicit (as we have noted above) in the contrasting qualities of

9. Thuc. I.22.1–2: ὅσα μὲν λόγῳ εἶπον ἕκαστοι . . . τὰ δ' ἔργα τῶν
πραχθέντων κτλ. The idea is clearly expressed by Plato *Tim.* 19c: the history
of a state consists of κατά τε τὰς ἐν τοῖς ἔργοις πράξεις καὶ κατὰ τὰς ἐν τοῖς
λόγοις διερμηνεύσεις πρὸς ἑκάστας τῶν πόλεων (where διερμηνεύσεις
means conferring, the exchange of speeches with the enemy); Ephorus *FGrHist*
70 F 9; Polyb. XIV.1a.3. Naturally speech and narrative (corresponding to
word and deed) require a particular stylistic treatment: Dionys. *De imit.* III.3;
cf. *Pomp.* III.6; *Thuc.* 25 and 55; Quint. *Inst.* X.1.101 and also Dionys. *History* VIII.6.4.

10. The exclusion of the traditional political class from decision making
would, according to the senatorial historians, lead to a drastic decline in historiography. Naturally the best warrior will be the one who has come through
the most battles and the best politician the one who is most experienced in
debate: Theopomp. *FGrHist* 115 F 342 = Polyb. XII.27.8.

11. Livy XLV.25.1; Gell. *N.A.* XIII.25.15; H. Peter, *Historicorum romanorum reliquiae* 1 : CXXXVI.

12. *Thuc.* 42 and 53; *Isoc.* 11.3; *Pomp.* 5 (= *De imit.* III.2; cf. *Isoc.* 2.6
and *Dem.* 32).

epideictic oratory and historiography. Such differences were not confined to discussions and theories on a stylistic level. Naturally the fact that the historian was required to be a practicing politician originally played no little part in the contrast that evolved. Certainly Dionysius confirms this idea in the introduction to his *History* (I.8.3). There he qualifies his work as an effort at a global picture made up of real historical materials, which, while being useful to the politicians,[13] still allows room for a philosophical or theoretical approach and may yet, it seems,[14] satisfy a reader seeking some pleasure from the text.

Given this parity in principle between word and deed, the problem that inevitably and immediately presented itself to the historian and the theorist of historiography (from Thucydides to Lucian)[15] lay in finding a method of inserting the speech into the historian's framework, a framework that had always had the search for truth and the narration of historical reality as its fundamental objective. It was not always possible to follow Cato's example. Thucydides' famous chapter on his methodology (I.22.1–3) distinguishes "things proclaimed" from "actions" and recognizes differing degrees of difficulty in establishing, with any exactitude, the reality of one as opposed to the other. There is little doubt that any speech (leaving aside the practical results it may have achieved) presents major problems of verification of a nature different from those involved with, say, a political or military event. The problem lies in the close connection between the speaker and the event of the speech. Political or military actions are normally the result of more numerous and less personalized coincidences and interventions and they often contain elements of collective involvement. In point of fact Thucydides declares his own wish to come as close as possible to the conception behind what was really said, whether or not he was

13. Probably in the sense of a practical utilization of the historical works.
14. In this passage the text is corrupted: I follow the correction of C. Jacoby.
15. *De conscribenda historia* 47 and 58.

present on the occasion of the speeches concerned.[16] Such an approach must have conferred a great latitude on his drafting of the text—and not simply (as was said above) from a stylistic point of view. One can see how Dionysius might accuse him of inventing not merely speeches but even the occasions upon which they were delivered.

The difficulties that confronted Thucydides continued to multiply for those who came after him. In the first place the general historical framework had broadened. In addition there was a growing tendency to write histories of a noncontemporary nature. The reasons behind this tendency cannot be dealt with here, but they are bound up with the very development of historiography and the political and cultural history of Greece. Ephorus had been perfectly conscious of the problem and all its implications.[17] The solution found by Thucydides inevitably moved toward an emphasis upon the personality who delivered the speech and the occasion of its delivery. This principle is very clearly outlined by Callisthenes.[18] The argument in Dionysius's *De Thucydide* is based on this same idea and was applied in his own *History*.[19] Nevertheless, even for the historian of a remote past who wished to write a readable history, a particular speech, as a definite part of a sequence of events, was an historical fact that could not be eliminated, but was easily imagined and recon-

16. I follow in this point Walbank's interpretation.
17. *FGrHist* 70 F 9: οὔτε τὰς πράξεις ἁπάσας οὔτε τῶν λόγων τοὺς πλείστους εἰκὸς εἶναι μνημονεύεσθαι διὰ τοσούτων.
18. *FGrHist* 124 F 44: μὴ ἀστοχεῖν τοῦ προσώπου, ἀλλ᾽ οἰκείως αὐτῷ τε καὶ τοῖς πράγμασι τοὺς λόγους θεῖναι.
19. The contemporary historian should, undoubtedly, be in a more secure position if he can base his work on a more or less direct and sound knowledge of what was really said. According to the eminent opinion of Walbank this was the case with Polybius, and one cannot really disagree, despite the frequent presence in the speeches of influences from Demosthenes (C. Wooten, "The Speeches in Polybius. An Insight into the Nature of Hellenistic Oratory," *AJPh* 95 [1974] 235–51). Certainly Polybius's boast of adhering to what was truly said (II.56.1c; XXXVI.1.4: τὰ κατ᾽ ἀλήθειαν λεχθέντα) gives greater weight to his arguments against the speeches in Timaeus.

structed. Once its existence was given, the speech could be composed according to the criteria laid down by Callisthenes.

The historian may, and indeed must, choose the occasions and speeches he uses. This, naturally enough, is done in accordance with the ends of the historical work and thus in relation to its compositional layout. This is why Timaeus is criticized by Polybius (XII.25.a–b), who held that the former took advantage of every event to interlard speeches in his work. It is certainly no easy task, however, to understand the why and wherefore of some selections made by Polybius himself, who, for example, chooses to omit any mention of the debates that accompanied the decision to wage the Third Punic War (XXXVI.1.7).

V

It is in this area that we find Dionysius in opposition to the methodological reasoning of Polybius. At the beginning of his work Dionysius had already noted with some disappointment the previous summary treatment of early Roman history and had proposed for his own programme a type of global, historical narration that would also avoid the monotony of sectional histories (I.8.1–3).[20] The same idea is repeated at VII.66.3 precisely in relation to the presence of speeches in historical writing. The whole chapter is fundamental to an understanding of the historiographical intentions of Dionysius. The politico-ideological motif predominates and persists through contrasts with the στάσεις of the Greek cities, many of which had become famous examples. At Rome, on the other hand, the most important controversies on the political plane were resolved through discussion and thus required a full treatment, articulated through the speeches that had helped in their resolution. It is clearly shown how the narration goes about following the develop-

20. Probably, in polemics against Polybius: S. Gozzoli, "Polibio e Dionigi d'Alicarnasso," *SCO* 25 (1976) 157–58. Dionysius frequently affirms that he leaves out political debates: X.50.3, 52.1, 55.3, 58.1; XI.53.3.

ments surrounding a particular event.[21] The political principles
that underlie the interpretation of events are taken from Greek
political thought and applied in a context largely derived from
the annalists. Thus there is a unity of methodological concept
and politico-ideological intent. The writing must follow all the
developments of an event with the same accuracy as is devoted
to unravelling the various phases of battles. Historians, however, were often more interested in military facts and skimmed
over the struggles and internal political movements of states.[22]

How can this type of historiography be defined? I am no
longer sure that it can be dubbed "rhetorical," a term with dis-
tinctly disparaging overtones that I have myself employed in the
past. The obvious evidence that historians, while drafting their
narrative sections and speeches, may have applied stylistic criteria and artistic modes peculiar to their era and thus given their
work a suggestion of rhetorical learning is not conclusive. Such
evidence is not sufficient to implicate the entire process of historiography in a judgment that ends in the negation of what has
always been the ultimate objective of history, the search for
truth. P. A. Brunt[23] has shown admirably how the clear distinction between history and rhetoric is an underlying factor in the
work of Cicero and the thinking of his period. The search for an
effective style and a lively presentation was never regarded as an
alternative to the exposition of truth. There is, moreover, always
a presumption of prior critical work to establish the veracity of
data. The expansion of the narrative is no rhetorical fraud.[24]

21. E. Noè, "Ricerche su Dionigi d'Alicarnasso: la prima stasis a Roma e
l'episodio di Coriolano," in *Ricerche di storiografia greca di età romana* (Pisa,
1979), 21–116.

22. With possible allusion to Polybius.

23. "Cicero and Historiography," in *Miscellanea di studi classici in onore
di Eugenio Manni* (Rome, 1980), 1:311–40.

24. T. P. Wiseman, *Clio's Cosmetics* (Leicester, 1979), 27 ff. and "Practice
and Theory in Roman Historiography," *History* 66 (1981) 375–93. Less ten-
able is his basic thesis that there is wide evidence in the annalists of rhetorical

This line of reasoning may be applied with equal justice to Dionysius, and not simply because of his dependence on the annalists of the first century B.C. The reason lies, rather, in the fact that this type of historiography, which aims at accomplishing as full a treatment of its subject as possible, had to be the norm for those works that adopted a global approach to history and did not simply restrict themselves to listing the outcomes of events.

At any rate, more light is thrown on the historiography of Dionysius and its underlying theoretical assumptions when one analyses the highly positive evaluation of the historical opus of Theopompus contained in the *Letter to Pompey* (6.1.8).[25] It has been known for some time that this historian and his approach to history supplied a model for Dionysius. Theopompus (as also Ephorus) had gone beyond the traditional geographical confines of the history of the *polis* toward a more universal conception embracing both Greeks and barbarians. The focus of contemporary history was seen in the personality and political activity of Philip II of Macedon. It was not simply a matter of a political and ethnic opening out; there was also a cultural universality. The faith placed in political and moral Isocratean ideals carried with it a projection of these same ideals onto a wider historical framework. In Dionysius there is a proleptic application of them to Rome, as a Greek *polis*, to prove their validity for the Imperial Roman state. One of the few criticisms Dionysius reserves for

---

invention, which, judged by the criteria for truthfulness, is seen as pure reelaboration, corresponding with the historian's political stance. He insists on "pleasure" as the aim of this form of historiography, primarily destined for public readings.

25. On Theopompus: A. Momigliano, "Teopompo," *RFIC* 59 (1931) 230–42, 335–53, now in A. Momigliano, *La storiografia greca* (Torino, 1982), 174–203; K. von Fritz, "The Historian Theopompus: His Political Convictions and His Conception of Historiography," *AHR* 46 (1941) 765–87; G. Bonamente, "La storiografia di Teopompo fra classicità e ellenismo," *AIIS* 4 (1973–75) 9–86. Cf. R. Develin, "Pompeius Trogus and Philippic History," *SS* 8 (1985) 110–15.

Theopompus concerns his frequent and wide-ranging digressions. The variety of their contents, covering ethnography, mythology, religion, politics, history, anecdotes, and paradoxes, is ample testimony to a new taste and to an even wider and newer circle of readers.[26] This is a characteristic of the Hellenistic era. In this sense there is justification for the observation that Theopompus allows a preoccupation with narrative and descriptive interest to prevail at the expense of an appreciation of events. In Dionysius, digressions are conceived quite differently and have a fundamental relation to their context.

The unitary vision that Theopompus had of the *oikoumene* embraced all aspects of human life and activity, exhibiting the influence of the Peripatetic school. It was, in a certain sense, an attempt at global history whose origins lay in the political collapse of the *polis* and its history in terms of hegemony. But it was also a conscious return to a type of Herodotean historiography, a wish to go beyond sectional interests and draw attention to individual and collective ways of life and the attainments of great personalities. Dionysius assumes the historical method but not, naturally, the political intent of Theopompus. For Dionysius the archaic history of Rome is important in all its aspects and implies the future destiny of Rome in the Polybian sense of a unity attained through hegemony.

Dionysius begins his critique of Theopompus with a highly appreciative recognition of the author's care and effort in research, his seriousness in the preparation and collation of materials, and his critical judgment. This was undertaken to such an extent that his work in historiography appears as a lifetime's total dedication. Strangely enough the praises of Dionysius are expressed, in part, through the same terminology used by Polybius in his arguments against Timaeus while clarifying the du-

26. E. Gabba, "True History and False History in Classical Antiquity," *JRS* 71 (1981) 50–62.

ties of the historian (XII.27–28). The usefulness of this type of historiography to those interested in political philosophy is much superior to its formative function. This is evident from the variety of its contents. The origins of nations, the foundations of cities, peculiar lifestyles, Greek and barbarian customs, legislation and constitutions, the biographies and deeds of personalities, the lives and deaths of kings—all combine to make up the rich material from which the coherent fabric of the narrative is woven. In this way Theopompus responds to a desire for cultural accomplishment typical of his time. A similar stock of materials would be examined by Dionysius for the history of Rome. But he would picture the origins of the city and the early centuries in the light of a model for political life provided by classical Greece and not according to the new Hellenistic outlook of Theopompus himself. In fact, Dionysius describes a society structured after the lofty model of Isocratean morality. His praise for Theopompus is directed at the rich complexity of the historical framework, not at the immediate scope of his historiography. Theopompus is the opposite of the sectional historians criticized by Dionysius.

What Dionysius finds even more admirable in Theopompus is the constant reference to moral and philosophical problems inserted in the numerous and fine speeches. Reference has already been made to Isocratean epideictic and political speeches in Theopompus. The praise for political interest is linked to the pedagogical and instructive functions of historiography. Dionysius finally reserves his praise for the capacity for psychological investigation demonstrated by Theopompus and maintains that this is the outstanding characteristic of the work and the reason for his superiority over previous and succeeding historians. There is little doubt that psychological analysis and the uncovering of vice and virtue rapidly inclines to harsh emotional judgments and moralizing. This, in fact, was the case with Theopompus, whom Dionysius nonetheless praises for his "parrhesia." This contrasts with the attitude of Polybius, who had reproved the historian for malignity. The interest shown by Theopompus in famous personalities is typical of the Hellenistic age and accompanies the flowering of biography. Psychological investigation enabled Theopompus to uncover the hidden causes underlying events and place them alongside more evident motives. We shall have to bear in mind this distinction between true and hidden causes when we later examine the very conception of cause in Dionysius himself.

VI

How Dionysius intended to write his historical work emerges through his criticisms of Thucydides and his praise for Theopompus. We should now, however, combine what we have learned so far with what can be culled from some reflections on method within the *History* itself. The essential passages are Chapter 8 of Book I and the first chapter of Book XI, which opens the second ten books of the work.

In the preface Dionysius establishes the subjects of his work: external wars and internal sedition, forms of government, customs, and the more important laws. Each subject was to be considered in terms of its causes, development, and outcome. This is clearly a Theopompan programme, as is confirmed by V.48.1, where he declares that it is the historian's duty to relate not only the military and political activities of famous people but also their personal lifestyles. At I.8.2 Dionysius concludes that he will, on the whole, show "the complete life of the city." On the surface this claim would seem to allude to the famous work of Dicaearchus, *The Life of Greece*. In fact, as we shall see, the anthropological outlook of the Peripatetic historian and philosopher had no significant influence on the work of Dionysius. However, the method and techniques used by Theopompus in presenting the history of Greek civilization are now adopted by Dionysius for his history of the society and state of Rome. Ro-

man history is thus understood as a global history of Roman society in its historical development, an epoch-making period in
the story of civilization. For this reason Dionysius adopts neither a historiography whose sole interest lies in wars and constitutional details nor an approach in simple chronicle form. Such
genres were too monotonous and boring for the reader. They
had only partial value as history and were less useful for the political and moral ends that Dionysius saw as part and parcel of
historiography. A rich, problematical approach along Theopompan lines was preferable because more profitable to his
audience.

As has been said above, it was the declared intention of Dionysius to combine the techniques of political debate, philosophical thought, and pleasing narration in his work as a response to
the demands of a threefold public. This circle was made up of
those interested in concrete historical facts and their concomitant political debate, those of a philosophical bent, and those
who found reading history a peaceful and useful way of passing
their spare time. In point of fact the first two categories have
utility as their ultimate goal; the object of the third category is
pleasure. These ideas are confirmed at XI.1, where we also find
utility and pleasure as twin objectives of history. But Dionysius
insists above all on the idea that a circumstantially detailed history may be of use to those involved in public affairs. This group
includes those who pursue philosophy as practical action and
not simply as discourse. Again in V.75.1 the notion is repeated
that history and its noble exemplars (and in particular that of
Rome as master of the world) are useful not only to legislators
and leaders of the people but also to all who aspire to participate in public life and govern the state. The past is always seen
in terms of the present.

A comparison with the reader Dionysius intended for his *De
antiquis oratoribus* reveals an identical perception of his audience. Even comparison with the public of Strabo shows that Dio-

nysius, like Strabo, pictures true politicians among his audience. These indications of the intended audience enable us to overcome the tangled problem of whether his readers were Greeks or Romans: Dionysius thought primarily in terms of Greek readership.[27] Certainly he had Roman friends in high positions to whom he dedicated certain of his opuscules on literary criticism; that is not to say that he had them solely or principally in mind as readers of the *History*. His audience consists of the upper classes of imperial society, above all those in the Greek cities. The great Isocratean model meant something to these people. It was a practical instruction, both political and moral, which was based on an imitation of epideictic oratory but which Dionysius had transposed, to his readers' benefit, in his reconstruction of the history of Rome.

VII

Historiography of this type, with its varied content and usefulness, was suitable for this readership mainly because of the way the material was approached. Dionysius insists particularly on this point. To such readers a mere mention of the event and its outcome is not enough. They require a detailed and circumstantial exposition of its causes, along with the overall develop-

27. If the passage at I.4.2 (Greek ignorance of Roman history) is indecisive and if the reference at I.6.4 to Roman degeneration from their forebears makes one think of a Roman public, nonetheless, II.63.1 and XVI.4.1 clearly indicate Greek readership (ἑλληνικαῖς ἱστορίαις can only have been written for Greeks). A Roman public was envisaged by J. Palm, *Rom, Römertum und Imperium in der griechischen Literatur der Kaiserzeit* (Lund, 1959), 10–11, and Bowersock, *Augustus and the Greek World*, 130–31. A more moderate position is found in B. Forte, *Rome and the Romans as the Greeks Saw Them*, 195–96. The comparison of Roman dating with Greek seasons (presenting its own difficulties) has to be understood as intended for Greek readers: I.32.5 (see the commentary of Cary, 1 : 104–5), 38.3, 88.3; IX.25.1. The Greek rendition of Roman political terminology is more complex. As a rule Dionysius uses Athenian terms: J. H. Oliver, *The Athenian Expounders of the Sacred and Ancestral Law* (Baltimore, 1950), 102–9 (dealing with the sacred colleges in II.73).

ment of events and even details of any eventual divine intervention, in order to ensure that they are left uninformed of none of
the circumstances that naturally attend those events (V.56.1; cf.
III.18.1, XI.1.2–6). In other words, the event must not simply
be the object of a mention, which allows an eventual political
reassessment. The paradigmatic importance of an event and
hence its formative and instrumental value lies, not simply in its
outcome (the Greek victory over the Persians, the subjugation of
Athens by Sparta after defeat), but precisely in following the development of its causes, the intentions of the actors involved,
and the manner of its accomplishment.

Writing history in this way is best exemplified in Dionysius by
the long narrative of the first struggle in Rome between patricians and plebeians after the fall of the kings. Introduced in
Book V, the episode is carried over to a great extent through
Books VI and VII and also encompasses the affair of Coriolanus. It was of great significance and was supposed to serve by
way of contrast to the στάσις at Corcyra in Thucydides. It allowed the conclusion that in Rome the gravest of civil discords
were resolved peacefully, while such was far from the case in a
Greek *polis*.

Such fullness of historical description achieved the aim of allowing the reader to partake in every detail of an event. The
chief praise given by Dionysius to the orator Lysias is, in fact,
for his success in organizing a speech without neglecting any of
the key elements and in presenting them so that the listener
could readily believe himself in conversation with those involved.[28] This type of participation, which Dionysius wished to
recreate in his history, is entirely different from the emotional
participation sought by the so-called dramatic or tragic historiography seen in Duris or Philarchos, of which Dionysius dis-
approved. It becomes easier now to see why Dionysius should

28. *Lys.* II.15.1–2, II.7.1–3.

reproach Thucydides for interruptions and obscurity. For Thucydides the thought that an event gave rise to was of even greater importance than the event itself.

This depiction of an event in its totality has the added advantage that the historian can make its causes absolutely explicit. Dionysius knows, however, that descriptive completeness does not suffice to explain how something came about. The ultimate reason for its genesis lies in the minds of men. It is at this juncture, in the search for hidden causes, that the capacity for psychological analysis, which Dionysius so admired in Theopompus, comes into play. This methodology may not measure up to the causal analysis found in Thucydides or Polybius, but one must remember that the historiography of Dionysius is different from that of an historian preoccupied with contemporary history.

For our historian one of the merits of his precision (ἀκρίβεια) lay in a richness of detail. Without a doubt Dionysius did not verify all the material he used. It has been said that he limited himself to a workmanlike synthesis of what his sources supplied and that he evaluated his information according to its inherent probability. It is true that he often makes a choice between two conflicting accounts on the somewhat dangerous grounds of verisimilitude. Such a negative appraisal, however, lacks justice insofar as it is restricted by our own critical parameters. Dionysius was often critical of his sources, especially when dealing with problems of chronology. Many of his arguments are of great value. His better qualities and his ἀκρίβεια emerge from his analysis of the authenticity of the orations in the fourth century B.C. His essay on Dinarchus is a model effort, where pseudo-epigraphical criticism is renewed on a scientific foundation.[29]

29. M. Untersteiner, "Dionigi di Alicarnasso fondatore della critica pseudepigrafica," *Anales de filología clásica* 7 (1959) 76–93; G. Marenghi, *Dionisio di Alicarnasso: Dinarco* (Milan, 1970).

In fact, the attainment of a complete exposition of an event entailed the necessity of filling possible lacunae in its genesis. So, for example, speeches might be introduced or quite naturally presumed on the basis of a general intuition of the fact itself and its context.[30] Such a procedure is fundamentally analogous to that followed by the late Roman annalists, who, in all seriousness and with a wholehearted belief in a substantial continuity of both problems and institutions, reconstructed the ill-known archaic phase of the city by following the political and ideological pattern of contemporary life. In a certain sense this is an upside-down application of the Thucydidean principle of an inevitable repetitiveness in history because human nature is in essence unchanging. The connection between the annalists and the law—historian and jurist were often one and the same person—seemed to confirm the method, inasmuch as they both sought and re-created in the past the origins and development of judicial and political institutions. Within a cyclical conception of history, which effectively ignored the idea of progress and insisted on the political and human value of its lessons for the future, it was a natural step to picture a substantial uniformity in historical problems over a long arc of time and hence to reconstruct the past from the present—all the more so when the continuity of political tradition in the exercise of power was guaranteed by the Roman ruling class itself. It is in this light that verisimilitude and convenience could pass for the truth in an historical reconstruction. Dionysius followed the Roman annalists closely, and it is quite probable that the greater part of

30. The problem can also be posed for modern historiography. G. De Sanctis, in his negative review of the first volume of G. Ferrero's *Grandezza e decadenza di Roma* (Milan, 1902) (*BFC* 8 [1901–2] 274–79 = De Sanctis, *Scritti Minori*, vol. 6, pt. 1, 37–42), criticizes, among other things, the description of the triumph of Pompey in 61 B.C. (p. 430) because it was not based on ancient evidence nor totally convincing. The English translation of A. E. Zimmern (New York, 1908), 1:278–79, leaves out the more disputed passages.

the speeches that he reelaborates according to his own rules had already been touched on or amplified in his sources. Indicative of this is the point, made at VI.83.2, that the famous speech of Menenius Agrippa featured in all the histories. Contrasting with the elaborate oration in Dionysius is the observation by Livy (II.32.8) that Agrippa delivered his speech in the rude tongue of his own time.[31] Livy, however, omits any quotation from the speech, perhaps as a reaction to the anachronistic reconstructions found in his predecessors.

A worthwhile example of "complete" narration may be found in the previously mentioned episode of the first Roman stasis and Coriolanus. A recent examination of this broad section of the work has shown the reelaboration of the vast material supplied by the annalists, according to Isocratean moral and political ideals that are congruent with the political objectives already present in the sources. This event was chosen by Dionysius to contrast with the episode at Corcyra in Thucydides and to uphold his thesis of nonviolent conflict in the political struggles of archaic Rome. Dionysius is well aware that matters proceeded differently after the Gracchi (II.11.2−3). By extending the narrative he can draw a wide range of important themes within the ambit of the episode, thus conferring upon it the value of a general paradigm. The themes were already present in the sources, but they acquire fresh relevance in the context of Dionysius. The principal problems dealt with include the *senatus consultum ul-*

31. Tac. *Dial.* 17.1; 21.7. As examples of falsification of speeches by the annalists, two cases may be cited: the speech of Tib. Sempronius Gracchus in Livy XXXVIII.56.10−13, where there are traces of Sullan and Caesarian elements (T. Mommsen, *Römische Forschungen* [1864−79], 2:502; P. Fraccaro, "I processi degli Scipioni," in *Opuscula* [Pavia, 1956], 1:328; G. De Sanctis, review of *Studies on Scipio Africanus,* by R. M. Haywood, in *Scritti Minori,* vol. 6, pt. 1, 506−8); and the speech by Servius Tullius in Dionys. IV.11.6, where we find a famous phrase of Caesar's (T. Mommsen, *Die römische Chronologie bis auf Caesar* [2d ed., 1859], 168 n. 328; E. Gabba, "Studi su Dionigi da Alicarnasso. II. Il regno di Servio Tullio," *Athenaeum* n.s. 39 [1961] 99−102).

timum; the tribunate of the plebs; the *iudicium populi* and the responsibility of the people in judicial proceedings, along with, in more general terms, the responsibility of the *comitia* in relation to the *auctoritas senatus;* the *frumentationes;* and the mixed constitution. To these are added certain topics peculiar to historiography of the first century B.C. but projected back upon the fifth century, such as the march on Rome by Sulla (Coriolanus) and the problem of debts.

VIII

Of necessity Dionysius had to rely on Roman historiography when writing his history of archaic Rome. Comparisons with the tradition of Greek historiography are not lacking. His excursus on the tyrant Aristodemus of Cumae (VII.3–11) is well known and rests on a Cumaean chronicle transmitted perhaps by Timaeus and regarded as truthful by A. Alföldi.[32] The great majority of the information on archaic Rome handed down by Greek sources is preserved for us by Dionysius in Book I. In fact the book presents a special case, and Dionysius had published it separately (VII.70.2). He had no high opinion of Roman historiography. The oldest authors, he felt, had treated archaic history summarily (I.6.2); errors in chronology were frequent and often highlighted in his work (II.74.5; IV.6–7, 30.2–3; VII.1.4–6). Dionysius places Roman historians firmly in the category of local historians, for whom he had, nonetheless, a certain regard, as he showed in *De Thucydide* 5 and 7. In these passages he mentions certain pre-Thucydidean logographers, probably known to him by way of Hellenistic "reprints." Such historiography, more than likely derived from models received from the Near East,[33] had continued to exist afterward, with dif-

32. *Early Rome and the Latins* (Ann Arbor, 1965), 56 ff.
33. S. Gozzoli, "Una teoria antica sull'origine della storiografia greca," *SCO* 19–20 (1970–71) 158–211; L. Troiani, "Contributo alla problematica

ferent ends in view, alongside mainstream historiography. The merit of these local histories lay in their making public much information relative to their cities that had been conserved in sacred and profane places, rich in legend, myth, and fable, a patrimony passed down from father to son. This legendary and mythical material had been eliminated by Thucydides, and Dionysius also rejects divine myth from his history, though still accepting human legend (I.77.3). Local historiography is deemed important because it preserves information from local historians who may be presumed better informed on indigenous facts and problems. This is, in fact, the case with the traditions preserved by Roman ἐπιχώριοι, of which the information in Cato and Varro on the Sabines is a typical example. Thucydides had already (I.20.1) called for a cautious approach to information handed down from tradition and on the necessity for its verification. Dionysius was also aware that local traditions required accurate assessment and confirmation (VII.70.2). However, he could not but accept data supplied by the Roman annalists, despite its leavening of antiquarian material.

On a problem of chronology Dionysius consulted the archives of a family of censors.[34] This type of documentation, preserved by noble families, must have given him some guarantee of the authenticity of such material, circulated as it was by historians in their works, particularly if these historians were also senators. Varro himself was led into error by the reconstructions of Valerius Antias.[35] The verification of information and the validation of sources for noncontemporary history obviously pre-

---

dei rapporti fra storiografia greca e storiografia vicino-orientale," *Athenaeum* n.s. 61 (1983) 427–38.

34. I.74.5; E. Gabba, "Un documento censorio in Dionigi d'Alicarnasso I 74.5," in *Synteleia, Vincenzo Arangio-Ruiz* (Naples, 1964), 486–93; the sacred and secret books quoted in XI.82.3 can be identified with the so-called *libri lintei:* Livy IV.7.12 and R. M. Ogilvie, *A Commentary on Livy, Books 1–5* (Oxford, 1965), *ad* l.

35. Wiseman, *Clio's Cosmetics,* 46.

sented greater difficulties than the judgment of facts occurring within the historian's own lifetime, concerning which he might be able to bear witness personally or at least be in a position to retrace contemporary testimony.

The reconstruction of Dionysius, however, is not the simple repetition of annalist lore. It represents the selection of material from the annalists and its insertion within the framework of a civil, political, social, and institutional history whose scope was to prove the "Greekness" of the Romans and underline this factor as the constant and characteristic element of their history. The Greekness of the Romans was the premise for their moral and political superiority over the other Greek city-states and hence their right to hegemony. Roman superiority to Athens and Sparta was explained by the Roman capacity to assimilate other populations, as opposed to the obtuse exclusiveness of the Greeks.[36] This parallels a willingness to adopt foreign institutions once their greater worth was recognised. This is an historical and political observation that runs from the inscription of Philip V of Macedon to the Larissans of 217 B.C., to the speech

36. I.9.4; II.17.1–2; XIV.6.2–6; a negative stance in P. Gautier, "'Generosité' romaine et 'avarice' greque: sur l'octroi du droit de cité," in *Mélanges d'histoire ancienne offerts à W. Seston* (Paris, 1974), 207–15, followed by Y. Garlan, *Les ésclaves en Grèce ancienne* (Paris, 1982), 96–97. The theory of Dionysius derives from his conception of slavery in the most ancient period of Rome, when the slave, as booty, was a conquered Italian enemy who could shortly be manumitted and incorporated within the citizenry: IV.22–24; Gabba, review of *Ancient Slavery and Modern Ideology,* by M. I. Finley, *Athenaeum* n.s. 60 (1982) 279 n.2; F. De Martino, "Intorno all'origine della schiavitù a Roma," *Labeo* 20 (1974) 163–93, reprinted in F. De Martino, *Diritto e società nell'antica Roma* (Rome, 1979), 130–61; E. Ferenczy, "Clientela e schiavitù nella repubblica romana primitiva," *Index* 8 (1978–79) 167–72 (relations between slaves and clients). At another point, indiscriminate manumission seems, for Dionysius, to be a reason for the corruption of the body politic. His line of argument reflects the discussions that led in 4 A.D. to the *Lex Aelia Sentia:* E. Pais, "Dionigi d'Alicarnasso e la legge Aelia Sentia," *RAAN* n.s. 18 (1904) 191–99; G. Fabre, *Libertus. Recherches sur les rapports patron-affranchi à la fin de la république* (Rome, 1981). Cf. G. Poma, "Schiavi e schiavitù in Dionigi di Alicarnasso," *RSA* 11 (1981) 69–101.

by the Emperor Claudius in the Senate recommending the admission of the Gauls to the *ius honorum* and the rewriting of the
same in the work of Tacitus.[37] To Dionysius the motif was a
canon of historical interpretation that could lead to a surmounting of the ethnic problem of Greekness and to the acceptance of
an antithesis between Greekness and barbarianism, the former
quality linked with intelligence and moral attitudes toward others, as well as a consequent respect for human nature.[38] This
motif of Greekness is supported by continuous reference to and
contrast between the institutions of archaic Rome and the Greek
world. The connotation of a somehow Greek Rome still persisted in the historian's own time and this Greekness was a living
and vital fact, not some erudite hypothesis. It was not a matter
of determining to what extent Rome had borrowed from Greece
but rather of proving the continuity of original Greek elements
in the Roman people, among whom, moreover, these elements
had undergone a development. These elements accounted for
Roman ascendancy.

Material from the annals thus loses, at least in part, some of
its original character. It assumes a new character within the
overall framework of Dionysius. Certain specific cases can be
pointed out as characteristic examples to demonstrate the new
function and reworking of the annals and antiquarian material.
In his description of the foundation of Rome and the constitution of Romulus, Dionysius runs a serious risk of obvious anachronism in order to show, for the purpose of argument, Greek

37. On the dating of the inscription *SIG* 543: C. Habicht, "Epigraphische
Zeugnisse zur Geschichte Thessaliens unter der Makedonische Herrschaft," in
ΑΡΧΑΙΑ ΜΑΚΕΔΟΝΙΑ (Thessaloniki, 1970), 273–79; on the speech of
Claudius (Tac. *Ann.* XI.23–25; *ILS* 212): A. De Vivo, *Tacito e Claudio:
Storia e codificazione letteraria* (Naples, 1980); Gabba, review of *Tacito e
Claudio,* by Arturo De Vivo, *Athenaeum* n.s. 59 (1981) 245–46.
38. XIV.6.2–6 (Roman generosity toward the Tusculans); XIX.9 (a Ro-
man embassy is mocked by the Tarentines for its poor command of the Greek
language and considered barbarian).

characteristics in the foundation of the city. The well-known chapters on the client system, placed in the context of the constitution of Romulus, are a remarkable adjunct to social history. The author has understood perfectly the political weight of the institution in its historic development, whatever its source or original context. The religious institutions of Numa played an important part in the anthropological framework that led to Roman civilization, with the intervention of great personalities as a constant determining factor. The description of the timocratic constitution of Servius Tullius and the resumption of oligarchic ideas in the wake of Sulla (concepts also found in Cicero and Livy) are reflections indicating a desire in Dionysius to filter an evaluation of the moderate tendencies of the upper classes through a reconstruction of the ancient model. We could go on listing examples, but at least one other case must be mentioned here to illustrate that the reelaboration of the available sources was not simply formal. I refer to the long excursus on the Ludi Magni (VII.70–73), about which I shall have more to say later. The passage is based almost word for word on the work of Fabius Pictor, with interspersed comments by Dionysius. This is not a literary artifice. Fabius Pictor's argument is worthy of the sharpest Greek ethnographical and anthropological criticism and was useful in the demonstration of the Greek origin of the Romans. It is upheld by the autopsy of Dionysius, who acts as a guarantor, here and elsewhere, of the validity and sincerity of the information.

Dionysius's observation and use in his historiography of such facts as the archconservatism of religious, as compared to civil, institutions and more marginally the diffusion of Roman cults in Greece, as well as the distinction made between the protohistoric and later Hellenistic periods in the hellenization of Rome, all reveal a noteworthy attention to facts and cultural history. His adherence to those facts is not under discussion here. His implicit judgment of the work of Fabius Pictor, whatever the purpose of the original passage recorded and analysed by Dionysius, indicates a close reading of the sources and a precise assessment of their cultural status.

What has been said thus far is not intended to transform Dionysius into an historian of the first rank. I have sought to understand his most fundamental ideas and his methods of work. The examination of Book I will clarify with greater precision the historian's critical capacity and the structure of his work.

Appendix: Comments on Polybius
XII.25a–25b

On this passage see F. W. Walbank, *A Historical Commentary on Polybius* 2:385–86. Polybius argues against Timaeus and here condemns speeches that neither exactly repeat what was said nor give a true sense of their original content. None of the three types of oration introduced by Timaeus satisfies his requirements. The meaning of XII.25a.3 is not at all clear: the speeches are key points in historical events and bind the entire history together (καὶ συλλήβδην πᾶν τοιοῦτο γένος ἃ σχεδὸν ὡσεὶ κεφάλαια τῶν πράξεών ἐστι καὶ συνέχει τὴν ὅλην ἱστορίαν). Thus their divergence from the truth is all the more serious. The phrase has general application on the basis of XIV.1a.3 and XII.25b.4, where speeches are τὸ τῆς ἱστορίας ἴδιον, and Polybius argues, from a superior point of view, against the non-adherence to truth and reality. The whole of XII.25b insists on the value of political speech as an essential element of history, even taking precedence over investigations into the causes of a negative or positive outcome of words and deeds. Polybius fully grasped the idea that the actor/narrator of a particular historical event speaks in a given oration and that the historian should, particularly in these instances, be able to relate the whole truth.

Section XII.25a.5 is important for an understanding of Timaeus and hence of Dionysius. Polybius reproves Timaeus for wishing to enumerate and reproduce speeches on every conceivable occasion and also for giving their contents according to what ought to have been said in the circumstances. This is precisely the theory and practice of Dionysius. Polybius reaffirms his own point of view in II.56.10 with words almost identical to those in XII.25a: there is no need to take advantage of every occasion to record a speech and its circumstances.

The passage in XXXVI.1.1–7 is also important. Polybius confirms his intention to omit any repetition of the speeches made on the occasion of the decision to enter upon the Third Punic War, despite the fact that he must have been familiar with extant material of great richness relevant to an occasion of exceptional moment. Just as a politician should not intervene at every juncture, so the historian must behave toward his readers, not parading his ability ostentatiously but rather making a choice, after the most accurate possible evaluation of exactly what was said, to relate the more vital and particularly effective parts. The reasons behind this Polybian renunciation may be various (also of a political nature: Walbank, *Commentary* 3: 651–53). In XXIX.12 the search for the essential is justified by Polybius in relation to the breadth of his work (Walbank: *Commentary* 3: 373ff).

CHAPTER FOUR

History and Antiquarianism

I

Cicero's wistful reflection on the history of archaic Rome, "sed obscura est historia Romana,"[1] is a fair indication of the difficulties facing any ancient historian seeking to give a complete and in-depth account of events in ancient Rome. Livy, as we know from his *praefatio,* wished to describe the history of the city from the time of its most obscure origins, through its subsequent development, until the inevitable spread of a corruption whose presence was all too dramatically apparent even in his own era. The writing of history was, for Livy, a reaction to contemporary disasters. By taking refuge in the past he could evoke and idealize the city of the Samnite and Hannibalic wars[2] and, while recalling the great civic and moral virtues that had supported the city in its ascent to power, pessimistically point up the contrast with the present age, even though he lived during the Augustan principate.[3] For Livy, writing history was a

1. *Rep.* II.33; E. Bickerman, "Some Reflections on Early Roman History," *RFIC* 97 (1969) 393–408, reprinted in E. Bickerman, *Religions and Politics of the Hellenistic and Roman Periods* (Como, 1985), 525–40.

2. Livy IX.16.19; XXI.1.2.

3. Livy's preface can be dated around 27–25 B.C.; but the pessimistic tone is spread over the whole work: P. Fraccaro, "Livio e Roma" (1942), now in

moral problem. His nostalgia for the past led inevitably to an identification with the ideals that guided the political actions of the traditional ruling class and were hence pictured as belonging to the entire Roman people.

Livy is well aware (*praefatio* 6) that the traditions of the city's foundation are fashioned from poetic fable. Only their great symbolic value justifies their partial acceptance within a narrative whose internal validity and historicity derives from a deep moral sense, which is evinced in the pathos of the historian's narration and which transcends the particulars. Thus Livy, who frequently underlines the obscurity that, almost naturally, veils the distant past, is aware of the unreliability of the entire historical tradition for the period prior to the burning of the city by the Gauls.[4] He realizes that one must at times be content with probability rather than truth[5] and that to investigate details is often a fruitless task. In such cases one should instead accept and hand on the tradition, however incredible, while occasionally expressing disappointment with those predecessors who were (as was often the case with Valerius Antias)[6] clearly lying.

Obviously this consciousness of tradition as something unreliable did not lead to discouragement or a renunciation of the act of writing. As we know from Herodotus, the historian must record notions and traditions even if he is not obliged to believe in them.[7] Herodotus was quick to point out that this attitude applied to every aspect of his work, whether recent (as in this

---

Opuscula, vol. 1 (Pavia, 1956), 81–102; R. Syme, "Livy and Augustus," *HSPh* 64 (1959) 27–87, now in R. Syme, *Roman Papers* (Oxford, 1979), 1:400–454; E. Gabba, "Literature," 17–18, and "The Historians and Augustus," 79–80.

4. Livy VI.1.1–3.

5. Livy V.21.9.

6. T. J. Luce, "Design and Structure in Livy: 5,32–55," *TAPhA* 102 (1971) 265–303, esp. 291 ff.; and *Livy. The Composition of His History* (Princeton, 1977), 248.

7. Hdt. VII.152; A. Momigliano, *Tra storia e storicismo* (Pisa, 1985), 20–23.

case) or remote from the historian's own time. Thus, centuries later, Plutarch, by entering a realm of prodigies and tragic legends inhabited by poets and mythographers, would not hesitate to go beyond the plane of history per se by telling of Theseus and Romulus, giving the legend an historical air.[8] Livy saw the necessity of reporting the legendary traditions of the past as all the more pleasing, insofar as the obscure and uncertain archaic history was richer in essentially true moral exempla. He had no need to embellish the origins of his city. His representation of Romulus and the foundation of the city is neither cosmeticized (as it is by Cicero and Dionysius) by ennobling artifice nor transformed with Greek cultural contributions. The companions of Romulus are the very bandits and vagabonds remarked on with such relish by those Greeks hostile to Rome, whom Dionysius was obliged to change into brave and honest people. One need only think of Dionysius's and Livy's divergent interpretations of *asylum*.[9] For Livy, the greatness of Rome with its inherent values and significance arose from its very foundations.

The work of Livy is never cited by Dionysius even though it is natural to assume that he knew it well enough. The pentads were published one after another during Dionysius's stay in Rome. Indeed, those books in Livy most related to Dionysius's own undertaking had already been published when he set about writing his *History of Archaic Rome*. One may even readily suppose that in many instances where Dionysius differs from Livy, despite, in the last analysis, their mutual dependence on the same sources in the annals, the difference is intentional, as in the case of *asylum* to which we have already referred, and in the interpretation of the Decemvirate. If there is never any open conflict, it may be because Dionysius was aware of a different spirit, intention, and perspective pervading the writings of Livy. In terms

8. Plut. *Thes.* I.1.5.
9. Livy I.8.4–7; Luce, *Livy* 246 ff.

of proportion, it is probable that the work of Dionysius was closer to the accepted models of the later annalists than Livy's efforts were.[10] Certainly Livy deals with the age of kings and the early republican era to a lesser extent than his predecessors. The decision to trim the narration to its essential elements, however difficult their verification, displays an awareness of the immense breadth of the historiographical task undertaken. On the other hand, these same elements were a sufficient indication of the progressive development of Roman history.

Dionysius follows his sources much more closely and presents a more diffuse text than Livy. There are many reasons for this. The historiographical method of Dionysius required, as we have already noted, a broad and articulated narrative that aimed at a complete account of the development of events. In addition to this Dionysius wished, by means of the historical narrative, to illustrate a political thesis. For this purpose a full treatment of the age of kings was essential. Unlike Livy, he never saw the past as a nostalgic allurement revealing the decline of the present age. For the Greek historian the entire past demonstrated a reality that was achieving its clearest validity in his own days. In short, Dionysius had no reason to doubt the credibility of the tradition he had before him. Even where such doubts may have arisen he was still subject to the principle elaborated by Herodotus: how could he not report what he found in the Roman sources? Of course there was no shortage of divergence in the traditions, and

10. T. Cornell, "Alcune riflessioni sulla formazione della tradizione storiografica su Roma arcaica," in *Roma arcaica e le recenti scoperte archeologiche: giornate di studio in onore di Ugo Coli* (Milan, 1980), 23. Livy and Dionysius are often compared in relation to particular details and their use of the sources (e.g., L. Peppe, *Studi sull'esecuzione personale*, vol. 1, *Debiti e debitori nei primi due secoli della repubblica romana* (Milan, 1981), 23–84. The essay of E. Burck, *Die Erzählungskunst des T. Livius* (Berlin, 1934; reprint, 1964) is deservedly well known and illustrates how the two authors generally adopted different approaches to material drawn from shared sources.

it was a matter of knowing how to choose according to the criteria of probability. Dionysius had no great regard for the Roman historians, but he knew that for the most part they had been, and indeed were, members of the ruling senatorial class. Thus, in principle, because they were actors in that history, but also by tradition, they should have known the history of their own city.

But there is more to it than that. Dionysius, in his intention to demonstrate politically and ideologically the Greek origins of Rome, was obliged in his work to introduce critical and archaeological arguments ranging over religious and political institutions, monuments, inscriptions, and linguistic and cultural data, providing ready contrasts with the Greek world. For this purpose Dionysius had to fall back on antiquarian research. According to a famous saying of Cicero's,[11] Varro showed Rome to the Romans in his *Antiquitates*. The work of Varro, as well as the burgeoning of antiquarianism at Rome in the first century B.C.,[12] which was paralleled in Greece and previously tapped by Dionysius for his literary studies, supplied concrete evidence and documentary information not to be found in earlier written histories. The antiquarian material is widely used by Dionysius and is not confined to Book I. This represented a direct intervention by the author with his rich cultural background and took the form of a commentary upon a work that, in essence, followed previous narrative sources. The antiquarian material functioned as a documentary support for the historical text. The combination of narrated history (facts and speeches) and antiquarian research on various levels, enriched through comparisons with Greece, must have given Dionysius and hence his readers a guarantee of certainty and authenticity transcending any doubts about the legendary material or the inherently more

11. *Acad. post.* I.9.
12. E. Rawson, *Intellectual Life in the Late Roman Republic* (London, 1985), 233–49 (Chap. 16, "Antiquarianism").

or less discordant hand-me-down versions. This combination of
history and antiquarianism is one of the main merits of the work
of Dionysius.

Book I of his *History* is in many respects very different from
the rest of that work. The type of narrative whose composition
and origins I have been describing above really begins with
Book II. The special position of Book I is underlined by the author himself when, in I.90, having given a brief synopsis of the
conclusions already reached (I.89), he underscores the value of
this section as an introduction to the overall work. From the evidence of VII.70.1 one might also conclude that the first book
was published separately. In the same way the methodological
preface to Book XI suggests that the opus was conceived as two
decads. If that is the case, Book I was nonetheless perceived as
part of the work's overall plan. The recapitulation at II.1 of conclusions reached in Book I illustrates a wish to strengthen the
ties between the two books, however different their methodology. The editorial technique employed has been well noted.
Naturally the preface (I.1–8), in outlining the aims of the *History,* demonstrates a cementing of the various parts.

II

In Book I Dionysius reconstructs the ethnogenesis of the Roman people, which, according to his own declared intent, must
precede the global, political history of the city. This history, this
"life of the city," is understood as a vital, uninterrupted, and active continuity of customs, laws, and institutions spanning 630
years. It takes its beginning from the moment when the first
king-legislator, almost by way of intrusion into history, had,
with the foundation of Rome, established the urban framework
and the social and constitutional order of the city. This is pictured by Dionysius in its globality as perfect. The whole process
is described according to the classic principles of Greek coloni-

zation.[13] This "life of the city" had in turn, however, its own evident roots in the formation of the Roman people themselves. This was a result of the progressive accumulation of waves of Greek migration to Italy, each of them acting as a carrier of the cultural patrimony that, from Romulus on, would become a hallmark of the Romans. This patrimony, despite momentary setbacks and successive renewals, was synonymous with the very legitimacy of the Roman people. The values of this Greekness, which had, as we know, attained exemplary and unsurpassable heights in the fourth century B.C., became, with their continued growth and refinement, the true underlying structure of Roman history and society. These values also explain the Roman capacity for assimilation, which ignored ethnic divisions.

Though the reconstruction of a people's ethnogenesis was a difficult task, there were plenty of models to hand for Dionysius. It was a matter of presenting an historical, geographic, and ethnographic picture of the proto- and prehistoric Roman, rather than Italian, ambit. Work of this type had, in fact, already been done on other areas of historical ethnographic research, Timaeus being one example.[14] Earlier still Ephorus and Theopompus had dealt with similar problems, as we learn from Dionysius's treatment of these authors. Traditional materials derived from so-called local historiography, that is to say rationalized myths and legends,[15] played a great part in these efforts. In both method and material the treatment differed from ethnographic research of the Hellenistic period, which was concerned with the description and analysis of new and little known contemporary peoples. Dionysius, as has been remarked, had the antiquarian research of the first century B.C. for a model, particularly the work of M. Terentius Varro, who is in fact one of the principal

13. II.2.4, 16.2.
14. T. S. Brown, *Timaeus of Tauromenium* (Berkeley, 1958), 21 ff.
15. Wiseman, "Practice and Theory in Roman Historiography," 391–92.

sources drawn upon by Dionysius. Despite the title of one of the Reatine's works, *De vita populi Romani* (recalling the βίος Ἑλλάδος of Dicaearchus), the differences between Varro and Dionysius run fairly deep. Varro, as is evidenced in many of his works, was interested in prehistoric Italy as well as prehistory in general. Of these works our main concern is with his *De gente populi Romani* and more specifically the *De vita populi Romani*.[16] In the latter, as far as we can tell from the fragments we possess,[17] Varro gave an historico-cultural outline, in broad terms, of aspects of the Roman state and society, covering public, private, religious, and domestic matters. The tone was for the most part moralistic, and there was a profound sense of decadence. His *De gente*[18] would seem to be closer to the vision of Dionysius. There, as indeed in the *Antiquitates,* Varro's aim was an explanation of Rome's civic and religious customs and an investigation of the city's earliest history. He insisted on the ancient ties between Greece and Rome, though he sought to preserve the distinct individuality of the Roman people. His intention to show "quid a quaque traxerint" (the Romans) "gente per imitationem"[19] is specifically indicated, though this was indeed a motive acknowledged, not without some pride, by all the Roman historians. Varro exploited the most recent Greek work on the chronology of the ancient universe and posited the entire archaic history (from Ogygus and the flood) as a premise to the history of Rome. As we also know from his *De re rustica,*

16. I accept the views of F. Della Corte, "L'idea della preistoria in Varrone."

17. B. Riposati, *M. Terenti Varronis De vita populi romani,* 2d ed. (Milan, 1972).

18. P. Fraccaro, *Studi varroniani. De gente populi romani* (Padua, 1907), 229 ff. On the chronology and the political meaning of the work: L. R. Taylor, "Varro's *De Gente Populi Romani,*" *CP* 29 (1934) 221–29, and N. Horsfall, "Varro and Caesar: Three Chronological Problems," *BICS* 19 (1972) 120–28. Dionysius could not like the euhemeristic motif connected with Caesar's deification.

19. Serv. *ad Aen.* VII.176 = fr. 37 Fraccaro.

Varro accepted the three stages of civilization that Dicaearchus had defined according to methods of subsistence (hunting, breeding, and tillage), though Varro understood them as stages of progressive civilization from an original savage phase. Dicaearchus, on the other hand, began with a primitive golden age, and his theory of three stages, with its account of the passage from each to the next, was taken as an explanation for the growing distance between man and his miraculous and irretrievable beginnings.

Dionysius produced a very different reconstruction, from which the perspectives of Varro and Dicaearchus are conspicuously absent. The very concept of βίος underlying the work of Dionysius is not in fact what Dicaearchus intended by the same term and has only vague similarities to Varro's ideas in the *De vita*. It appears more closely related to the "quae vita, qui mores" in the preface of Livy.[20] This notion, whatever connection it may have with a biological conception of history (understood as development and enrichment), is nonetheless apparently far removed from any cyclical theory. This is because the power of the Roman state is always perceived in a moment of vitality and magnetism.

The description of ethnogenesis in Dionysius is also profoundly different from the concept that dominates those first famous chapters of Thucydides that led Dionysius to criticize their author because he judged them extraneous to the body of the work. Dionysius knows and insists that his own ethnographic perspective is a major component in his approach to his task as historian. Nevertheless, at a conceptual level and in his evaluation of method, Dionysius was quite noticeably influenced by the Thucydides of the *archaiologia*. In his desire to prove that

20. On the meaning of βίος, followed by a determinative, to distinguish stages of civilization: R. Joly, *Le thème philosophique des genres de vie dans l'antiquité classique* (Brussels, 1956), 133 ff.

the Peloponnesian War occurred at the highest point in Greek history, Thucydides places it at the culmination of the development of human civilization in Greece, taking the most primitive conditions of social life as a starting point. Ideas of scientific and technical development, both in political and military institutions, are employed to interpret the past. They are a means of describing the various phases of human civilization, which coincided with a gradual and progressive increase in stable and settled living conditions, maritime power, security, the building of walls, commerce, the growth of wealth, and the foundation of cities. The passage of history is thus explained by the historian, who sees his own time as the peak of a development that even the future will not rival. The rise and expansion of the Athenian empire in the fifth century B.C. provided Thucydides with an historical framework within which he could picture and reconstruct the most ancient phases of Greek history.[21] But Thucydides had also been able to devise or, in certain cases, to reelaborate old myths and legendary traditions (the Pelasgians, Minos, Agamemnon). He accomplished this by rational thought and intellectual method and hence deduced arguments, comparisons, and proofs ($\tau\epsilon\kappa\mu\acute{\eta}\rho\iota\alpha$) of potential interest to the history of human civilization. Important historical and ethnographical concepts were skillfully employed to encompass and historically evaluate and criticize traditional data: for example, emigration and its causes, instability and stability in communities, the changing of a people's name, insecurity and security in life, and settlement.

The intuitions and methodological principles of Thucydides later became canons of interpretation for history. In the case of Dionysius, this was often at the level of a terminology that enabled him, just as certainly as it did his predecessors, to orga-

21. J. de Romilly, *Histoire et raison chez Thucydide* (Paris, 1956), 240ff.

nize, recast, compare, and interpret those lost mythic and legendary materials of Greece and Rome, relevant to Roman and Italian prehistory, that he had been able to gather by great toil and learning. To give only a couple of examples, it is well-nigh self-evident that the theory of emigration, when applied to the formation of the Roman people, furnished an adequate explanation of their undeniably composite character, while at the same time prefiguring the subsequent politics of a Rome that was open and nonexclusive as far as the rights of its citizens were concerned. Again, there was the institution of *asylum*, which was a notoriously controversial point in discussions on the composition of the original group around Romulus. *Asylum* meant that fugitives from all sides could find safety, and it is described by Dionysius as a clever device of the king's to attract and welcome persons (on condition that they were freemen)[22] on the run from other Italian cities governed by tyrants or oligarchs. Here Dionysius has transposed to Romulean Rome the process that had seen the growth of Attica through the support of the best exiles, who had been hunted out of their own homelands for political reasons.[23] The subsequent growth in population later stimulated the Athenian drive to colonize Asia Minor.

From another point of view, where Italian ethnology was concerned, Dionysius had found historically based grounds for the theory of emigration that were linked to the Thucydidean assertion (I.2.3) that with the occupation of better lands emigration is a definitive factor for growth and power. According to the ancient custom of the *ver sacrum*,[24] which Dionysius felt he could trace in both Greek and barbarian peoples, a small band of young men were sent forth by their parents to seek a livelihood. In this

22. II.15.3–4; cf. III.47.2.
23. Thuc. I.2.5–6.
24. As described in I.16.1–3: E. Gabba, "Mirsilo di Metimna, Dionigi e i Tirreni," *RAL*, 8th ser., 30 (1975), 46 nn. 28–29.

phenomenon there was a correspondence between population growth and a shortfall in soil productivity, an insufficiency that could be due to even temporary climatic factors. Dionysius did not hesitate to use this Italian tradition to explain analogous cases in the Greek world, and indeed the Pelasgian dispersion from Italy, for example, is presented as a *ver sacrum* (I.24).

While the principle of emigration was thus awarded such a highly privileged position in the story of the formation of the Roman people, the opposite principle of autochthony, a matter of great pride to the Greeks and especially to the Athenians, was in no way downgraded. This is clear from its implementation in Dionysius's treatment of the Etruscans.[25] It was simply the case that the principle of autochthony could not be applied to the Roman people, even though there was a clear recognition that their development, up to a certain point, was confined to a fixed geographical ambit first occupied by Aborigines and Pelasgians (I.9.3). Here, the concept of settled stability reappears as a favoured element for civic development. This had already been the case with Thucydides, though he had connected this concept to autochthony in the strict sense and not, as here, to an unwillingness to shift residence. It is obvious that beyond the confines of Greece autochthony could only signify non-Greekness and hence barbarianism. But for Dionysius even these terms had no negative connotation in the Italian sphere. This is apparent from his own conception of Greekness, which had no ethnic limit, and also from his inclusion of Italian peoples whom he held in high regard (specifically the Umbrians and Etruscans) among the barbarian tribes. In other words autochthony has an altogether different value in Italy from what it has in Greece,

25. The Umbrians had a large part in the history of the Aborigines and are numbered among the Italian barbarians, even if ancient and powerful people: I.19.1; also in their case autochthony was attested: II.49.1 (from Zenodotus of Troezen).

but, I repeat, it is not for all that a negative element. It simply could not be applied to the Roman people.[26] To qualify the Etruscans as autochthonous did not imply being anti-Etruscan.

The fundamental difference between the description of ethnogenesis in Dionysius and the civilizing process in Thucydides lies in the very idea that is at the root of Thucydides' thinking. The process in Greece, according to the latter, had its starting point in a period of great backwardness. Such is not the case with Dionysius. He does indeed describe the ethnogenesis as a progressive growth of civilization and a series of victories for the Greek emigrants over the barbarian peoples of Italy, who are successively hunted out and subjugated. But he does not envisage an initial savage phase for this process. The emigrant Greek components, whatever their differences, are already presented in fairly developed stages of civilization. The starting point for his ethnogenesis is advanced to begin with. There is no room for the stages imagined by Dicaearchus and accepted in turn by Varro, in which there were different methods of subsistence related to different states of progress. When Dionysius describes (I.36–38) the traditions of Saturn in Italy, with praises for the land of Italy that include the richness of its soil and the methods of subsistence, he thereby cancels the usefulness of the stages contrived by Dicaearchus, since his own descriptions are couched in contemporary terms. The Saturnian βίος appears as a fact of life, an original facet of the Italian land onto which the Greek emigrations were grafted. These privileged conditions justify and legitimize Italy's position as the seat of world dominion.

The fundamental element that articulates and accompanies

26. I.89.4: Opicans, Marsians, Samnites, Tyrrhenians, Bruttians, Umbrians, Ligurians, Iberians (cf. I.22.1), and Gauls are all considered barbarian peoples. The Etruscans are autochthonous (I.26.2 and 30.2) and so are the Umbrians (above, n.25) and the Sabines (II.49.2–4). Even the Sicels are implicitly considered an autochthonous population: I.9.2.

the phases of formation of a people who will later be sovereign is religion, with its cults and rites and the construction of its temples. These all provide Dionysius with a rich seedbed for comparisons between the Greek and Roman worlds, whether in the field of religion itself, in archaeology, or in architecture. Above all they allow him to support the idea of continuity and the survival of original Greek elements in Roman civilization. They also helped him to devise a complex anthropological theory of the greater resilience shown by religious elements against external influences. The rejection of human sacrifice (a custom connected, in a sense, with the Pelasgians) is a moment of particular importance in the refinement of these religious practices. The step is attributed to Hercules and was not a new theory, being already present in Varro. It allowed Dionysius to give a rationalized interpretation along Greek lines of the Argei rite (I.38.2–4), which in turn contributes to subsequent very important arguments at VII.72 à propos the description of the *Ludi Magni* and the *circensis* procession.[27]

Along with the interpretive canon on emigration, the integration of similar ethnic groups arriving in different waves quickly gained significance for Dionysius. These, while accepting ever more advanced lifestyles, finished by founding religious institutions and laws. This pacific and voluntary acceptance entailed a certain self-denial of personal traits, but most importantly it represented an assimilation in which everyone shouldered his own obligations and surrendered his personal autonomy.[28] There were no subjugations or conquests among the five waves

27. On Hercules and human sacrifices in Varro: Lactant. *Div. Inst.* I.21.6 ff.; Macrob. *Sat.* I.7.28–32; F. Schwenn, *Die Menschenopfer bei den Griechen und Römern* (Giessen, 1915), 118, 152 ff. On the *Argei:* G. Maddoli, "Il rito degli Argei e le origini del culto di Hera a Roma," *PP* 26 (1971) 153–66; B. Cardauns, ed., *M. Terentius Varro. Antiquitates rerum divinarum* (Mainz, 1976), fr. 244.

28. I.20.5, 33.5, 44.2, 60.2.

of Greek emigration that came to Italy, and hence no violent cultural transformations. The most important surrender was that of specific denomination. From Herodotus on, name changing (μετονομασίαι) was an integral function of Greek ethnography and historiography.[29]

III

A simple review of the Dionysian text clearly shows us that the process of emigration and cultural growth took the form of a progression. The Aborigines, whose preferred origin in Dionysius's eyes was Arcadian rather than autochthonous, were part of a wider pattern of emigration and colonization led by Oenotrus and prompted by internal political developments (I.11.3). A large part of Italy was occupied, though mainly in areas with little or no population. The Aborigines finally settled on land taken from the Umbrians (I.3.3, 16.1, 19.1), which lay in mountainous regions and where their settlements were scattered and without walls. This was a typical form of primitive settlement (I.9.2–3, 13.3).[30] This information contrasts with I.26.2, which deals with the Etruscans and Tyrrhenians, who, according to proponents of autochthony, had been the first to build fortified settlements protected by roofs and walls (τύρσεις), whence they derived their name.[31] The Aborigines then, along with the Pelasgians, came down into the plains and ejected the Siculi, founding cities[32] and occupying, with little alteration, the places that

29. The Romanization of the Etruscan Lucumo, the son of the Corinthian Demaratus, who emigrated to Rome from Tarquinii under the king Servius Tullius, is made complete by the change of his name to Tarquinius: III.48.2.

30. These settlements are called πόλεις in 14.1, but in 12.1 Dionysius maintains their archaic type.

31. This theory requires that their indigenous name, Rasenna, was unknown (I.30.3).

32. This is a typical stage of progress and security contrasted with settling on mountains: Plato *Leges* III.682b–c.

would later form the geographical base for Roman dominion (I.9.2). The expansionist drive of the Aborigines was bound up with the practice of *ver sacrum* (I.16).

The next wave of emigration, a Pelasgian contingent coming from Thessaly but originating in the Peloponnese, also cooperated with the Aborigines in territorial expansion and the foundation of cities (I.20.5, 23.1). For Dionysius this cultural phase is exemplified by the temple of Falerian Juno and the Pelasgians' vast Argive connections (I.21.1–2). In a variety of ways they were associated with human sacrifice. Their growth in population, cities and wealth (I.23.1), maritime activity, and military capacity (I.25.1) were a provocation to divine anger and disaster.

The Arcadians of Evander, though small in number, played an important role in the ethnographic framework of Italy, because they were traditionally associated with the transmission of many cults and religious ceremonies of lasting significance. More than anything else they were responsible for the introduction of the Greek alphabet,[33] music, and laws (νόμοι), and for a way of life that was, by contrast, more civilized than the previous, predominantly savage (θηριώδης) lifestyle. They introduced crafts, professions, and other ideas of benefit to the community (I.31–33). They thus form a true benchmark in the progress of civic development.

As for the advent of Hercules and the settlement of a nucleus of his Peloponnesian followers (I.44.2), Dionysius saw fit to choose a version (I.41–44) that, in reality, involved the whole of Italy. Above all it was a political fact, an event of social and political consequence. It entailed the destruction of tyrannies and their aggressive policies, the elimination of the residues of a primitive lifestyle (human sacrifice), and the establishment of legal monarchic governments, which constituted a traditional

33. Gabba, "Il latino come dialetto greco"; D. Marin, "Dionisio di Alicarnasso e il latino," in *Hommages à Marcel Renard* (Brussels, 1969), 595–607.

advance over early, more primitive forms of individual rule. Along with these came the introduction of new social models, as well as modifications in land use, with their potential benefits to mankind. More than an "Augustan"[34] programme, the vision accepted the traditional image of Hercules as the bringer of civilization that had served as a model for many renowned conqueror-kings.

The arrival of the final wave of Greek emigration in the guise of Aeneas and his Trojans (I.45–60) enters the plane of Greek history within the limits defined by the Greek historians. Dionysius can limit himself to demonstrating the Greek character of Aeneas and the Trojans (I.5.61–62). With the successors of Aeneas, the kings of Alba and Romulus, we are confronted by material that, though legendary, has its own historicity.

The ethnographic complexities of Rome are recapitulated against an Italian background (I.89.1ff.). The conclusion reached, that is, the original Greekness of the Romans, disregards the typical Greek tendency to reflect the traditions of peoples with whom they came into contact back to an essentially Greek referent.[35] To forestall the accusations of barbarity, the controversial concept of Rome as a Greek city is adopted. Rome is seen as even more Greek than other cities, because it was willing to share its benefits and welcome outsiders (κοινοτάτην). The historian himself, as we shall later see, assumes a meaningful political position that goes beyond historiography.[36] The recognition (I.89.3) of the mingling of Romans and barbarian elements, Ital-

34. P. M. Martin, "Héraklès en Italie d'après Denys d'Halicarnasse (A.R., I, 34–44)," *Athenaeum* n.s. 50 (1972) 252–75; cf. Martin, "La propagande augustéenne dans les Antiquités romaines de Denys d'Halicarnasse (livre I)," *REL* 49 (1971) 162–79.

35. E. Bickerman, "Origines Gentium."

36. According to King Pyrrhus, the Romans were ὁσιοτάτους Ἑλλήνων καὶ δικαιοτάτους (XX.6.1, Struve's correction is unhelpful and mistaken). In reality Pyrrhus exploited the Trojan origin of the Romans to confirm his own purpose in coming to Italy to fight against them as a descendant of Achilles.

ians and non-Italians, as well as the partial obliteration of certain archaic institutions, reinforces a certain sense of wonder. The wonder was that the introduction of customs, lifestyles, and strange languages had not in fact modified the ancient disposition of the city, given that other Greek groups, placed in a barbarian context, had suffered assimilation and loss of identity. In the final chapter of Book I (I.90) this capacity for maintaining the old Greek framework and above all the constitutional order (which is a pivotal argument in other books: II.3) is singled out as the reason behind Rome's good fortune, which is thus divorced from chance and bound to the reality of social and political life. This framework is not a consequence of the conquests of the third and second centuries B.C. but is inherent in the formative Greek origins of the Romans.

The reconstructed Roman ethnogenesis becomes, in fact, part of a broader picture that includes and indeed defines, in a particular way, almost all Italian ethnography. We are presented with a slow but continuous prevailing of Greek over autochthonous Italian elements that comes to fruition in the establishment of Roman power in the historic period. The Greek element is, however, considered only in its Roman incarnation. That is not to say that Dionysius wished to restrict the Greek presence in Italy to a Roman orbit, ignoring the cities of Magna Graecia; it merely means that to Dionysius as an historian of Rome the problem of the Greek origins of the dominant city was of prime importance. In this perspective the indigenous Italian peoples who came into contact with the waves of Greek emigration had a different historical role. They succumbed to Greek dominance (the Siculi disappeared altogether from the peninsula) only to be later subsumed, after a long process of assimilation, into the Roman union in the historical period. This was possible because of the superior moral and political capacities that the union (perhaps better described as Greco-Roman) had been able to preserve: it was thus a matter of functionally subordinate elements within an overall historical framework. There was, however, no reason to abuse the indigenous Italian peoples or tarnish their image, despite the fact that some of these peoples would, during the centuries of struggle against Rome, inevitably assume an historical role and so an importance that the historian of Rome could deal with only from a Roman perspective.[37]

In this context the Etruscans clearly presented a major difficulty. It was a problem that had assumed particular significance in Dionysius's own time. There had been a growing interest in Etruscan culture, both its history and its sacred and profane literature. This interest perhaps owed something to the growing influence of noble Etruscan families who were being admitted in ever greater numbers to the Roman ruling class.[38] Dionysius himself shared this interest and demonstrates a good knowledge of Etruscan lore. In I.30.4 he promises us a complete treatment of the Etruscans, which is to be inserted (following a well-known technique) in the appropriate place at a later point in his *History*.[39] He knew them to be different, both in language and lifestyle, from other Italian peoples. As J. Heurgon has demonstrated, he adopts a tone of sympathetic goodwill; so indeed had Posidonius before him.[40] Dionysius was well aware of the obsti-

37. Such is the case with the Etruscans, to whom the Roman annalists were naturally hostile: D. Musti, *Tendenze nella storiografia romana e greca su Roma arcaica. Studi su Livio e Dionigi d'Alicarnasso* (Rome, 1970).

38. T. Cornell, "Etruscan Historiography," *ASNP*, 3d ser., 6 (1976) 411–39; M. Torelli, "Senatori etruschi della tarda repubblica e dell'impero," *DArch* 3 (1969) 285–363; idem, *Elogia tarquiniensia* (Florence, 1975).

39. There is no reason to suppose a separate book as D. Briquel does in his "L'autochtonie des étrusques chez Denys d'Halicarnasse," *REL* 61 (1983) 70 and n. 22. There was ample opportunity in the books following X for this insertion of an excursus, as in Book XII, for instance, which deals with the taking of Veii and where Dionysius develops some of his thoughts on the Etruscans.

40. J. Heurgon, "Les penestes étrusques chez Denys d'Halicarnasse (IX 5,4)," *Latomus* 18 (1959) 712–23.

nate Etruscan hostility to Rome. Thus when Veii is destroyed at
the hands of Camillus he does not fail to record that the Etruscans were the most prosperous and important of the Italian
peoples and that Veii itself, a rich and renowned city, had for a
long time been Rome's rival for hegemony.[41]

With Italian ethnography there was a different problem. Here
it was a matter of rebutting theories that linked Greece with
Etruria and the Etruscans of the historical period, as well as
others that saw Rome itself as an Etruscan city (I.29.2). Dionysius squarely confronts the problem in I.26–30. He refutes any
identification of the Tyrrhenians (= Etruscans) with the Pelasgians, an idea that had been touted authoritatively for some
time. He does this by means of an involved argument that uti-
lizes the famous passage in Herodotus I.57.1, a disputed reference to the Italian Pelasgians. This refutation was extremely important to Dionysius because he accepted that the Pelasgians
had participated in the formation of the Roman people and that
they were of Greek origin. The well-known Herodotean theory
of a Lydian provenance of the Etruscans is denied by Dionysius.
He refers us to the work of a local Lydian historian, Xanthus,
who, though probably writing at an earlier date than Herodotus, knew nothing of such a theory (I.28.2). Dionysius approves
the idea, already present in the historical sources he consulted,
of Etruscan autochthony. His argument inaugurated the "Etruscan question." Evidently his opinion was already determined by
the historical and political assumptions of his work. Uncovering
the incongruities and weaknesses of his argument on the basis of
our own knowledge and methods is an absurd and certainly
fruitless task. There is some benefit, however, to be gained from
a reconstruction of the complex articulation of his argument in
the light of the traditions he had at his disposal. Fully conscious
of what he was doing, he completely distorts the theories of his

41. XV.3.9; XII.14.19, 15.21.

principal source, Myrsilus of Methymna, in order to adapt them to his own ends.[42] It should be obvious that Dionysius invents nothing. He simply chooses from the theories he has found ready-formulated, basing his preference on the general premise of his own work and a close internal analysis of the texts themselves.

Another characteristic example of his approach to ethnographic and archaeological material is apparent in his treatment of the Aborigines.[43] In this instance the historian is confronted by a variety of theories whose authors he groups into two categories: those favouring an autochthonous, Italian origin (I.10), and those who believed the Aborigines had come from Greece (I.11.1). Those plumping for an Italian autochthonous origin were of three different opinions, of which two were based in part on etymological explanations of the name Aborigines. According to one theory it referred to family foundation (*ab origine*); according to another they were homeless vagabonds

42. I have examined the problem posed by Dionysius's chapters on the Pelasgians and Tyrrhenians in "Mirsilo di Metimna, Dionigi e i Tirreni." I think that Dionysius found the theory of Tyrrhenian and Etruscan autochthony in Myrsilus, though there is a possibility that local tradition may have been the ultimate source. This interpretation is discussed with some caution by D. Musti, "Etruschi e Greci nella rappresentazione dionisiana delle origini di Roma," in *Gli etruschi e Roma: Atti dell'incontro di studio in onore di Massimo Pallottino* (Rome, 1981), 32–41 (in my opinion, however, the passage in Dionysius [I.28.4] remains decisive: *vide* my article, note 45). D. Briquel, on the other hand, rejects my interpretation in his article "L'autochtonie des étrusques," which upholds the position already found in his *Les pélasges en Italie. Recherches sur l'histoire de la légende* (Rome, 1984): the autochthonous position goes back as far as Philistus, where it would have served an anti-Etruscan function to combat the propaganda that accused Dionysius of Syracuse of attacking the Greeks in Italy (Justin XX.1.1–16 = Theopomp. *FGrHist* 115 F 316). I suspect that Briquel has not understood the meaning of autochthony as an ethnographic description for a non-Greek region. According to P. M. Martin, "Denys d'Halicarnasse et l'autochtonie des étrusques," in *Colloque histoire et historiographie Clio* (Paris, 1980), 47–59, Dionysius found the autochthony theory in Xanthus.

43. J.-C. Richard, "Varro, l'Origo gentis romanae et les aborigènes," *RPh* 57 (1983) 29–37.

(Aberrigines, from *aberrare*), like the Leleges of Greece (I.10.1–2); and according to the third they were Ligurian colonists whose autochthonous origin lay in Italy or Gallia (I.10.3). The theory of autochthony was upheld by Varro in his *Antiquitates rerum humanarum.* He located the Aborigines in his own Sabine region, from which they descended with the Pelasgians on what was later to be Rome and expelled the Siculi.[44] The damaging theory of a people with no fixed abode was championed by Saufeius.[45]

According to Dionysius, Cato proposed a Greek origin in his *Origines*[46] and shared the idea with many others, C. Sempronius Tuditanus among them (I.11.1). They opted for Achaia[47] and put the date at many generations before the Trojan War. They did not, however, provide a precise location, date or leader. Dionysius supposed this theory to have a Greek source, though the Roman authors do not provide any references. This is the hypothesis that he himself accepted, however tenuous he thought its foundation. He takes it upon himself to specify its details and, as we have already noted, he identifies its origin in a wave of emigration led by Oenotrus (I.11.2), in support of which he cites several Greek sources (I.11.3–13.2). An Aboriginal participation in this emigration was all-important. Dionysius is convinced that he has given a solid basis to the imprecise Catonian theory. No earlier westward movement is known before Oeno-

44. Della Corte, "L'idea della preistoria in Varrone," 113 ff.
45. Nepos *Att.* 12.3 = fr. 2 Peter.
46. W. A. Schröder, *M. Porcius Cato. Das Erste Buch der Origines. Ausgabe und Erklärung der Fragmente* (Meisenheim am Glan, 1971), frr. 5–6 (with the commentary at pp. 102–10); C. Letta, "L' 'Italia dei *mores romani'* nelle *Origines* di Catone," *Athenaeum* n.s. 62 (1984) 424–28; J.-C. Richard, "Ennemis ou alliés? Les troyens et les aborigines dans les Origines de Caton," in *Hommages à Robert Schilling* (Paris, 1983), 403–12.

47. It is not clear what Achaia means for Dionysius: at I.27.3 the region is a part of Haemonia; but at 25.5 it coincides with Peloponnesus: I suspect that even in this case the historian refers to this area.

trus (I.11.2). Yet our historian later (I.13.4) shows an awareness that the simple discovery of legendary tradition for the Oenotrian movement is no decisive confirmation of Cato's opinion. He invites the doubtful "to suspend their judgment until they are in a position to make a correct choice of the most likely theory." In saying this he was perhaps sincerely revealing his own awareness of the risk involved in contradicting the autochthonous theory held by Varro.

His refutation of Varro on this score does not, however, prevent his total acceptance of the author's topographical and archaeological descriptions of the Sabine region, as if the latter were the area of Aboriginal settlement. Chapters I.14 and 15 in Dionysius, which are exceptionally important, rely on Varro,[48] but one should perhaps give credit to the assertion that a direct investigation had been made in the locality. Chapter I.16, dealing with the practice of *ver sacrum,* must also depend on Varro. Following a precise historiographical technique by which archaeological evidence is adduced to support narrative assertions, the sequel to the history of the Sabine region, dealing with the Sabines of the historical period, is inserted in Book II in connection with Titus Tatius of Cures (II.48–49). Even in this instance the problem is one of origins.[49] Varro proposed a divine and indigenous origin for the founder of Cures. Zenodotus, the Greek historian, held that the Sabines were an autochthonous group of Umbrians who, when they were hunted from their native lands by the Pelasgians, had, in their new homeland (the true Sabine territory), changed their name.[50] Cato was, it appears, more precise and could name the locality from which the

48. Della Corte, "L'idea della preistoria in Varrone," 115 ff.; E. C. Evans, *The Cults of the Sabine Territory* (Rome, 1939).

49. Letta, 418–24.

50. Strabo V.3.1 supports the autochthonous theory. The passage is obscure: Briquel, *Pélasges* 459 ff.

Sabines originally came before moving to Reate, ejecting the Aborigines, occupying Cutiliae and colonizing the whole area with unwalled settlements (II.49.2−3). Cato insists upon the central position they occupied between the Adriatic and Tyrrhenian seas. Dionysius finally recalls the tradition recorded by local historians that gave the Sabines a Spartan origin and dated their emigration to the time of the Lycurgan laws (II.49.4−5),[51] providing an explanation for the traditionally severe Sabine lifestyle. Our historian, however, does not seem preoccupied with providing a Greek provenance for the Sabines even though it was potentially useful for his own thesis. There had, after all, been a complete fusion of the Sabines of Titus Tatius and the Romans under Romulus (II.46). Dionysius records all the different versions without taking sides, not, be it noted, through any fear of contradicting his predecessors, but rather as a downright understatement. At any event this excursus on the Sabine origins gives us some indication of the form that the lost history of the Etruscans may have taken.

Dionysius's reconstruction of the Roman ethnogenesis ultimately poses the political problem of its position in relation to the Augustan intellectual climate. Providing Greek roots for the Romans runs somewhat contradictory to the Virgilian interpretation of Italian ethnography and Virgil's solution to the problem of Greek and Trojan reconciliation. In the *Aeneid* this reconciliation is accomplished on Italian soil through the mediation of Evander, leader of the Greeks already established in Italy (the followers of Hercules), and Aeneas the Trojan. The theory of a Trojan "return" to their original country apparently gave

51. The Spartan origin was supported, as it seems, by Gn. Gellius (fr. 10 Peter, from Serv. auct. *ad Aen.* VIII.638) and Cato (fr. 51 Peter), even if the latter is not quoted in Dionysius among the supporters of the Greek origin. Peter *HRR* I² cxxxiv supposed that Cato quoted but did not accept the local version (in the same sense Letta, 432−38; different position in Briquel, *Pélasges* 463−64).

Aeneas' arrival in Italy a form of legitimacy (*Aen.* VII.205, 240). It is probable, however, that this idea derived from Etruscan sources and was based on traditions of the Etruscan nobility.[52] It was thus of little or no use (if anything, counterproductive) for the reconciliation of the Greeks with the Romans, and all the less useful to Dionysius. Dionysius's attempted reconstruction outdoes Virgil's proposals and provides an even more definitive solution to the problem. Within the overall framework of Italian ethnography the distance separating Virgil and Dionysius may indeed be smaller than one might expect at first glance. The reason for this is the clearly expressed awareness, in both writers, of a capacity in the Greek nucleus of the Roman people for cultural attraction to other populations who are little by little absorbed into a unitary complex. From this point of view Dionysius is not at odds with Virgil's vision, even though we may burden the latter with a heavy superstructure of Augustan ideology. The Etruscans, who are divided by Virgil into friends and enemies of Aeneas, are assigned a decidedly positive role by Dionysius, who leaves aside their historical action in the story of Rome rather than eliminate it entirely. Even regarded in this light, his position cannot be construed as opposed to the Rome of Augustus.[53]

The labours of Dionysius, who toiled with such diligence over critical and mythical material relating to the origins of Rome, had their final result in his demonstration of the political theory proclaiming Rome's Greekness. This is the basic reason why he could not follow Livy in eliminating the fables of a poetically colourful tradition that predated the foundation of Rome and

52. G. Colonna, "Virgilio, Cortona e la leggenda etrusca di Dardano," *ArchClass* 32 (1980) 1–15.

53. H. Hill, "Dionysius of Halicarnassus and the Origins of Rome," *JRS* 51 (1961) 88–94; D. Marin, "L'opposizione sotto Augusto e la datazione del 'Saggio sul sublime,'" in *Studi in onore di Aristide Calderini e Roberto Paribeni* (Milan, 1957), 1:157–85.

described that very foundation. Instead Dionysius chose a path
that Polybius had rejected, one whose main concerns were ethnography and the foundation of cities. The merit of his work lies
in its use of a rich stock of antiquarian material within a complex historiographical vision with a political orientation. In this
way he outdid the interests and methods of Hellenistic local historiography, though these too were well known to him and were
not without their own facets of political importance.[54]

IV

There is one very important point to be noted in this vast reorganization and rationalization of legendary material undertaken by Dionysius: he has sought, as far as it lay within his
power, to leave aside any myth involving divine intervention in
human affairs. This principle of his was also applied to the narrative portion of his history. He has even seen fit to give some
thought to the matter, and his conclusions, containing material
of historic interest, cover some interesting aspects of methodology. Especially interesting is the high profile given to religion and religious institutions in the interpretive framework,
both historical and anthropological, of his opus. The main focus
of Dionysius's reflections can be found in II.18–20. These chapters form the nucleus of the portion of his work dedicated to the

54. Gabba, "Storiografia greca e imperialismo romano." I believe the
problem of the extent of Dionysius's knowledge of the authors he quotes has,
after so much lengthy and futile debate, been overcome. It was an enquiry that
had already been made in relation to his knowledge of the archaic authors
cited in *Thuc.* 5 and was a continuing cause of curiosity as regards the many
Greek and Roman sources he uses in Book I. Philologically, his direct or indirect acquaintance with the sources cannot be demonstrated, as the diversity of
critical opinion shows. Even the individual examination of each particular
case does not lead to any firm conclusions; the very methods of Dionysius,
whereby the information of his sources is arranged to follow his theories,
obliged him to choose and incorporate those passages most pertinent to his
own ideas. For my own part I accept the sincerity of I.6–7. At any event, there
are no major contradictions between the views we find in Dionysius and our
other evidence about the same authors.

religious institutions that were to be laid down by Romulus in his work as legislator (II.18–23).[55]

The fundamental idea in Dionysius[56] is his assertion that the moral roots of a state's development are not dependent on a casual spontaneity but derive primarily from the goodwill of the gods. It is an idea that he extends to Romulus at this point in the work (II.18.1–2), basically suggesting that the practice of honesty and other civic virtues should be encouraged by appropriate measures, specifically those concerning the cults of the gods and daemons. Thus Romulus built temples, sanctuaries, altars, and statues. He decreed the attributes and appearance of the gods and laid down regulations for the various institutions "basing his ideas on the best existing legislation of the Greeks." On another level, "he forbade all those myths that condemned or insulted the gods, deeming them sacrilegious and damaging, indecent, and unworthy not alone of the gods but of every decent human being. He laid down that all men should speak and think of the gods in the most fitting way possible without attributing actions to them that were inappropriate to their divine natures" (II.18.3).

The proof for this assertion is offered in the following chapter (II.19). Dionysius recalls the repulsive Greek myths of Uranus and Cronus, which were unknown to Roman religion, as were the more indecorous or disrespectful Greek rites and myths. This rejection continued even after corruption had set into Roman customs. Dionysius had great admiration for the wise political decision that refused to accept foreign rites and deities

55. The following text is in substance a translation of my own article, "Dionigi, Varrone e la religione senza miti," *RSI* 96 (1984) 855–70. On the chapter devoted to Romulus: Gabba, "Studi su Dionigi da Alicarnasso. I. La costituzione di Romolo," *Athenaeum* n.s. 38 (1960) 175–225. Different interpretations in Hill; G. Ferrara, "Commenti al dopoguerra aziaco," *La Cultura* 8 (1970) 22–39; J. P. V. D. Balsdon, "Dionysius on Romulus," *JRS* 61 (1971) 18–27.

56. Gabba, "Studi su Dionigi da Alicarnasso. I," 190.

into the official state religion, this despite the tremendous influx of foreigners who all practiced their own traditional cults at Rome. When a foreign cult was accepted in Rome, as had happened with the Magna Mater, the Roman officials would celebrate the games and sacrifices according to their own traditions, leaving the foreign rites of the cult to Phrygian celebrants and forbidding the participation of Roman citizens.

If I am not mistaken, the thoughts of Dionysius in this section represent the first and almost unique example in antiquity of the realization that Roman religion was substantially lacking in myth. Dionysius drew this conclusion for the simple reason that he was in a position to compare Roman and Greek religious institutions and rites and so posit a Greek origin for Roman practices; he was not, however, able to find anything in Roman religion corresponding to the lavish pantheon of the Greeks, with its cosmological and genealogical elaborations. He also, quite justifiably, recognized that Roman religion was a complex of rites and cults rigorously controlled by political force. This had been the case from the beginning, and Dionysius knew that the political control exercised by Romulus and likewise by Numa in the religious sphere had led to the imposition of a network of regulations that were numerically far in excess of anything found in other Greek or barbarian cities (II.63.1–2). Dionysius thus had little hesitation in picturing an original political decision that, while accepting Greek models for deities, divine imagery, and rites, excluded the mythology, thus acknowledging the grave moral reservations expressed on many sides. In an important essay L. R. Taylor held that a link could be perceived between this voluntary repudiation of mythology and the prohibition of divine images that was the distinguishing trait of the most archaic phase of Roman religion.[57]

57. L. R. Taylor, "Aniconic Worship among the Early Romans," in *Classical Studies in Honor of John C. Rolfe* (Philadelphia, 1931), 305–14.

This lone observation by Dionysius did not escape the attention of Eusebius of Caesarea. Books I and II of his *Praeparatio evangelica* contain a refutation of polytheism and a critique of the tales of the gods devised by Greek and Phoenician writers and poets who were concerned with sacred matters. The criticism extends to attempted philosophical explanations of these writings. In II.8 Eusebius records the long passage in Dionysius from II.18.2 to 21.1, precisely because the inherent criticism that Dionysius implies in the attitude of the Roman legislator and king provides a convenient means for demonstrating the worthlessness of Greek theories on the gods: the Romans had in fact, he pointed out, rejected them years before. In comments made at the end of Book I and repeated at the beginning of Book III, Eusebius expresses satisfaction that his own views were reflected in the antipathy to Greek myths that he discerned both in the greatest of Greek philosophers (Plato of the *Timaeus* and *Republic*) and in the early founders of the Roman empire, which he held in such high esteem. On the other hand the text of Dionysius is explicit: the Romulean rejection applied to counterproductive mythology, anything whose crudeness or unsuitability could distort man's image of the gods. Here Dionysius, following in the footsteps of Plato (particularly *Republic* II.377ff.), is part of a critical succession that pilloried both Homer and Hesiod for their representations of the divine world. Xenophanes had been the most famous case.[58] But because Dionysius does not extend his remarks to religion itself, or indeed to the efficacy of its political operation, his critique does not include anthropomorphism.

Because of his awareness of the lack of mythology in Roman religion and his proposed explanation, Dionysius is obliged, in II.20, to forestall any possible objection based on well-known

58. M. Untersteiner, *Senofane: Testimonianze e frammenti* (Florence, 1956), frr. 11–12, 14–16, pp. cxix ff. Cf. Cic. *Nat. D.* I.42, II.70.

theories of the usefulness of myth or indeed the reasons behind its origin. The advantages of mythology lay in its ability to provide an allegorical explanation of natural events, its consolatory effects on distressed human beings, its capacity for freeing the soul from disturbances, fears, and bad ideas, and in other useful designs for which it had been devised. Dionysius confronts these undoubted benefits with great caution, and it is Roman theology that lies at the root of his caution. He realized that the Greek mythology could only be of use to those few who had studied and understood it, in other words, philosophers. The majority of the people, who had no philosophical background, understood it in its worst sense and as a result fell into two errors: either they despised the gods for being caught up in so many mishaps, or they excused their own lack of restraint and shameful deeds by pointing to the example offered by the gods.

This explanation betrays a measure of unease, which, as we shall later see, derives to a great extent from his being obliged to reconcile a known and verified fact (the lack of mythology in Roman religion) with his own vision of early Roman history—indeed, on a broader plane, his own conception of history.

Dionysius, who later (II.21.2) quotes Varro (probably the *Antiquitates rerum divinarum*),[59] must have known the Stoic doctrines adopted by the Roman in the first book of his work. These doctrines claimed that religion had been invented by man, in fact by *civitates* (fr. 5 Cardauns), and they developed the idea of a tripartite theology, or rather three ways of viewing the gods. There was the natural or physical approach (proper to philosophy), the mythical (for the poets), and a civic attitude (for legislators) (frr. 6–11 Cardauns). At Rome this theory had earlier been accepted by Q. Mucius Scaevola and then by Varro him-

59. Cardauns, M. *Terentius Varro. Antiquitates* 1 : 62 (see the commentary at 2 : 182); cf. fr. 60 Cardauns (= Dionys. II.62.5) with the commentary at 2 : 168. It is not necessary to suppose that Dionysius's comments on the foreign cults in Rome derive from Varro *Antiq. rer. div.* frr. 45–46 Cardauns.

self. The theory was part of a complicated cultural debate involving the criticisms of poetry made by the philosophers and, in turn, the counterattacks made against the philosophers. The debate highlighted the civic facet of theology and therefore the political significance of the tripartite division.[60]

Varro explicitly acknowledged a Roman mythology, which he considered to be an invention of the poets and a great influence on mankind (fr. 19 Cardauns and the comment in Cardauns 2:148). He upheld the usefulness of the euhemeristic theories (fr. 20 Cardauns) and gave equal weight to concealing many truths from the masses or, frankly, deceiving them (fr. 21 Cardauns).

In reality none of this can be found with any certainty in Dionysius. The necessary provision of religious institutions in Rome by the legislator did not mean that Dionysius adhered to the doctrines of Critias, shared by Polybius (VI.56.6–12), that held that religion was exclusively a means of reining in the ignorant masses.[61] Though Dionysius might admit a civic purpose, at least in Greece, behind the invention of some myths that might benefit mankind, such was not the case in Rome. The legislator had, in fact, excluded myth from the cultural and political organization of society and the state. Yet Dionysius takes a very firm stance against atheistic philosophy, especially the Epicureans (II.68.1–2, VIII.56.1), primarily because they denied that the gods took the slightest interest in man. As has already been remarked, he considered the religious institutions (in their broad-

60. P. Boyancé, "Sur la théologie de Varron," *REA* 57 (1955) 57–84, now in Boyancé, *Etudes sur la réligion romaine* (Rome, 1972), 253–82; B. Cardauns, "Varro und die römische Religion," *ANRW* II.16.1 (1978) 80–103; G. Lieberg, "Varros Theologie im Urteil Augustins," in *Studi classici in onore di Quintino Cataudella* (Catania, 1972), 3:185–201, and "Die theologia tripertita in Forschung und Bezeugung," *ANRW* I.4 (1973) 63–115. On Scaevola: A. Schiavone, *Nascita della giurisprudenza* (Bari, 1976), 5 ff.

61. D. Stephans, *Critias. Life and Literary Remains* (Cincinnati, 1939), 67–69, 76–78; L. Perrelli, "Epicuro e la dottrina di Crizia sull'origine della religione," *RFIC* 33 (1955) 29–56.

est sense) laid down by the legislators to be a direct reflection of the benevolence shown by the gods toward Rome, hence a recognizably divine intervention in history. This was an argument that the Romans themselves had exploited as a justification for their dominion, but it could also be seen in a sense as limiting their merits. It was this recognition of a divine intervention in history that sparked off his arguments against the atheists. It also caused him to adopt a definite methodological stance toward history whenever a divine presence meant the acceptance of myth or fantasy as part of the narrative, especially when dealing with remote periods.

As far as divine epiphany was concerned, Dionysius limited his acceptance to those already present in the writings of the Roman historians that found credit with the people. Earlier, when dealing with the problem of relations between Numa Pompilius and the nymph Egeria (II.60.4–7), Dionysius acknowledges that some historians rejected the fabulous, seeing it as a simple expedient invented to facilitate the acceptance of laws as if they had come from the gods (following the Greek examples of Minos and Lycurgus: II.61.1–2). He nonetheless refuses to pursue a specific discussion of the gods or mythology and restricts himself once again to recording what was to be found in Roman histories. This attitude—one might almost call it agnosticism—is typical of Dionysius. In I.77.3, where he deals with the violence suffered by Rhea Silvia, Dionysius is loath to attribute improper deeds to the gods. He holds that they are not capable of such actions,[62] and he cannot bring himself to accept the theory of an intermediate race of daemons between man and the gods,

---

62. The same attitude was held by Varro in *De gente pop. rom.* (August. *De civ. D.* XVIII.10 = Fraccaro fr. 18): "Et tamen Marcus Varro non vult fabulosis adversus deos fidem adhibere figmentis, ne de maiestatis eorum dignitate indignum aliquid sentiat. . . . Haec [Paris's adventures with Juno, Minerva, Venus] Varro non credit, ne deorum naturae seu moribus credat incongrua."

who, joined with either, produced heroes.[63] Even here he refuses to discuss the value of these types of mythic tale, while acknowledging their existence by recounting them as he found them. The fact that he rejects theoretical discussion fits in with his narrative conception of historiography.

In other words, Dionysius accepts the patrimony of myth, which in fact could not be eliminated, given that it was to be found in many of the Roman histories and was believed by the people. It was, moreover, a patrimony that recorded the interventions of the gods in the affairs of man and had thus its own historicity, whatever degree of rationalist reelaboration it may have undergone.

V

The position adopted by Dionysius on the relation of myth to history may be clarified, and certainly given a better perspective within the culture of his own age, by a comparison with certain ideas dealing with the same problem that we find in the writings of Strabo and Diodorus. Diodorus confronts the problem at the very beginning of his own work. He asserts (I.3.2) that many historians have omitted τὰς παλαιὰς μυθολογίας (mythic tales and ancient fables) because they were difficult to work with. For

---

63. For the ideas on daemons: Plato *Symposium* 202 and ff.; Xenocrates fr. 225 Isnardi Parente; Plutarch *De Is. et Os.* 25–31 and *De def. or.* 10; cf. J. G. Griffiths, *Plutarch's De Iside et Osiride* (Cambridge, 1970), 26 ff., 383 ff. The theory of daemons is opposed to euhemerism, which was in a certain sense partially atheistic. Dionysius is loath, in the case of Romulus, to accept the tradition of his assumption into heaven, even though he is obliged to accept that the traditional connection of his death with the festival of Poplifugium gave weight to the supporters of the euhemeristic theories (II.56.2–6), which he clearly did not share. As far as Dionysius is concerned there was a more credible version of Romulus's death in his assassination at the hands of senators for his later tyrannical attitude (Gabba, "Studi su Dionigi da Alicarnasso. I," 221–22). According to W. Burkert, "Caesar und Romulus-Quirinus," *Historia* 11 (1962) 365–76, the saga of Romulus's death symbolized a ritual myth concerning the murder of the king.

his part, he promises (I.6.1, referring to Book IV) a separate work
on the ideas of those who first taught respect for the gods, as
well as more ample accounts, whenever necessary, of the fantastic traditions relating to each deity. The treatment would be
divided into distinct sections and would omit nothing of importance to the history under consideration, which would thus be
circumscribed by demigods, heroes, and benefactors of humanity. A distinction is, however, already clear in Diodorus,
and he readily accepts the historicity of heroic and semidivine
mythology.

Diodorus returns to the problem in IV.1.1ff. Once more it
stems from the author's awareness of the difficulties faced by
historiography in the treatment of ancient mythology. The difficulties involved are a result of the antiquity of tradition, the absence of any chronology, and the variety found in genealogies of
heroes, demigods, and other famous characters. This confusion
lay at the root of the discrepancies in the preserved tradition and
gave grounds for uncertainty. It was also the reason (IV.1.2–3)
why more recent historians (Ephorus, Callisthenes, Theopompus) had excluded the ancient mythology. Diodorus, on the
other hand, confronted this attitude to the ἀρχαιολογία. According to him, the deeds of heroes, demigods, and famous men
were both exemplary and significant; they were deserving of
their heroic or semidivine cults because they were innovators
and benefactors to mankind. At the very least they should be
praised in history. And this is, in fact, the theme of Book IV
(IV.1.5). The ultimate purpose behind this treatment of history,
that is, the inclusion of mythology, though this was limited to
heroes and demigods, is made explicit in IV.8 with the case of
Hercules. This famous character presented particular difficulties
to anyone wishing to recount the ancient mythologies, because
of the fame of his actions and their magnitude in space and time.
It is true to say that the antiquity and extraordinary nature of his
deeds had given rise to scepticism, but silence could only dimin-

ish the divine glory, while a full account would make the history incredible; one was thus faced with two dangers. Scepticism and incredulity are seen as errors of judgment (IV.8.3). The error lay in a conception of truth that was measured, in degree and type, according to the yardstick of the reader's own day rather than that of ancient times. Diodorus was convinced that a different truth existed for the heroic age, which was not susceptible to the measures and methods appropriate as criteria for the verification of more modern events, that is, in the historic period. In addition, the strength of Hercules could not be judged from the weakness of modern man. Hence one could not search in mythology for an historical truth (IV.8.4) whose precision was achieved at any cost. Myth must be accepted in history as it was in the theatre. Just as their predecessors (IV.8.5) had, for their own benefit, endowed Hercules with divinity (Diodorus gives an accurate account of euhemeristic theories), so Diodorus's contemporaries must continue to reverence the god. As he asserts in IV.77.9 in a passage concerning Icarus, myth must not be excluded on the basis of absurdity or strangeness.[64]

One may finally add that the system of thought found in Diodorus is part of a theoretical outlook on history that regarded the biographies of gods and heroes, and famous men who might later undergo a beatifying process, as part and parcel of "true" history.[65]

We now turn to Strabo in *Geography* I.2.8. Here he practically overturns the arguments and proposals found in Plato's *Republic* (II.377ff.), which aimed at limiting the pedagogical influence of mythological fables found in the poets. As we saw in Chapter 2, Strabo recognizes that poetry, with its fabulous char-

64. P. Veyne, *Les grecs ont-ils cru à leur mythes?* (Paris, 1983), 57 ff. The best comment on the passages of Diodorus and Strabo here cited will be found in the essay of B. Fontenelle, "De l'origine des fables," in *Oeuvres* (Amsterdam, 1764), 3:160–75.

65. E. Gabba, "True History and False History in Classical Antiquity," *JRS* 71 (1981) 54 and n.15 (on Sextus Empiricus *Math.* I.253–55, 258–61).

acter, takes chronological precedence over history and philosophy. Its precedence is due to the gradual nature of cultural diffusion and the manner of its reception. Strabo maintains that the
acceptance and spread of myth was not so much an invention or
artifice of the poets as a calculated political fact based on the
natural disposition of man, with his inclination to learning and
curiosity for the new and unexpected.

Within a complicated anthropological framework this drive
to awareness is modulated according to the era, the ability to
learn, and the level of instruction. Different types of truth correspond to these factors, or rather different methods of presenting
the narrative, which is not, in effect, primarily concerned with
expressing reality. Instead it seeks receptiveness by using novelty
and the pleasure it arouses. The desire for learning is, nonetheless, still present, for the strange and marvellous are an incen-
tive. It is only in a second phase that reality can be learned by
those who have strength of mind, proceeding beyond this early
stage and the lures that were a necessary preliminary to reason.

Moreover the marvellous, which is a basic element of myth
and fable, encourages the majority of people to goodness while
discouraging them from evil, and thus fulfills a pedagogical role.
The poets accomplish this end by their exposition of the noble
deeds of a Theseus or a Hercules, telling of their rewards from
the gods, while painting and sculpture present analogous episodes. Fear, based on the menace of divine retribution as seen in
writings or images, drives women and the ignorant masses to
believe in the reality of punishment and thus compels them to
respect the gods and observe religious piety. The fear of the gods
is inseparable from the whole apparatus of wonder and fable
that attends the manifestation of divinity, and which characterizes primitive theology. The legislators exploited this fear to
dominate the masses. In poetry this patrimony of myth answered social and political ends, whereas history and philoso-

phy were the preserve of the few (though early historians and investigators of nature were also writers of myth).

Strabo adds that artists can supplement the real facts they sing of with fabulous adornments specifically because these are of pedagogical value and import. (In the particular case at issue here, which prompted Strabo's digression, these are the reasons given for being able, indeed being obliged, to retrieve the nucleus of historical and geographical truth that lies at the heart of Homer.) For Strabo, myth definitely belongs to the province of religion. Because he is concerned with arguing against Eratosthenes and defending the "scientific" validity of the Homeric text, he does not at this point pay any attention to the immoral aspects of myth or human representations of the gods that had initiated the Platonic rejection of Homer, Hesiod, and poets in general.

Despite a number of similarities, Dionysius and Strabo occupy two quite separate positions on the basis of fundamentally different assumptions. As Dionysius saw it, the essential historical and moral validity of a traditional narrative history, where divine and human actions are confounded, is far removed from what Strabo, when working on Homer, had in mind as the basic and scientifically sound nucleus to be found at the heart of fantastic and wonderful poetic texts. Dionysius is clearly, and understandably, closer to Diodorus, even if he cannot, again understandably, bring himself to accept the necessity of a different set of historical criteria for the archaic period in Rome, as opposed to later epochs.

The absence of mythology in Roman religion is still a problem of great importance to modern historians and their research, though the methods, assumptions, and developments of today are quite different from those facing Dionysius; comparison of the two approaches might well prove interesting. The following brief indications will provide some idea of the direc-

tions research has taken. G. Wissowa[66] always maintained that
the traditional Roman mythology was a mixture of second-hand
ingredients, poetic invention, and the translations of Greek sagas.
He denied the existence of an ancient, popular core. K. Latte
reached a similarly negative conclusion[67] from a "primitivist"
perspective of the most remote phase of Roman religion, which
examined both the minor deities (who are seen as an Italian representation of the divine, so dispersed in its concrete manifestations as to defy speculation or the elaboration of fantastic
myths) and the major gods. The assumptions of Wissowa and
Latte found an important successor in the justly celebrated research on Roman Jupiter by C. Koch, who worked with the
methods of the Frankfurt school.[68] An examination of the strata
of tradition allows one to recover traces of a mythology that
in the later historic period are reflected in elements of the Roman religious system. Having evaluated the evidence found in
Dionysius in II.19.3 (dealing with the political controls on foreign cults), and by specifying the links between cults and mythology, Koch manages to detect a process of "demythicization"
in the state religion that was both conscious and unconscious.
Divine power at Rome manifested itself not in the field of myth
or at some past time, but in history. Demythicization signified
the elimination of everything extraneous to the common ground
of state and history, that is, whatever was uncontrollable or
rather outside the orbit of humanity in history.

66. "Römische Sagen" (1888), reprinted in G. Wissowa, *Gesammelte Abhandlungen zur römischen Religions- und Stadtgeschichte* (Munich, 1904),
129 ff.; *Religion und Kultus der Römer* (Munich, 1912).

67. "Ueber eine Eigentümlichkeit der italischen Gottesverstellung," *ARW*
24 (1926) 244–58; *Römische Religionsgeschichte* (Munich, 1970) 18 ff.,
264 ff.

68. *Der römische Juppiter* (Frankfurt am Main, 1937); see R. Syme's review in *JRS* 29 (1939) 108–10. According to Burkert, 356–59, the identification of Romulus with the god Quirinus (and so the reintroduction of the myth
in the state cult) was an initiative of Caesar.

Dumézil too,[69] in his opposition to primitivist tendencies and their related interpretation of the divine at Rome (Latte), has set forth the complex and coherent idea of a lost and forgotten mythology that may yet be rescued by recourse to the rites and by contrast with other Indo-European systems.[70] This loss is attributed to the intrusion of Greek mythology and its assimilation, which forced the vestiges of the old divinities into oblivion. Along with his recognition that the more important gods at Rome had no background mythology, Dumézil makes some very astute observations on the transition from mythology to history, that is to say on the tendency, already existing in the archaic period, to use myth and epic legend to reconstruct the protohistory of the city.

It might appear that, given the existence of myth, demythicization ought to have been recognized. The process of writing history, however, is not always a consequence of or an alternative to demythicization. At any event, the reasons or methods that may have operated in this instance are not clear to us unless we admit Taylor's succinct proposal of a deliberate intention to demythicize state religion. We would still, however, have to account for the decision to displace part of the myth in the reconstruction of Roman protohistory. Certainly "the coincidence between various moments in the pseudo-history of Rome and the mythic dimension"[71] has no bearing on those myths concerning the major gods that were eventually lost and may never have been historicized: these cases are the object of Dionysius's arguments and Wissowa's denials.

69. *La réligion romaine archaïque* (Paris, 1966), 39 ff., 46 ff., 60 ff., 72 ff., 106 ff.

70. G. Camassa, *L'occhio e il metallo. Un mitologema greco a Roma?* (Genoa, 1983), on the relationship between the prehistoric Latium and Mycenean or post-Mycenean Greece.

71. G. Pittaluga, *Terminus. I segni del confine nella religione romana* (Rome, 1974), 11.

The historicizing of certain myths is a recognized procedure that also occurs in ancient times, but it is not adequately explained even by Bayet.[72] He does, however, grant that the Roman mentality was, by comparison with other Indo-European peoples, to a great extent hostile to myth, and that the fund of Indo-European mythology was much depleted by the time it reached Rome. This weakness of the mythic and genealogical imagination would also explain the late transition to anthropomorphism in Roman religion, which in turn acts as a factor for this very weakness. Bayet, following traditional data, links anthropomorphism to Etruscan domination at Rome in the fourth century B.C. The problem is also of great importance to modern historians, because it provides a means for measuring the distance between Dionysius and Varro on this key matter of interpreting archaic Roman religion.

In Book I of the *Antiquitates rerum divinarum* Varro declares that during the first 170 years from the city's foundation the Romans used no images in their adoration of the gods.[73] This observation must have been made in the light of a threefold development in the performance and status of divine cults. From an aniconic phase without temples and with only provisional altars there must have been a transition to the first simple temples (though still without any images of the deities) in the age of Numa and thence, through Etruscan and Greek influences, to an anthropomorphic representation of the gods and larger temples.[74] The end of this 170-year period brings us to 584 B.C., the beginning of the sixth century, in the reign of Tarquinius Priscus,

72. *La réligion romaine: Histoire politique et psychologique* (Paris, 1976), 45 ff., 110 ff.

73. August. *De Civ. D.* IV.31 = Varro fr. 18 Cardauns; Plut. *Numa* 8.18. According to L. R. Taylor, "Aniconic Worship," Varro thought that the Romans, like the Jews, were not allowed to represent the divinity.

74. Tert. *Apol.* 25.12 = fr. 38 Cardauns; Varro *De vita pop. rom.* I.13 Riposati.

when Vulca, who was responsible for the clay statues of Jupiter and Hercules, was called to Rome (Pliny *NH* XXXV.157). The Jupiter statue would have been in the temple of Capitoline Jupiter, which is thus dated to the period of the first Tarquin (Dionysius III.69.1–2).

The opinion of the archaeologists is all-important in any consideration of these problems, and they in fact concur that Varro's reading of the chronology coincides with reality.[75] Nonetheless, the Varronian version of the development of Roman religion, so far as it may be discerned from this theory of its transition from an aniconic to an anthropomorphic stage, presents us with difficulties that both Boyancé and Dumézil remarked.[76] At this juncture these difficulties do not concern us; what should be noted, however, is that the admission of an aniconic phase in Roman cult might, evidently, have affected the problem of the absence of a mythology (hence the reservations of Dumézil); but Varro, on the one hand, shows little interest in pursuing this line, and Dionysius, on the other, refrains from any comment on this primitive aniconic phase.[77] Thus Dionysius (II.18.2) makes the explicit assertion that Romulus founded temples, sacred precincts, holy statues and images and symbols of the gods, and so on. Only in this way, that is, through the affirmation of an original anthropomorphism based on an available and already very ancient Greek model, could he sustain his thesis of a voluntary, contemporary elimination of the mythic patrimony for reasons of civic and religious morality.

75. G. Colonna, "Tarquinio Prisco e il tempio di Giove Capitolino," *PP* 36 (1981) 46–48, 51–59.

76. Boyancé, "Les implications philosophiques des recherches de Varron sur la réligion romaine," in *Atti del congresso internazionale di studi varroniani* (Rieti, 1976), 1:137–61.

77. The aniconic theory of the gods, attributed to Dionysius by Cyril *Adv. Jul.* p. 193 Spanheim (= *PG* 76 col. 796), is a mistake: Taylor, "Aniconic Worship," 306 n. 2.

This view is confirmed by Dionysius's treatment of the Trojan Penates (I.67–69).[78] In I.67.4 he argues indignantly against Timaeus (*FGrHist* 566 F 59), who, trusting the inhabitants of Lavinium, had claimed that the sacred objects brought by Aeneas were in fact iron and bronze emblems and a vase of Trojan ceramic. For Dionysius, the Penates were the great gods of Samothrace, identified with the Dioscuri, whose statues he had seen in the *aedes deum Penatium* on the Velia. Varro (*Antiquitates rerum humanarum* II, fr. 8 Mirsch), however, did not accept a link with the gods of the Velian Temple and, following Timaeus, held that the Penates were indeed *sigilla lignea vel lapidea*.[79] As aniconic symbols of the gods they fitted well with his own theory of Roman primitive religion. Dionysius does not exclude the possible existence, in inner sanctums of the Vestal Temple forbidden to the profane (I.69.4), of other sacred objects brought by the Trojans, but he has no doubts of his identification of the Penates with the Dioscuri.

Dionysius cannot afford such doubts because Roman religion is a cornerstone of his reconstruction of history as a demonstration of Rome's original Greek character. It is worth recalling the arguments in VII.70—a key passage for an understanding of Dionysius's historiography and in its own way a very helpful guide to the development of ancient anthropology. Dionysius, whose principal aim, it must be repeated, was to establish the Greekness of the Romans, sets out in VII.72 to describe the religious procession preceding the *Ludi Romani Maximi* (VII.73), which took place for the first time in 490 B.C. Dionysius openly

78. G. Wissowa, "Die Ueberlieferung über die römischen Penaten" (1886), reprinted in *Gesammelte Abhandlungen zur römischen Religions- und Stadtgeschichte* (Munich, 1904), 95–128. Cf. S. Weinstock, "Penates," *PW* 19 (1937), cols. 451–56. The problems concerning the Penates have been completely reinstated by the discovery of the famous inscription of Castor and Pollux in Lavinium (end of the fifth century B.C.?): Degrassi, *ILLRP* 3; F. Castagnoli, *Lavinium*, vol. 2 (Rome, 1973), 441–43.

79. Serv. auct. *ad Aen.* III.148, I.378.

acknowledges Fabius Pictor, the first Roman historian (*FGrHist* 809 F 136), as his main source. He is sure that he can show these games and ceremonies to be of Greek origin, and a key point in this demonstration is his examination of certain passages in Homer. Our point in this case is unaffected by the fact that archaeological investigations have shown that comparisons with Greek examples do not correspond with reality and that there is a predominance of Etruscan influences.[80] Fabius Pictor was not chosen at random as a source, and the description of the procession is calculated for effect. Fabius Pictor precedes the period marking the Greek cultural invasion of Rome (VII.71.1, 72.4), which Dionysius sees in relation to the Roman military conquests and the consequent achievement of hegemony over Greece and the Greek world. In his eyes the phenomena of cultural fertilization are a result of subjugation. The comments of Dionysius, interspersed in the text of Fabius Pictor, are in fact comparisons with the Homeric text and are intended to confirm that intuition. Thus he distinguishes the Greek cultural fertilization of Rome in the second century B.C. from another phase of Greekness that he pushes ever backward in time, specifically to locate it at the very origin of Rome. He does this so that it may be understood less as an acquired characteristic than as a primary factor in itself, essentially at one with the provenance and ethnic character of the various peoples who, by their fusion, had laid the foundations for the birth of the Roman state. In this sense I.90.1–2, which we have already cited, is of fundamental importance.

In VII.70 Dionysius asserts that, by comparison with other systems, religious institutions in both the Greek and the barbarian worlds are as a rule more consistent in maintaining their original character and suffer less modification, because of the

80. J.-P. Thuillier, "Denys d'Halicarnasse et les jeux romains (Antiquités romaines VII 72–73)," *MEFRA* 87 (1975) 563–81.

conservative tendencies induced by the natural fear surrounding religious matters. Only conquest at the hands of a superior foreign race can lead to the forgetting or transgression of elements in the traditional religious rites—the old giving way to the new. As this had never happened at Rome it was to be assumed that its rituals had been preserved intact from the past and, rather than the reverse, in all likelihood it would have been to the advantage of those conquered and ruled by Rome to embrace its religious traditions. If the Romans had been barbarians the world that subsequently fell under their sway for seven generations would have been barbarized. As this quite evidently did not occur, one could confidently affirm that the rites celebrated at Rome corresponded to those of antiquity; they were characteristically Greek, and this trait could be attributed to the peoples who had cooperated in the formation of the Roman people.[81]

These were the grounds for the great prominence given to re-

81. This vision of archaic Rome and the recognition of an ancient Greek presence in Rome and Latium is encountered in modern theories, based as much on archaeological material as on linguistic evidence, that propose a wide Greek influence (Mycenean or post-Mycenean) in ancient Latium. It must be stressed that, at least as far as method is concerned, the references to Dionysius that are often used to prove or support such theories are in no way conclusive and even substantially unjustified (I am thinking particularly of the many investigations by E. Peruzzi and most recently his *Myceneans in Early Latium* [Rome, 1980]). This inconclusiveness results either from the cultural and methodological assumptions underlying the modern work or from the origins and reelaboration of the material dealt with by Dionysius, a material that has significance within the author's own concept of historiography even when it can be shown to date back to ancient Greek or local traditions. In any case a preliminary analysis of the ancient historiographic text is essential. This should aim at defining the possible significance or original source for the material in question as well as the degree of reelaboration it has undergone within an assumed political and ideological perspective that must in its turn be clarified. There is no doubt that the coincidences with certain modern theories, based on a different type of documentation and different methodological criteria, are suggestive. Even the comments Dionysius makes when mentioning monuments or ancient documents should be understood, however, within the framework of his own ideas, his criteria for judgment, and the themes on which he intends to use them.

ligion within the overall plan of Dionysian historiography, for
it guaranteed preservation and the continuity of tradition. Its
Greek qualities were the surest proofs of the original Greek
character of Rome. Roman religion is understood and depicted,
in its gods, cults, rites, and institutions, as similar in all respects
to its Greek counterpart. Wherever this is not the case, as, for
instance, in the absence of mythology, some autonomous political decision must necessarily have intervened to deliberately
create the difference.

We can trace to this position the Dionysian tendency to give
scant regard to a theory whose greatest proponent was Cicero in
the *De re publica* (II.34). He held that a massive Greek penetration of Roman culture was felt with the first Etruscan king,
Tarquin, whose Greek origins even Dionysius was compelled to
acknowledge. Another example is even more revealing. Greek
religious rites connected with the cults of Ceres, Liber, and
Libera had been introduced to Rome at the beginning of the republican period in the wake of plebeian sedition. Their introduction is well attested in a variety of reliable historic sources
and marks a significant step in the social, religious, and cultural
history of Rome and also in her renewed relations with the area
of Magna Graecia. In these circumstances Dionysius merely
mentions the building of a temple as a result of a vote (VI.17.2,
94.3; 496 and 493 B.C.). In reality, as far as he is concerned, the
Greek rites of Ceres, unchanged by the years, had their origins
in an even older goddess of that name brought to Italy by the
Arcadians before the foundation of Rome (I.331).[82] The Arcadians, as a civilizing influence, are the people principally responsible for the introduction or inception of other divine cults in

82. H. Le Bonniec, *Le culte de Cérès à Rome. Des origines à la fin de la
république* (Paris, 1958), 213 ff., 248 ff. Intentionally I avoid the discussion of
whether an Italic Ceres existed before the coming of the Greek goddess, because the question is irrelevant for the reasoning of Dionysius.

Italy or Latium, starting with those of Hercules, and these cults
had continued uninterrupted to the historian's own time (I.32.5,
33.2–3, 40.2).

The prominence given by Dionysius to Roman religion as a
religion without myth must be situated within the perspective of
this complex vision of history. His observations derive from a
comparison, inevitable for the historian, with Greek religion,
which showed a close resemblance to the Roman system. In
the midst of all these similarities, identities, coincidences, and
derivations, here was one exceptional difference that Dionysius
alone had known how to grasp, precisely because of the direction he had given to his work in historiography. This observation of his, and to an equal extent the answer offered, have their
raison d'être in the framework of his historiography and must
be judged in that context. Our own explanations of the same
problem, based as they are on different mental outlooks, cultural demands, and research methods, must not be imposed in-
discriminately on an historian from the age of Augustus.

VI

It is clear from this and other examples that the rich antiquarian material that Dionysius used to outline the ethnographic framework of Book I is also employed, though somewhat differently, as a vehicle for comments of varying length and
substance to reinforce his thesis of a Greek origin for Rome. His
observations are often of a documentary nature. For example,
the mention of an ancient Roman inscription, which Dionysius
believed to be written in an archaic Greek alphabet, is of particular significance in the reconstruction of the earliest stages in
Roman culture. For the most part these ideas are based on the
historian's own investigations.[83] The Aeolic origins of Latin en-

83. IV.26.5 (*lex arae* of the temple of Diana Aventinensis); cf. II.54.2 and
I.87.2; III.1.2; X.32; on the problem: A. Stein, *Römische Inschriften in der
antiken Literatur* (Prague, 1931), Stellenregister s.v. Dion. Hal.

able him to introduce a learned aside on the digamma in the course of his examination of the word "Velia."[84] Archaeological and artistic observations, with this type of documentation, serve to support the theory of the Greek character of Rome.[85] In the main, the monuments cited have been visited by Dionysius himself. Archaeologists are well aware of how important the contents of Dionysius's work are for an understanding of the topography of the Comitium in the Roman Forum.[86] Another extremely interesting example is found in the information (I.64.5) on the hero shrine at Lanuvium, which was dedicated to Aeneas, even though his name did not appear in the monument's inscription. In all probability this is the same monument that was recently excavated near Castel di Decima. Here, as elsewhere, one must presume that Dionysius had indeed personally visited the site.[87]

The discussions on public law interspersed throughout the *History* of Dionysius rank in importance alongside the famous "staatsrechtlichen Exkurse" of Tacitus.[88] Naturally they are included for quite different reasons, but one cannot exclude a common source in authors, perhaps historians, of the late republican period who had a fertile interest in history and law. These discussions are enriched in Dionysius by comparisons with Greek institutions, and through them archaeological research is endowed with a precise political value. A typical case is

84. I.90.1 (Aeolic Dialect); I.20.3 (digamma); Gabba, "Il Latino come dialetto greco."

85. A. Andrén, "Dionysius of Halicarnassus on Roman Monuments," in *Hommages à Leon Herrmann* (Brussels, 1960), 88–104; C. Ampolo, "La storiografia su Roma arcaica e i documenti," in *Tria corda. Scritti in onore di Arnaldo Momigliano* (Como, 1983), 9–26.

86. F. Coarelli, *Il foro romano*, vol. 1, *Periodo arcaico* (Rome, 1983), 161 ff.

87. Cassius Hemina fr. 7 Peter maintains that Aeneas was worshipped as *Pater Indiges*. On Aeneas and Lanuvium: A. Momigliano, "How to Reconcile Greeks and Trojans," *MAWA* n.s. 45 (1982), no. 9, 238.

88. F. Leo, "Die Staatsrechtlichen Exkurse in Tacitus' Annalen" (1896), now in *Ausgewählte Kleine Schriften* (Rome, 1960), 2:298–317.

found in his arguments (V.64) regarding the nomination of the first Roman dictator. The date is 498 B.C., and the office of dictator is linked to internal undercurrents caused by the problem of debts and their remission.[89] The whole passage is rich in speeches in which echoes of the Catiline affair and Gracchan overtones are readily discerned (for example, V.64.1–2, 65.5, 68), and these reflect differing political positions of an extreme or a moderate type. In V.70 the Senate passes a motion aimed at outflanking the law of Valerius Publicola on *provocatio* that had incited the populace to disobedience. As the laws could not be repealed, they adopted the artifice of suspending the consulate and instituting a new magistracy with absolute powers and no restraints save a time limitation of six months. The nomination was, naturally, to be in the hands of the Senate, but their decision and deliberations on the new office would have to be ratified by the people for the nomination to be authorized. Because this was clearly an aristocratic ploy, the tradition relied on by Dionysius is forced to assert that the people, in giving their authorization, had been deceived (a similar operation is found in IV.20.1 and 21, dealing with the aristocratic interpretation of the Servian system).[90] Dionysius, however, repeatedly insists on the idea that the new office is a true and proper "voluntarily chosen tyranny."

The overall procedure leading to the nomination of the first dictator is skilfully integrated within the general attempt to account for many essential details. The Senate's nomination, which receives a significant mention in Cicero's ideal constitution[91] and is intended to emphasize the repressive political force of the office, encountered some difficulties in its practical appli-

89. Peppe, 42–46. In these pages I follow the reasonings advanced in my article, "Dionigi e la dittatura a Roma," in *Tria corda. Scritti in onore di Arnaldo Momigliano,* ed. E. Gabba (Como, 1983), 215–28.

90. Gabba, "Studi su Dionigi da Alicarnasso. II," 109.

91. Cic. *Leg.* III.9; E. Rawson, "The Interpretation of Cicero's 'De legibus,'" *ANRW* I.4 (1973) 350.

cation. In the end it was decided to entrust the appointment to a consul (V.71.3). Naturally, no explanation is given as to why an individual should succeed where the Senate had failed, but we should not ask too much of a tradition that had to reconcile the realities of institutional practice with the political intentions behind the office. As the choice had to be made between the consuls themselves, there was a genteel contest in modesty that led to Q. Cloelius's nominating T. Larcius, the other consul, as dictator. The description of the complex procedure and the subsequent nomination of the dictator is accompanied by two thoughtful chapters (V.73–74). Having proposed some possible explanations for the title "dictator," Dionysius emphasizes two ideas that subsequently assume a very precise role: on the one hand lay the desire to avoid any odium attaching to the title (as to "king"), on the other that it should be a true and proper elective tyranny (V.73.2). This conclusion allowed Dionysius to develop the theory of a Greek origin for the dictatorship. The comparison is made with the αἰσυμνῆται who feature in Theophrastus's work *On Monarchy,* where they are seen as elective tyrannies insofar as they were a response to a particular situation and, though necessary for a time, were restricted in their duration. Pittacus provides a clear example.[92] Dionysius, along with Theophrastus and indeed Aristotle[93] before him, places this type of office within the historic development of monarchy (V.74.1–3). The central idea was that, once the power of the king had been abolished because of corruption and abuses, there was an awareness of the necessity for a force above the law as a last recourse in unusual circumstances, such as unforeseen misfortunes, crises, or periods of corruption: that force, be it king or tyrant, would intervene with independent and swift remedies. After this comparison between the Greek and Roman

92. On the relationship between Theophrastus and Dionysius: Gabba, "Studi su Dionigi da Alicarnasso. I," 194–96.

93. *Pol.* 1285a29, 1286b38.

worlds Dionysius naturally rejects the theory of an Alban origin for the dictatorship, which had been advanced by the historian Licinius Macer (V.74.4 = fr. 10 Peter), who held that the annual offices replaced the extinct dynasty.

Dionysius's description of the manner in which T. Larcius exercised power is typical of the themes he judged beneficial to his readers, who were not simply political thinkers but members of the imperial political classes (V.75.1). There was a complete reorganization of the state, which ended with the termination of the office before its appointed time (V.75–77.1). Dionysius asserts (and here, perhaps, he is following Licinius Macer) that the moderate use of dictatorial powers continued uninterrupted right up to the third generation before his own time, that is to say until the advent of Sulla (V.77.2–3). This conduct on the part of the dictators was responsible for the concept of dictatorship as a last resource for salvation in a state of crisis.

These are thoughts of some importance to history because they are evidence for a positive evaluation of dictatorship as an unusual office whose task was not simply to quell by repression an internal and, by its nature, populist sedition, but rather to correct a situation that had become politically compromised. The dictatorship of Scipio Aemilianus in 129 B.C. must have been seen in this light as it came to grips with the crisis in the Roman state and its relationship with the Latin and Italian allies,[94] and this must also apply to the later dictatorship of Pompey between 54 and 52 B.C. The information we have from Cicero's *De re publica* shows that some time toward the end of the second century B.C. a relatively new idea of dictatorship was gaining ground, new at least as far as the final examples in the Hannibalic War were concerned; implicit in these ideas was the suggestion that the practice be resumed. Polybius, writing of

94. Cic. *Rep.* VI.12; C. Nicolet, "Le De re publica et la dictature de Scipion," *REL* 42 (1964) 212–30; cf. App. *BCiv.* I.67.

the Roman constitution only a short time before, had in fact made no mention of dictatorship. This idea of a possible role for the dictatorship must certainly have influenced the historiographical interpretation of the origins and historic development of the office, for example by underlining its interventions in internal politics in contrast to its original military role. Dionysius must already have found many examples in the annalists encouraging his own interpretation of an identical function and purpose underlying the role of the *aisumnetai* in Greece and the Roman dictators.

It was Sulla who showed the Romans that dictatorship could turn to tyranny. Sulla was the first and only dictator to act with bitterness and cruelty (V.77.4). The tyrannical exercise of dictatorial powers obscures but does not eliminate the fact that Sulla, in acting as he did, was in strict conformity with the concept of the office as a means of reorganizing and reestablishing the state; the title itself, *dictator legibus scribundis et rei publicae constituendae*,[95] is a sufficient indication that the office was a "constituent" dictatorship. The Sullan reforms are viewed negatively by Dionysius as aspects of a tyrannical power (V.77.5) despite, it must be said, a certain hesitation on his part, which is admitted in his declared unwillingness to pursue the problem of whether these reforms were beneficial or necessary to the Roman state. From his point of view it was the exercise of power that brought odium to the title of dictator (V.77.6). There is a probable allusion to Caesar in this. The dictatorship of Sulla is thus judged by Dionysius to be a deviation from a highly respectable tradition, a deviation that resulted in the diminution of the aristocratic and repressive character of the office while highlighting the operation of the magistracy in order to reestablish the rule of law, which had been compromised.

The constituent function of dictatorship is already outlined in

95. App. *BCiv.* I.462.

Dionysius from its earliest origins on another historic occasion, the Coriolanus episode, which, as we have already noted, is extremely important to the work of our historian. In Dionysius's depiction of this matter M'. Valerius, the brother of the famous Publicola, delivers a speech (VII.54–56) based on the themes of civic concord and the participation of all the elements of society in the running of the state. The speech is perhaps the fullest theoretical presentation of a programme advocating a mixed constitution for the Roman republican state, and as such it has received a great deal of attention in modern political thought. The mixed constitution is judged to be the sole worthwhile remedy against the degeneration of individual forms of government. The latter are described as undergoing a circular development involving a degeneration and a transition from one form to another, monarchy to oligarchy and in turn to democracy, one after the other, determined by the resolute interventions of individual citizens or groups who reestablish the new authority. He foresees the possibility that even the best oligarchy may be transformed into a tyrannical monarchy by the machinations of the powerful and their factions in senatorial circles. This concern, which obviously alludes to the situation in the first century B.C., is repeated at VII.56.1, but this possible outcome is balanced by the opposed possibility that a great personality, guilty of disturbing the oligarchic equilibrium, could, like Coriolanus, be called to account before the people if they had any say in government.

Another scenario might see the people, surfeited with power and seduced by demagogues, conspiring against the better citizens. The remedy in this case lies with the senatorial nomination of a dictator who, equipped with absolute and unfettered powers, would operate on the city's malaise in order to eliminate and prevent infection. His reforms would bring improvements in customs, laws, and the underlying concepts of life; he would institute offices for the wise administration of the state and would eventually step down from power and return to private life within six months (VII.56.2). In other words, even within the terms of a mixed constitution there existed the potential for a breakdown in the state's mechanisms as a result of degeneracy or the predominance of plebeian elements. This would be corrected by the dictator, as an instrument of senatorial power, gifted with moral superiority and political wisdom, who would not, however, restore the Senate to supremacy but, while putting a brake on popular agitation, act in the interests of the common good. His duty was, in fact, to reestablish the mixed constitution, the ideal form of government, and to initiate a recasting of the ethical principles for civic cohabitation. The dictator was thus a necessary cog in the constitutional works, someone who could resolve the problems that come at moments of crisis.

The presentation of the mixed constitution in the speech of M'. Valerius shows traces of discussions in the first century B.C., after Sulla and probably prior to Caesar, on the possible use of dictatorship. Despite reservations concerning Sulla's conduct, there is a recognition of the constituent function of the dictatorship, which was put into effect for the first time in Sulla's case. Its theories are set out within a general constitutional perspective as, in a sense, is the case in Cicero's *De legibus*. Dionysius knows how to exploit this institutional complexity, inherent in the very roots of dictatorship, as a means of developing his arguments (politically precise, if secondhand)[96] concerning the Greek origins of the office and the contrast with the *aisumnetai*. In other words, the political motivations already present in the annalistic models are integrated perfectly into the politico-philosophical thought of Dionysius.

From the many examples available, one other case will demonstrate our historian's ability to receive and assimilate an historical tradition in which the traditional event has already undergone a reelaboration inspired by recent problematical developments.

---

96. On the matrimonial rules of Dionysius, see the Appendix to this chapter.

Dionysius dedicates three involved chapters to the trial of Spurius Cassius (VIII.77–79; 485 B.C.).[97] The historian is familiar with the two versions of the event and sees fit to relate both, though his preference is for the first, which took the form of *iudicium publicum*. The minutely detailed discussion that Dionysius gives to information already present in his sources reflects the close relationship between historiography and the law that is found in the reconstructions of the annalists in the first century B.C. The condemnation of Spurius Cassius did not affect his two brothers in any way, and their complete security was guaranteed by *senatus consulta* (VIII.80.1). At this point it was difficult to avoid a comparison with the situation found in Rome after the civil war, when Sulla denied *ius honorum* to the sons of those whom he proscribed. This act contravened the general principle, held up to that time, that sons should not be liable for their fathers' misdeeds. The arguments that we find in the text at this point are directed not so much at Sulla as against those who, after 80 B.C., had blocked any reparation for such a monstrous and unprecedented injury by opposing any repeal of the iniquitous clause. As Dionysius notes, these opponents did in time receive a fitting punishment: they lost the great power they had acquired, and by Dionysius's own period there was no trace of their male lineage (VIII.80.2).[98] As we know, the sons of those proscribed by Sulla were given justice by Caesar in 49 B.C. with

97. Gabba, "Dionigi d'Alicarnasso sul processo di Spurio Cassio," in *La storia del diritto nel quadro delle scienze storiche. Atti del 1. congresso internazionale della società italiana di storia del diritto* (Florence, 1966), 143–53.

98. The text is not specific at this point and in all probability refers to Pompey rather than to Sulla's descendants (Gabba, "Dionigi d'Alicarnasso sul processo di Spurio Cassio," 150 n. 30). After Sulla, no Roman personality, with the exception of Crassus (II.6.4), is mentioned in Dionysius. The names of Augustus and Tiberius are recorded for the purpose of dating: I.7.2, 3.4; see VIII.87.7 and I.70.4. I believe Dionysius is following in this the practice of Cato, who, as we know, omitted the *imperatorum nomina* from his work (Nepos *Cato* 3.4; Pliny *NH* VIII.5 = fr. 88 Peter). The omission must only have applied to contemporary events, otherwise it would be difficult to ac-

the passage of a law by Antony. Here Dionysius has preserved echoes of the lively debates that must have taken place in Roman political circles. He then concludes the chapter in VIII.80.3 with a comparison between the usual Roman behaviour and the very different Greek custom, where the sons of tyrants were executed with their fathers or condemned to exile. Dionysius leaves his readers to decide which is the better course. He himself would have been quite familiar with Greek legislation against tyrannies and the rich philosophical and political thought that had developed around the problem, drawing on religious, legal, social, and political conceptions about the responsibilities falling to the descendants of a criminal father. As we know from an exchange of letters between Cicero and Brutus in 43 B.C.,[99] this very problem had dramatically reappeared in the realities of the civil war that had followed the death of Caesar. Only in the reacquired tranquillity of the Augustan age could Dionysius recall the legal rights: what had been a matter for debate on the plane of political reality now became an argument subject to antiquarian and historical analysis.

---

count for the exemplary status of great personalities with which we are presented in the preface to his work (frr. 2 and 118 Peter). For an excellent analysis of the preface *vide* Letta, 25–30.

99. Cic. *ad Brut.* I.12, 13, 15.

Appendix: The Matrimonial Norms Established by Romulus

Even Dionysius accepts (II.24.2) the basic principle that the family unit is the formative element of the state (Arist. *Pol.* 1252a), as indeed had been recognized by all those who had previously established constitutions among the Greeks and barbarians.[1] The regulation of family affairs was thus given an importance transcending the privacy of the individual citizen. The able politician, be he legislator or king, was obliged on this account to lay down standards that would make the life of the citizen both just and temperate. According to Dionysius (II.24.3), however, some politicians had been mistaken in their treatment of the very basics. Indeed (II.24.4) at the very heart of the matter, that is to say marriage itself or the relations between a man and a woman, they had taken the beasts as examples and allowed a free and promiscuous relationship to develop so that the results of passion and jealousy, and hence their ruinous effects on both state and individual, could be avoided. Others (II.24.5) had instead instituted monogamy but had made no provisions to preserve matrimony or to ensure the chastity of women, almost as if this were an impossible undertaking. The idea that women are ultimately responsible for society's ills is already quite clearly expressed in this passage.[2]

1. W. Erdmann, *Die Ehe im Alten Griechenland* (Munich, 1934), 87 ff. (monogamy), 112 ff. (state and marriage); W. G. Becker, *Platons Gesetze und das griechische Familienrecht* (Munich, 1932), 31 ff. (state and marriage).
2. Similar objections were advanced against Augustus's proposals in 18 B.C.: Cass. Dio LIV. 16.1–7.

Others again had forbidden sexual relations outside matrimony (though the barbarians were not averse to this)[3] and did not neglect to safeguard their women (the Spartans, on the other hand, were remiss in this respect), going so far as to lay down rules to restrict women and even instituting an office to regulate feminine εὐκοσμία. These regulations, however, had shown their insufficiency in cases where the woman was not virtuous by nature. As a matter of course the norms established by Romulus (II.25) proved excellent. When Dionysius describes the "sacred marriage" (the *confarreatio,* II.25.2), he also considers its later consequences and provides us with the information (the only source before the *Institutiones* of Gaius) that the wife inherited the estate on the husband's decease as a daughter would her father's estate.[4]

The anthropological and ethnographic arguments in II.26 touch on the serious problem of relations between the state and the individual in the matter of a citizen's private life and in particular the institution of matrimony. The necessity for the state's intervention in matrimonial affairs is legitimized, though it had been conspicuously absent from classical Roman law up until the fifth century B.C.[5] Dionysius's comments conclude by restricting themselves to the specific problem of the greater or lesser liberty of women and the safekeeping of their morality and behaviour. The excessive freedom given to Spartan women was a familiar theme in this context. The allusion to an office to oversee these matters refers to the γυναικονόμοι, which were, according to Aristotle (*Pol.* 1299a22; cf. 1322b39), already a feature of archaic legislations and in any event typical of tem-

3. On women's promiscuity: Hdt. I.215 (Massagetes); IV.172 (Massagetes and Masamones); Diod. V.18 (Balearians); Caes. *BGall.* V.16 (Britons); Theopomp. *FGrHist* 115 F 204 (Etruscans).
4. E. Volterra, "La graduum agnationis vetustissima descriptio segnalata da Cujas," *MAL,* 8th ser., 22 (1978), fasc. 1, 59–61.
5. R. Villers, "Le mariage envisagé comme institution d'état dans le droit classique de Rome," *ANRW* II.14 (1982) 285–301.

perate aristocratic states; the office would later assume different functions.[6] Such an office had never existed in Rome, but Dionysius (XX.13.7) has some interesting things to say about the broader powers available to the Roman censors enabling them to intervene in and regulate the life of the private citizen, powers which indeed were unknown in Athens and Sparta. The passage recalls a fragment of Cicero's *De re publica* (IV.6.6): "nec vero mulieribus praefectus proponatur, qui apud Graecos creari solet, sed sit censor qui viros doceat moderari uxoribus." Here we have yet another proof of the links between Cicero's *De re publica* and the work of Dionysius.

On the other hand, the basic arguments of Dionysius (II.24.4) are clarified by a comparison with Plutarch *Numa* 25 (containing a comparison between Lycurgus and Numa). There Plutarch compares the Lycurgan institutions[7] for matrimony with those at Rome. Both aimed at eliminating jealousy, but they envisaged different methods for the same end. In Plutarch the comparison is not completely to the disadvantage of Sparta, even though a deal of space is given to the excessive freedom enjoyed by Spartan women. Plutarch also concludes (25.13)[8] by recalling the divorce of Spurius Carvilius also found in Dionysius (II.25.7). Plutarch, who knew and used his Dionysius well, did not fail to make his own additional contribution. The direct attribution of the regulations for matrimony to the first king, albeit as part of his general activities as a legislator, assumed particular significance, specifically because Roman matrimony had never required state intervention. There is an air of special pleading in the use of philosophical and political thinking on the origins of family status, which, when combined with the historic

6. Claude Wehrli, "Les gynéconomes," *MH* 19 (1962) 33–38 (Dionysius's text is not quoted).

7. Described in Plut. *Lyc.* 14–15, esp. 15.11–16. The rules are declared in conformity with the laws of nature and of the state.

8. See Plut. *Rom.* 35.4 (= *Comp. Thes. et Rom.* 3).

and ethnographic comparisons made, underlines the difference between philosophical thinking and practical legislation on the matter. It is interesting to recall that Augustus himself, in a passage from the speeches attributed to him by Cassius Dio on the occasion of the Lex Papia Poppaea of 9 A.D. (LVI.6.4), mentions a law on matrimony that was instituted at the very origin of the Roman state and later regulated by the Senate and people. (Romulus is mentioned at LVI.5.4.)[9]

Lastly, Tacitus took the proposals made in 20 A.D. to modify the Lex Papia Poppaea as a starting point for one of his famous excursus on public law, which deals with the birth and development of law and legislation (*Ann.* III.25–28). Matrimonial legislation is seen as the greatest interference with personal freedom and as the logical conclusion of any and every state intervention. For Tacitus this was part of an ever-increasing drift from the optimum conditions of a natural state and indeed a move away from the laws of the Twelve Tables, the "finis aequi iuris." Tacitus held that Romulus had governed "ut libitum" and that true legislation had only commenced with Servius Tullius. According to Pomponius (in *Dig.* I.2.2), Romulus had legislated only in the latter half of his reign.

9. L. Ferrero Raditza, "Augustus' Legislation Concerning Marriage, Procreation, Love Affairs and Adultery," *ANRW* II.13 (1980) 278–339; E. Badian, "A Phantom Marriage Law," *Philologus* 129 (1985) 82–89.

CHAPTER FIVE

Dionysius on the Social and Political Structures of Early Rome

I

There is a certain static quality in the work of Dionysius. One cannot expect to find in him the pathos and national pride that animate the writing of Livy. Dionysius himself rejects, on principle, any emotional involvement in the facts narrated, though historiography as manifested by Duris and Philarchos had deliberately adopted such an involvement. Dionysius, on the other hand, aims at placing the reader *in medias res* and arousing his interest, while supplying him with as much information as possible for an understanding of the facts under consideration. This method had previously been applied by Lysias in his forensic orations, and indeed Dionysius reserves warm and appreciative praise for the orator.

The reasons for this immobility in the exposition of our author's history are varied. These need to be taken into consideration because they ultimately condition the very character of the narration, especially where the oldest period of the city's history is concerned. They form an integral part of the narration and as such are a conscious expression of the historian's intentions. In the first place, the entire history of Rome is guided by an ideological and historiographical schema that has been rigidly predetermined. This schema's ultimate and unerring aim is the demonstration of Roman superiority. The history of Rome is seen by Dionysius as a continuous exemplum of political, military, and civic virtue and thus as a proof of Rome's right to world domination. The not infrequent references to a decay in time-honoured customs and to civil wars in the post-Gracchan era are marginal and are never developed in Dionysius's historiography. They never impair the veracity of his evaluation of Rome in its earliest period.

The initial consequence of this approach is that all the personalities who intervene in the history have a fixed role. This role is most apparent in the speeches, which are both long and frequent because each orator is required to explain and justify his position in the historical and political context in which he acts out his part. The occasions for such interventions were, as we have said, numerous and chosen by Dionysius in relation to their importance. In accordance with the historian's overall intuition of the general historic context and the particular situation, with its probable but ultimately necessary development, each personality plays his part. In this perspective even Romulus and Tullius Hostilius and Servius Tullius deliver long speeches that are programmatic of their political actions, as indeed is the case with Brutus, Spurius Cassius, Manius Valerius, Coriolanus, and the Decemviri.

Even the motif of the essentially Greek character of Rome as a city, though central to the historiography, eventually becomes monotonous. Not only is it constantly reaffirmed, but it inevitably entails the necessity of a series of proofs that rely upon erudite comparisons of customs and institutions and discussions of constitutional and archaeological problems. The discussions of archaeology, always pertinent and important, are in truth direct interventions of the historian in the course of the narrative. Both in their aims and in their content they call to mind a certain analogy with the "staatsrechtliche Exkurse" of Tacitus. Not only has the historian arranged and approached his narrative material according to his ultimate aims, he also intervenes on a critical level to document and explain the notions he propounds. In terms of composition these personal interventions of the historian are well dispersed and integrated within the text. From an artistic and literary point of view, however, they weigh upon the narrative and break its flow. Theopompus had preferred to give separate books to his digressions, with distinct titles. Dionysius wished to follow another method by inserting his critical and expository commentaries of an archaeological nature in the very body of the historical text.

Dionysius's understanding of the birth of Rome as a colonial foundation of the Greek type brought with it the necessity of positing all or almost all of the institutional apparatus of the state and its civic complement as complete at the city's very origins. Above all, this implied the fundamental structure of a society based on agriculture and war, with a precise delineation of classes and their various functions. This design facilitated an historical perspective that envisaged Romulus as *the* legislator, someone, that is, who had given the populace its constitution or, at the very least, established from the beginning social, political, and religious norms that were valid and binding for all the subsequent history of the city. In other words, many of the city's later historical phases were concentrated in or anticipated by Romulus and his independent political activity.[1] Since his laws and those of his successor Numa Pompilius were only partially written down (II.24.1, 27.3) one could uphold the theory that a great deal of Rome's subsequent legislation had been formed from norms already in existence, or from customs of the Romulean age that were eventually put into written form.

1. Musti, "Etruschi e greci," 41–43. Romulus left the decision on the form of the state's institutions up to the people, and they chose monarchy: II.3–4. After the *auspicia,* II.5, Romulus was elected king of the people: II.6. The type of constitutional system mentioned in section 14 is a mixed constitution. In 14.3, Dionysius does not tell us whether he regarded the popular assembly's freshly acquired independence as an improvement.

Even the wealth of legislation attributed to other kings is found to have its roots in the activities of Romulus (II.23.6). This approach evidently leads to a prevalent blandness in the historic development of Rome and consequently in the exposition of Dionysius's historiography. It seems likely that this bland aspect of the history, whereby critical periods in the city's evolution were restricted in their importance in the light of an anachronistic reassessment of the first king, was the object of the criticisms we read in the *Ineditum Vaticanum*. The veracity of such an historicized legendary patrimony would later be refuted by Plutarch.

Comparisons with Cato, Cicero, and Livy are inevitable. The historical portion of Cicero's *De re publica* (in Book II) presents, in its contents, a variety of analogies with the work of Dionysius but is different in its import. The political and constitutional history of Rome, to the time of the *provocatio* and the laws of the Twelve Tables, is seen as a progressive development toward the attainment by the populace of a greater degree of political freedom and participation. Hand in hand with this democratic development went the ever-increasing social and economic evolution of Roman society. Cicero naturally recognizes the high cultural level of the early period from Romulus on (II.18–21, I.58),[2] and the various reigns are seen as moments of historical progression in the acquisition of ever-greater powers for the people, regardless of intermittent returns to authoritarianism. For Cicero the final object of all this lay in the mixed constitution. Cicero himself, at the beginning of Book II of his work (II.1.1–3), cites a famous saying of Cato's, which probably represents the direction that author intended for his *Ori-*

2. According to Cicero, in that period of already remote antiquity, from the time when Romulus became king, Greece had already entered the historical era and was in a state of advanced civilization in which myths were no longer given credence. Rome is mentioned in the same breath. The permanence and continuity of the institutions in this instance is both an indication and a guarantee of their worth.

gines. According to Cato the constitutional and hence the historic development of Rome came about in total contrast to that of the Greek cities. In the latter, a single legislator laid down once and for all the constitutional norms for the state. The Roman state, on the other hand, was the historic outcome of the work of many hands through many generations, with the continuous application of much thought and experience over the years. Even for Livy, the monarchic period and the first republican era had seen a progressive development of Roman society, its institutions, and the concept of *libertas.* The historian stresses this development in Book II.[3] The interpretation of archaic Roman history displayed by the emperor Claudius in his speech to the Senate, which has been partially preserved for us in the inscription of Lugudunum (*ILS* 212) and which was rewritten by Tacitus (*Ann.* XI.23–25.1), is heavily qualified, because it was Claudius himself who was reassessing the early events of Roman history.[4] The emperor considered the many innovations and institutional changes of the monarchic and republican eras as positive and vital aspects of the history of the Roman people.[5]

Cato's viewpoint, which left the way open to fresh developments in the future, is totally confounded in the work of Dionysius. According to our historian, the individual kings were either legislators, whose work stemmed from Romulus and contributed to the exertions of their royal predecessors (such is the case with Numa and his nephew Ancus Marcius: III.36.3–4), or they represented in their speeches and political activities certain definitive aspects of Roman history. The latter is the case with Tullius Hostilius, who, in the great debate with the Alban Mettius Fufe-

3. H. Tränkle, "Der Anfang des römischen Freistaats in der Darstellung des Livius," *Hermes* 93 (1965) 311–37; T. J. Luce, *Livy,* 26–27, 244 ff.
4. Gabba, review of *Tacito e Claudio,* by Arturo De Vivo.
5. The comparison with the beginning of the *Annals* of Tacitus is obvious: F. Leo, "Die Staatsrechtlichen Exkurse in Tacitus' Annalen."

tius (III.7–11; cf. III.23.18–21), is seen as the theoretician for assimilation, upholding the right of the strongest to command rather than racial purity. The great figure of Servius Tullius is ambiguous because Dionysius is forced to combine two opposing interpretations of his achievements. Servius Tullius is ultimately, however, the legislator who rationalized the social and political system already existing at Rome and created the Latin League (IV.25.3–26).

This viewpoint accounts for Dionysius's great interest in the *leges regiae,* particularly those of Romulus and Numa, which are the subject of wide-ranging antiquarian comment, vying in importance with the laws of the Twelve Tables. Dionysius, adhering to his theory of a Greek origin for the Romans, has an interest in minimizing the Greek character in the legislation of the Decemvirate, even though he was aware of the tradition that spoke of a Roman embassy to Magna Graecia and Greece itself.[6] The laws of the Twelve Tables are seen as a fusion of Roman customs and written laws with Greek laws (II.27.3, X.55.5, 57.5; cf. X.55.3 and 60.6). No fewer than three of the prescriptions laid down in the Twelve Tables are dated by Dionysius back to the administration of Romulus.[7] The Decemvirate is understood and interpreted as an instance of internal sedition, rather than a fundamental political development.[8] The Roman

---

6. E. Ferenczy, "Römische Gesandtschaft im Perikleischen Athen," *Oikumene* 4 (1983) 37–41; "Le legge delle XII tavole e le codificazioni greche," in *Sodalitas: Scritti in onore di Antonio Guarino,* 4:2001–12; S. Tondo, "Ermodoro e Eraclito," *SIFC* 49 (1977) 37–67; M. Ducos, *L'influence grecque sur la loi des douze tables* (Paris, 1978).

7. S. Riccobono, *Leges,* vol. 1 of *Fontes iuris romani anteiustiniani,* ed. S. Riccobono et al., IV.2 b = Dionys. II.27.1–4; VIII.21 = II.10.3; IV.1 = II.15.2. A. Watson, "Roman Private Law and the Leges Regiae," *JRS* 62 (1972) 100–105, and *Rome of the XII Tables. Persons and Property* (Princeton, 1975).

8. E. Täubler, *Untersuchungen zur Geschichte des Decemvirats und der Zwölftafeln* (Berlin, 1921), 40 ff.; G. Poma, *Tra legislatori e tiranni. Problemi*

people remain somewhat anonymously in the background without ever assuming the role of protagonist.

In fact, even in the republican period, the actual protagonists of the history are prominent personalities through their respective speeches. The narrative centres on them and their intentions, behaviour, and actions. This arrangement owes much to the influence of Theopompus, in whose work, as we have already noted, the biographies of the personalities involved play a leading part. This, however, is linked to Dionysius's own conception of the political struggle at Rome as an essentially peaceful process, where the oratorical interventions of prominent people were granted a privileged reception.[9]

If we are to find in Dionysius's work a cultural development of Roman society other than simple territorial expansion, then we must look to his ideas on the Roman capacity for assimilation. Through this ability the Romans could accept, imitate, and improve the more advantageous institutions of those people with whom they came into contact. As has been widely noted, this was a matter of general acknowledgment and the subject of historical debate. The Romans themselves saw it as a matter for self-congratulation. Otherwise Dionysius's vision of Roman history, despite the imposition of the Greek model city, maintains its autonomy from Greek affairs; it is the historian who synchronizes events and establishes the connections. A definitive conclusion on this point is, however, hindered by the well-nigh total loss of the second half of the work.

---

storici e storiografici sull'età delle XII tavole (Bologna, 1984), 135 ff; F. D'Ippolito, "Le XII tavole; il testo e la politica," in *Storia di Roma,* ed. A. Momigliano and A. Schiavone, vol. 1 (Torino, 1988), 397–413. I suspect that the methodological statements proposed by Dionysius at the beginning of Book XI, i.e. of the second decad, hint at the description Livy gives of the Decemvirate.

9. A typical case is the speech of M'. Valerius on the best mixed constitution in VII.55–56; at VIII.5–8 Coriolanus, talking before the Volscians, defends the aristocracy.

II

To balance the possibly restrictive impressions of the judgments made up to this point on the work of Dionysius, it is essential to underline the fact that his exposition depends to a great extent for its character on the sources that he was constrained to use. As Dionysius himself records (I.6.2), the earliest Roman historiography had treated the history of the city, after its foundation, rather summarily. It could, indeed, be argued that more ample treatment was given to the pre-Romulean period. In areas such as this there was a rich supply of material from Greek sources on the prehistory and origins of Rome. The monarchic age and certainly the first republican period, at least until the first sacking by the Gauls, had been dealt with somewhat abruptly. Historical treatment becomes fuller when periods closer to or contemporary with the authors' lifetimes are concerned. This is a common enough hallmark of ancient historiography. The reasons for this dearth of history from the early stages of the republican era lie, however, in the scarcity of documentation and tradition available to the historians of the period. They were not the only ones to suffer in this way, for the poets too lacked information, as we see, for instance, with Ennius. In addition to this it must be remembered that, because of new contacts between the Greek and Roman worlds from the fourth century on, contemporary history lent itself better to the political purpose for which the Roman historians, who were politicians rather than men of letters, wrote. From the middle of the second century B.C. their political objectives were less in evidence, since Rome had achieved hegemony in the Mediterranean world. The goals of Roman historiography then changed drastically, as did the language in which it was written; formerly Greek for Greek readers, it became henceforth Latin.

Two important moments in the development of historiography occurred in the years of the Gracchi and of Sulla. The historians, who were virtually always politicians, concentrated to a much greater extent on the internal history of the city. Within the parameters of an outlook that recognized the repetitive character of history in line with the constants of human nature, the clashes between the Senate, knights, and plebeians, then between *optimates* and *populares,* could be seen as similar or analogous to the ancient conflicts between patricians and plebeians from the time of the origins of the republic until the laws of Licinius and Sextius. What had previously been an historical vacuum in early historiography was now filled by means of reconstruction and reinterpretation in the light of political problems in the second and first centuries B.C.[10]

The early history of the city, thus rewritten, now assumed a strong dramatic presence. Roman history had also been acquiring a more personal character throughout the second century B.C., particularly through the work of the Latin poets and the Greek historians. From the *Annales* of Ennius to Sallust and Livy and then to the *elogia* of the eminent dead in the Forum of Augustus,[11] there is an uninterrupted line that also includes the birth of the individual portrait and of Latin autobiography in the second century B.C. Cato's artifice in crediting the merits of Roman conquest to the Roman people as an impersonal whole, without mention of the commanding nobles (applied, perhaps, only to contemporary history), was a vain effort to resist this

10. Gabba, "Considerazioni sulla tradizione letteraria"; Cornell, "Alcune riflessioni." Above in the text I accept partially and not without hesitation the corrections Cornell has proposed to my interpretation, although I am not sure that with κτίσις τῆς πόλεως Dionysius did not intend even the royal age of the city.

11. Ennius *Ann.* 500 Vahlen: "moribus antiquis res stat Romana virisque"; Sall. *Cat.* 53.4: "ac mihi multa agitanti constabat paucorum civium egregiam virtutem cuncta patrasse"; Livy *Praef.* 9: "per quos viros quibusque artibus domi militiaeque et partum et auctum imperium sit"; L. Braccesi, *Epigrafia e storiografia* (Naples, 1981), 39 ff. on the *elogia.*

new approach in historiography and politics where the emphasis was laid on the preeminent personality. In the post-Sullan era
the role of individual personalities in the development of Roman
history was stressed to an even greater degree. This accentuation
paralleled the growing importance of powerful individuals as
well as of military influences in the political life of the late republican era. Historiography was profoundly affected by such
tendencies, and also by the widespread production of committed
political propaganda and the histories of individual families.

The historical depiction of the monarchic era, the individual
kings and their legislative actions and reforms, was also influenced by the self-assertion of individual power. Above all, there
was the birth and influence of the notion of *pater patriae,* the
new founder of the city, which began with Marius and Sulla and
continued during the first century B.C., with the imperial cult as
its final result. Noble Roman families boasted of their own origins among the ancient kings, and their effigies appeared on
coins. The kings were not the only ones to undergo the effects of
these new attitudes, for even perfectly historical personalities,
such as Camillus, were transformed.

The political and historiographical attitude of the Romans toward their kings has a curious history.[12] Roman hostility to the
monarchy was always basically linked to the person of the last
king, even though the image of Tarquin the Proud in historiography owed something to Greek antityrannical traditions.
Though the Romans had never concealed the element of fratri-
cide, it would appear that the feeling against Romulus had,
under Greek influence, penetrated from the second half of the
fourth century B.C. onward. It is possible that the antimonarchic

---

12. M. A. Giua, "La valutazione della monarchia a Roma in età repubblicana," *SCO* 16 (1967) 308–29; P. M. Martin, *L'idée de royauté à Rome,*
vol. 1, *De la Rome royale au consensus républicain* (Clermont-Ferrand, 1982).

propaganda against the Hellenistic kings of the second century B.C., which was spread by Rome through Greece and Asia,
may have influenced the historical traditions concerning the Roman monarchs and had an indirect effect on contemporary Roman politics. The poetry and historiography of the second century B.C., however, redrew the portraits of Romulus, Numa,
and Servius Tullius in a kinder light. Scipio Africanus was probably accused of royal aspirations on account of his air of proud
superiority. Such attitudes were naturally related to the over-
prominence of his powers within the oligarchic regime, with
which they were incompatible. Similar accusations would later
be levelled against Tiberius and Caius Gracchus. Such accusations would become the customary political slogans of the first
century B.C. as descriptions of the urge to personal political
power in opposition to the oligarchic and senatorial regime.
Possible and presumed revolutionary and demagogic ventures
in the early history of the republic were interpreted or reconstructed as *adfectatio regni,* though little solid information was
available for such an interpretation.

It has for some time been recognized that Dionysius's description of Romulus's reign was based on an historical source with a
political bias in favour of the Senate. This source naturally propounded a particular standpoint regarding relations between the
Senate and the people. It contained a full treatment of Romulus's
formative influence in the areas of public, religious, family, and
penal law. It dated the greater part of Roman political and social
institutions back to Romulus. This outlook carried great weight
in the historiography of the first century B.C. The dating of this
reconstruction is disputed, with the age of Caesar and the reign
of Augustus being put forward as likely dates. For my own part,
I think it best fits the era of Sulla or immediately afterward because of its general approval of an oligarchic regime. Dionysius
has personally reelaborated this viewpoint by adding comparisons with Greek institutions, an aspect that must have been

lacking in the source material. He has also, as he himself tells us, made his own selection from the vast legislation attributed to Romulus.[13]

This particular interpretation of the first king was consonant with the reorganization of the state undertaken by Sulla. One should not forget that Sulla's political programme was not a simple, moderate restoration of the regime of the Senate: it was also, indeed above all, an attempt to confront, by fresh means, the new conditions prevailing in the Roman state after the concession of citizenship to the *socii Italici.* On the other hand Roman society was, and would remain for some time, in a precarious and uncertain political and constitutional state with regard to the activities of the *comitia.* In this light it is quite understandable that normative archaic models should be imagined or created (originating with Romulus, Servius Tullius, the *leges regiae* in general), based on primitive and solemn sources of law that the kings typified.[14] Dionysius, with his conservative tendencies, was naturally in complete accord with such an outlook, and thus his receptive approval of its tone and contents may be readily understood. But this view of Romulus as king-legislator also had its influence on the interpretation of Romulus found in Cicero's *De re publica* (II.12–16), which

13. Gabba, "Studi su Dionigi da Alicarnasso, I." Having considered these texts over many years I think I have arrived at a better understanding of two aspects of the problem. On the one hand is the cohesion and unity of Dionysius's treatment of the monarchic era; on the other is the problem of establishing the chronology of the tradition on which he depends. While I would agree that there are decisive arguments confirming the politico-ideological context of the treatment within the period from Sulla to the second Civil War, nonetheless I would no longer hold that Romulus's "constitution" was originally in the form of a political manifesto. I would maintain that (as is the case in Dionysius's treatment of the matter) it formed part of a global reconstruction of the history of the monarchic era. I attempted to illustrate the tone of this reconstruction some years ago and I am emphasizing it here. Cf. also J.-L. Ferrary, "L'archéologie du *de re publica* (2,2,4–37,63): Cicéron entre Polybe et Platon," *JRS* 74 (1984) 87–98.

14. Mommsen, *Staatsrecht* 2:10.

provides us, among other things, with precious clues to chronology. This latter viewpoint of Cicero's partially contradicts the Catonian theory, which he nevertheless praises at the beginning of his work.

This was no isolated reconstruction of Romulus. It was indeed closely connected with already existing, strongly ideological interpretations of King Servius Tullius and his political activities.[15] The timocratic system under Servius and the system of centuriation cemented new social classes who were in the economic ascendant in comparison with the patrician class, and who were creating a more "secular" state. Naturally these classes could be interpreted in a popular sense, as indeed they already had been in the second century B.C. The traditional story of the king's slave origins played a part in this portrayal. In the *Brutus* of Accius, Servius Tullius is a popular and liberal king.[16] Much of this interpretation is found in our own tradition. According to Livy (I.60.4), the first consuls had been created "ex commentariis Servi Tulli." In Dionysius, Servius appears as a democratic king, and his reign is judged with this in mind. One cannot exclude the possibility that Dionysius's source in this instance may have been Licinius Macer, an historian with populist leanings. The latter even propounded a popular and antisenatorial refiguration of Romulus, traces of which may also be found in Livy.

The opposite and rigidly conservative view of Servius Tullius, which was historically more firmly based, emerged after Sulla. As far as can be discerned Sulla drew up his own constitutional reforms with Servius in mind (Appian *Bella civilia* I.266). In the face of social and political upheavals in the first century B.C. and above all with the decay of traditional political life, any recalling of or promised return to the centuriation arrangements

15. Gabba, "Studi su Dionigi da Alicarnasso, II." Cf. J.-C. Richard, "Recherches sur l'interprétation populaire de la figure du roi Servius Tullius," *RPh* 61 (1987) 205–25.

16. Gabba, "Il 'Brutus' di Accio," *Dioniso* 53 (1969) 377–83.

of Servius was a potentially strong ideological weapon. In fact, political rights and civic duties under this system were precisely graded according to the economic standing of the citizens. Servius Tullius and his administration became idealized, conservative models for society and politics within a balanced framework of freedoms in which the *gradus fortunae dignitatisque* were guaranteed (Livy I.42.4). The purpose of this arrangement was, as Cicero tells us (*De re publica* II.39), "ne plurimum valeant plurimi" and that power should lie "non in multitudinis sed in locupletium potestate." Cicero confirms these ideas in the late fifties, and I would not rule out the possibility that this nostalgically idealized institution, which was, however, firmly rooted in reality, may have been one of the points at issue in Sallust's polemic against the influence of riches in Roman political life.

The first result of using the centuriated system for ideological purposes was the increased prominence that the king's personality continued to acquire. In the history written by Dionysius this conservative interpretation is juxtaposed with another, more democratic viewpoint and reveals the historian's uncertainty when confronted with versions so radically different. As usual he lends weight to his text with archaeological arguments, which, however, enable us to understand more easily his own political stance, one of approval. At any event, his sources undoubtedly already contained this representation of Romulus and Servius Tullius as king-legislators of the Greek type.

Dionysius's insistence on the *leges regiae* also shares this tendency. The learned archaeological treatment given by Varro to Numa Pompilius's character provided material for the history of Roman religious institutions. Indeed, in all probability, in the years following 50 B.C. and therefore after the publication of Cicero's *De re publica,* a selection of laws attributed to King Numa Pompilius was circulated. These laws were distinct from the legislation of Romulus and were instead identified with the *ius Papirianum,* a collection of laws linked to King Ancus Marcius. We are still dealing with the political and historiographical traditions that facilitated Dionysius's theory that the entire structure of the Roman state dated back to the monarchic era and was the work of king-legislators. It would, moreover, have been very difficult for our historian to reject the complex and articulate reconstruction proffered by his sources. These were, more often than not, the work of historian-senators, at one and the same time writing history and participating in it, with lengthy family traditions behind them. For Dionysius they represented a guarantee of his work's accuracy.

III

The examination of a specific problem, the utilization of land and its ownership, can illustrate the complexity of the material that Dionysius received from the annalists and incorporated in his own work.

The division of his people into three groupings called tribes was basic to the makeup of Romulus's social and political schema. Each tribe was then subdivided into ten *curiae* and each *curia* in turn into ten *decuriae*. Each of these divisions was allotted a leader (II.7.1–4).[17] Corresponding to the division of people was a division of territory. The land was divided into thirty segments, which were assigned by lot to the thirty *curiae*. A portion of the land was reserved, however, for cult requirements and for temples, and some was left for public use. "This division of people and land constituted the largest common ἰσότης" (II.7.4). In this instance one must understand ἰσότης in the sense of greater overall equality and proportionality between

17. Varro *De ling. lat.* V.55: "ager Romanus primum divisus in partes tres, a quo tribus appellatae, Titiensium Ramnium Lucerum." Verr. Flac. *apud* Gell. *N.A.* XVIII.7.5: "tribus et decuriae dici et pro loco et pro iure et pro hominibus." The internal divisions of the *curiae* do not coincide with the *gentes*: Mommsen, *Staatsrecht* 3 : 12 n. 3; a different interpretation, I. Hahn, "The Plebeians and Clan Society," *Oikumene* 1 (1976) 54.

the territorial areas assigned by lot to the *curiae* and those areas belonging to the *curiae* themselves.[18] Dionysius does not intend to indicate that equality existed in the individual patrimonies within the *curiae*. For one thing, such an hypothesis would require that tribes and *curiae* should contain an equal number of citizens in order to envisage each individual member receiving a land allotment equal to that of each of his fellows.[19] There is thus no contradiction with the following chapter (II.8), which describes the division of the populace into patricians and plebeians, rich and poor.[20] The patricians were citizens eminent by birth, valour, and means (such as were available in those times); the plebeians were the undistinguished poor of the lower orders. The distinction corresponded to that in Athens between the εὐπατρίδαι (the rich nobles to whom the rule of the city was entrusted) and the ἀγροῖκοι (citizens as well but with no political weight).

In line with this fundamental distinction Romulus appointed the nobles as patricians, priests, officeholders, and judges; in other words, he shared the administration of the city with them. Because of their incompetence and the fact that their poverty allowed them no leisure, the plebeians had been excluded from these positions and were consigned to labour in the fields, husbandry, and other manual professions (II.9.1). In addition, the plebeians were to become clients of the patricians, thereby avoiding otherwise inevitable social discord (II.9.2–3).

18. On ἰσότης: Arist. *Pol.* 1317a; κοινή means "belonging to the community."

19. In Varro's theory concerning the *bina jugera* (foreword n. 30) the distribution of the land in equal shares can be imagined just because it occurs within an agrimensorial unity precisely defined, as is the *centuria*.

20. A. Momigliano, *New Paths of Classicism in the Nineteenth Century* (Middletown, Conn., 1982), 4; R. von Pöhlmann, *Geschichte der sozialen Fragen und des Sozialismus in der antiken Welt*, 2d ed. (Munich, 1912), 425; R. E. A. Palmer, *The Archaic Community of the Romans* (Cambridge, 1970), 32–33.

A similar description, intentionally much abridged, occurs in Cicero's *De re publica* II.16, though the author quite deliberately emphasizes that the wealth of the *principes* lay at that time "in pecore et locorum possessionibus, ex quo pecuniosi et locupletes vocabantur."[21] A rigid distinction is made between two categories of the people, one of which shares in the exercise of power with the king because a surplus of wealth frees it from labour. The members of the other group, by contrast, are variously employed as artisans and farmworkers, and are thereby unprepared for political power and unfitted for such responsibilities. Such a distinction runs contrary to every traditional account of the archaic Roman economy and its society, where the patrician character, as portrayed in many famous instances right down to the third century B.C., is that of the peasant smallholder.[22] In reality, what was involved was a simple transfer of the qualities of a state as pictured and described by Aristotle in his *Politics,* particularly in Book VII (1328b–1329a). In this description the functions of government in the ideal state are not assigned to every section of the civic body. Those involved in commercial and manual labour (incompatible with the exercise of virtue), as well as in agriculture, were excluded from office because they lacked the leisure necessary to develop virtue or to participate in political life (a reference to the peasant smallholder). The exercise of political power in the hands of priests and judges was to be reserved for those citizens possessing sufficient economic resources to allow them to dedicate themselves entirely to political life. They alone could be called citizens in the fullest sense of the word. Their political functions matched the leisure available to them, and the latter was dependent on

21. Pliny *NH* XVIII.9–11; Festus p. 262, 22 Lindsay. Cf. L. Capogrossi Colognesi, *La terra in Roma antica. Forme di proprietà e rapporti produttivi,* vol. 1 (Rome, 1981).

22. E. Pais, *Storia di Roma dalle origini all'inizio delle guerre puniche,* 3d ed. (Rome, 1926–28), 2:385.

their possession of land, which was, naturally, cultivated by agricultural slaves or barbarian servants (περίοικοι). The distinction between these agrarian land owners and the peasant smallholders lies more in the quality of their role than in the extent of their holdings.

As has been well noted, Aristotle was aware that political capacity was linked to economic resources.[23] He also realized that the stability of the *polis* could be maintained if the majority of its citizens were smallholders who participated in democracy without being excessively interested in an exaggerated use of its various institutions, as, for example, the assemblies (*Pol.* 1292b25–30, 1296a7–10, 1318b10–17). While these conditions of ownership persist and the same economic circumstances are productively maintained, the *polis* remains politically stable. Aristotle also knew, however, that historically these conditions of political and social equilibrium were subject to disturbance and alterations for a variety of reasons, in particular the development of a mercantile form of wealth. He had Athens itself as an example. The formation of large patrimonies of land was thus a reality demanding fresh solutions. While Aristotle recognized and described the complex articulation of society according to the economic activities of each group, in substance he reaffirmed the role of the peasant smallholder as the basis for political stability, even if the smallholders did not exercise their political power. The exercise of power he assigned to the rich agrarian class, which was free from all forms of manual labour and thus available on a full-time basis for the responsibilities of political life. Aristotle aims, in his description, at an ideal state, but his ideas are derived from the historical realities of the Greek *poleis* and, in particular, the example of Athens in the years following the Peloponnesian war. The thoughts contained

23. F. Calabi, "Sulla proprietà della terra in Aristotele," *RSF* 32 (1977) 195–203.

in Book VII of his *Politics* also provide us with a unique key for the interpretation of the prevailing historic conditions of the second and third centuries B.C. and Rome's attempts at a political solution to the inherent problems.

The fact that the Romulean scenario in Dionysius II.8–9 is an almost verbal repetition of Aristotle's theories[24] poses the difficult problem of the acceptance and use of Aristotle's works in Rome after the age of Sulla.[25] But even more important is the fact that this global rethinking of the political and social structure of Rome should be dated back to the city's origins; it is thus pictured as an organic complex open only to subsequent elaboration, as in the instance of Servius Tullius's constitution. Without the possibility of being checked against the true circumstances of archaic Rome, this picture answered (as has already been remarked and will be seen more clearly later) the political and ideological exigencies of the post-Sullan era. For all that, it is somewhat contradictory to other data provided by Dionysius in the same context. According to the historian (II.28.1–2) Romulus consigned slaves and foreigners to the sedentary and manual crafts, which were held in low esteem, and this was a source of the contempt felt by the Romans toward a kind of work that the citizens had not practiced for some time. The free citizens were entrusted instead with the activities of war and agriculture, not as separate but rather as complementary duties. The relation of this passage to the preceding description in II.8–9 is not clear,[26] though even here the influence of the Aris-

24. See also X.1.4: the patricians live in the town and therefore they know the law; the populace, engaged in tilling and trades, comes to Rome only on market days and is not acquainted with politics.

25. I. Düring, *Aristotle in the Ancient Biographical Tradition* (Göteborg, 1957), 337–38, 412ff., 420ff. C. Nicolet, "L'idéologie du système centuriate et l'influence de la philosophie politique grecque," in *La filosofia greca e il diritto romano* (Rome, 1976–77), 1:111–37.

26. I tried wrongly to reconcile the two passages in "Studi su Dionigi da Alicarnasso. I," 198 n.64.

totelian text is evident. The assignment of manual tasks to non-citizens corresponds to the precepts of Aristotle found in *Pol.* 1328b39–41; the identity between agrarian proprietor and warrior may be compared to *Pol.* 1329a3–18. This is, of course, also found in the reality of the Roman peasant-soldier, who, although in basic terms an endangered species in the second century B.C., had lost nothing of his force as an ideal. The disdain for manual and commercial activities is found elsewhere in Dionysius[27] and was also worked into a theory, as is well known, by Cicero in his *De officiis* according to the model of an aristocratic ethic adapted to contemporary circumstances.[28]

Being equated with the client class, the plebeians were destined to agricultural labour and, in reality, also to work the lands of the patricians. The client system, however, since the clients were freemen, is quite distinct from those forms of servitude found in the Greek and Etruscan world that formed a halfway house between freedom and slavery (II.9.2, IX.5.4). A tradition preserved in Festus (*Pauli excerpta*, p. 289, 1–2 Lindsay) confirms that it was the patricians (*senatores*) who assigned plots of land "tenuioribus ac si liberis propriis," and that this was the origin of their being called *patres*. These plots would have been bequests of precarious title. By integrating this information into the work of Dionysius one could extrapolate the theory that the first distribution of land under Romulus was to the patricians alone, and that the allocations to the plebeians, or clients, came only subsequently. This theory, in itself attractive, is certainly at this point[29] extraneous to the historian's

27. III.36.3 (speech of the king Ancus Marcius); IX.25.2.
28. Cic. *Off.* I.150–51: Gabba, "Riflessioni antiche e moderne sulle attività commerciali a Roma nei secoli II e I a.C.," *MAAR* 36 (1980) 95–97.
29. Instead, Dionysius in V.40.5, dealing with the granting of citizenship to Clausus and some five thousand of his clients, asserts that the Senate and people gave an area of the city to the Sabine for the building of houses (thus it was not Clausus alone who lived at Rome), as well as *ager publicus* between Fidenae and Picentia so that he could share land among his followers. In Plut.

thought, and this becomes all the more evident once we establish its dependence, however tenuous, on the theories of Aristotle.

At any event, one thing emerges clearly from these first chapters of Dionysius, as well as from the passages we have cited in Cicero's *De re publica*. This is that an original egalitarian division of the land by Romulus is totally neglected, despite the fact that it is presupposed by the tradition that recorded an allotment of two *jugera* of land to every follower of the first king. This plot of land was identified with the *heredium* and was thus recognized as part of the inheritable estate.[30] As Mommsen previously noted, this tradition is present only in texts of an archaeological type and in gromatic material, not in historiography. The reasons for this are evident, for if one were to admit a social and economic parity among Romulus's subjects one would be confronted with the insoluble problem of having to explain the subsequent change. Moreover, the distinction be-

---

Publ. 21.10 it is the Roman state that assigns two *jugera* to each of Clausus's followers (cf. Livy II.16.4 and Serv. *ad Aen.* VII.706). The problem has rightly been linked to other instances of nobles who, being integrated, along with their clients and wealth, into the Roman state, came to live in Rome although they continued in possession of properties in their original homeland: II.35.6 (Romulus and the Caeninenses-Antemnates); III.29.6 (Tullius Hostilius and the Alban nobility); III.38.2 (Ancus Marcius and the Latins of Tellenae); III.49.6 (Tarquinius Priscus and Crustumerium); IV.58.3 (Tarquinius Superbus and Gabii): E. Hermon, "Réflections sur la propriété à l'époque royale," *MEFRA* 90 (1978) 7–31, attempted to place the agrarian history of the monarchic era within the geopolitical context of Latium in the iron age. He also attempted to match the phases of this history to the types of land presumed to have existed during the same era (Varro *De ling. lat.* V.33).

30. Varro *De re rust.* I.10.2; Pliny *NH* XVIII.7 and XIX.50; Siculus Flaccus p. 153 Lachmann; Festus *Pauli excerpta* p. 47, 1–2 and p. 89 Lindsay. As I attempted to show in "Per la tradizione dell'heredium romuleo," *RIL* 112 (1978) 250–58, the origin of this tradition is most likely to be found in the land-surveying methods of the republican period, which were applied in the oldest methods of land distribution in the Roman colonies and then pictured as also applying to the foundation of Rome. In the colonial situation, the two *jugera* were granted in conjunction with the use of common land. Cf. L. Capogrossi Colognesi, "La figura dell'heredium nella storiografia di fine 800," *BIDR* 85 (1982) 41–75.

tween patricians and plebeians (however the latter were identified) was understood to be connected with the very origins of the city. There was an obvious political reason for this resistance. Certainly the subject of the equal division of patrimonies is seldom heard in Roman political debate, and it is also a rare occurrence in theoretical and historiographical thought.[31] Nonetheless, when it does occur it is not simply a reflection of Greek thought. In the arguments of Scipio Aemilianus in *De re publica* (I.49), the condition of civic parity in the state is arrived at by equality before the law from the moment when *pecunias aequari* is no longer convenient and *paria ingenia* are impossible. More decisive is Cicero's quotation (*De officiis* II.73) of the famous speech in 104 B.C. (?) with which the tribune L. Marcius Philippus supported an agrarian proposal: there were fewer than two thousand people in the state with patrimonies (perhaps only among the upper classes?). The insistence on a disparity in the patrimonies led to a proposal for some form of redistribution: "capitalis oratio est, ad aequitatem bonorum pertinens; qua peste quae potest esse maior?" As we know, Cicero's arguments are developed further on, in II.78–85, with some noteworthy references to the history of his own times, when he refers to those who "aut rem agrariam temptant ut possessores pellantur suis sedibus, aut pecunias creditas condonandas putant" and thereby "labefactant fundamenta rei publicae." Besides, Cicero had outlined in *De officiis* I.21–23 the transition from a primitive natural state, when goods were held in common, to a state characterized by private ownership. In doing this he pointed out the historical roots of the latter and, moreover, its natural tendency to promote social solidarity.[32] But individual, private property is certainly never thought of as being equally dis-

---

31. D. Asheri, "La declamazione 261 di Quintiliano," *Studi in onore di Edoardo Volterra* (Milan, 1971), 1:309–21.

32. E. Costa, *Cicerone giureconsulto*, 2d ed. (Bologna, 1927), 91–93.

tributed; indeed, as Cicero had theorized in the *De re publica*, social and political inequality are elevated to a natural and just basis for the state.

After the time of the Gracchi, demands for a fairer distribution of wealth were not wanting in Rome. The Catiline episode was a key event in this respect. It had its origins in the dramatic social realities of the period, which the agrarian proposal of Servilius Rullus had attempted to remedy. Sallust, the historian of the conspiracy, described the social and economic inequalities of that reality in terms not far different from those that he himself depicts the chief conspirators, Catiline and C. Manlius, using to describe the situation (*Cat.* 13, 20, 33). The argument against wealth is a central theme in the so-called *Epistulae ad Caesarem senem de re publica* attributed to Sallust; some have spoken of a proletarian polemic. Among other things, the *Epistulae* hold that in archaic Roman society even the economic differences between patricians and plebeians were not a cause for political dispute until the rich began to expel the poor from their lands (II.5.1–4; cf. II.7.3–10). Among the proposed practical remedies was the idea of superseding the system of voting used in centuriation, which was rigidly based on the census classes; by instituting a lottery system among the *centuriae* of all classes, an idea already put forward by Caius Gracchus, the privileges of the rich would have been destroyed (II.8.1–4).

Precisely because private property and the political and social differences inherent to economic disparity are thought of by Cicero in *De officiis* as fundamental to a well-ordered state, he views Caesar's actions, from his involvement in the designs of Catiline in 63 B.C. to his schemes of dictatorship,[33] as exhibiting a continuous revolutionary tendency. Caesar was no "leveller" by nature. When, however, he recounts the agrarian communism of the Germans in *De bello Gallico* VI.22, his explanatory

33. Gabba, "Per un'interpretazione politica del de officiis."

comments recall the arguments that would later be used by
Sallust to denounce the serious inequalities in Roman society.[34]
It is difficult to avoid the conclusion that in his portrait of the
agrarian conditions peculiar to the German lands, he also had
in mind prevailing Roman political conditions.[35]

When dealing with the period immediately following the
city's foundation and the post-Romulean era, the tradition followed by Dionysius views the agrarian problem in terms of a
retrospective projection of later issues and problems down to
the age of the Gracchi (as R. Pöhlmann has already shown). This
reconstruction, where certain definite dates can be recognized,
demonstrates how the initial disparity became more acute, for
good or ill, in Roman society and the organization of the state.

In the meantime, Rome's armies had conquered other territories, of which some became royal possessions and others public
property. The plebeian population had also increased, due to
the influx of those seeking *asylum,* which had been instituted

34. Caes. *BGall.* VI.22.1–4: "Agri culturae non student, maiorque pars
eorum victus in lacte, caseo, carne consistit. neque quisquam agri modum cer-
tum aut fines habet proprios, sed magistratus ac principes in annos singulos
gentibus cognationibusque hominum quique una coierunt, quantum et quo
loco visum est agri adtribuunt atque anno post alio transire cogunt. eius rei
multas adferunt causas: ne adsidua consuetudine capti studium belli gerendi
agri cultura commutent; ne latos fines parare studeant potentioresque hu-
miliores possessionibus expellant; ne accuratius ad frigora atque aestus vitan-
dos aedificent; ne qua oriatur pecuniae cupiditas, qua ex re factiones dissen-
sionesque nascuntur; ut animi aequitate plebem contineant, cum suas quisque
opes cum potentissimis aequari videat." The words *ne qua . . . nascuntur* are
expunged by J. Lange, "Beiträge zur Caesar-Kritik," *JCP* 41 (1895) 815, followed by Meusel. The subject of *adferunt* is normally considered either the
Germans or *magistratus ac principes:* in this case the reasonings, which in
Rome are flung in the face of the leading class, are attributed here to the German chiefs. Cf. IV.1.3–10 (Suebi).

35. Pöhlmann, 3d ed. (Munich, 1925), 2:451–52; G. Walser, *Caesar und
die Germanen* (Wiesbaden, 1956), 60. On the problem even in comparison
with Tac. *Germ.* 26: D. Timpe, "Die Germanische Agrarverfassung nach den
Berichten Caesars und Tacitus'," in *Untersuchungen zur eisenzeitlichen und
frühmittelalterlichen Flur in Mitteleuropa und ihrer Nutzung,* ed. H. Beck
et al., *AAWG,* 3d ser., 115 (1979) 11–40.

after the foundation of the state (II.15.3−4).[36] Thus a fresh plebeian grouping was created of peasant-soldiers, who lived in the countryside and were distinct from the slave artisans or foreigners, as well as from the original plebeians who were identified with the clients. These latter could be understood as city folk, even though they were heavily involved in agriculture. And so there was a continuous expansion of the private property sector, which, however, did not result in a change in the original organization of the state.

All the same, after the death of the first king there remained a small segment of the plebeians who had not been able to enjoy the fruits of Romulus's military campaigns, as much as anything because they had only been citizens for a short while. They represented a potential social danger and were hostile to the "haves" of their society. Numa the king, the mythic predecessor of the Gracchi,[37] assigned to these citizens a "small portion" of land from the territories that had belonged to Romulus and from the public possessions (II.62.3−4). This small allotment may be pictured, if one wishes, as consisting of two *jugera.* The measure, however, is simply to illustrate that there was no resultant modification in the socioeconomic and political structure of the civic body. Further on (II.74.2−4), Dionysius speaks of the religious legislation of Numa and of the institution of the *Terminalia,* recalling the cadastre of Numa and the precise determination of the boundaries of private property and public possessions. In Cicero's interpretation in *De re publica* II.26, Numa distributed the lands conquered by Romulus *viritim* to show the advantages of peace for agriculture and to instil sentiments of *iustitia* and *fides* in the citizens. A similar argument is outlined

36. The chapter offers some contradiction with II.7−8; it is not clear who are the ἐλεύθεροι: perhaps patrician clients as after with Servius Tullius. Cf. Cic. *Rep.* II.15; Plut. *Rom.* 17.3 judges these distributions as acting against the Senate.

37. Pöhlmann, 3d ed., 2:420.

by Plutarch in *Numa* 16, regarding the complete cadastral *terminatio* of Roman public lands accomplished by the king, who was also held responsible for the distribution of Romulus's territorial conquests among the poorer citizens.[38]

IV

At this point the structure of Roman society is complete, consisting of patricians, client-plebeians, rural plebeians, slaves, and foreigners. Even the agrarian system now seems fully defined. This sector was made up of the original private property of the patricians and the client-plebeians. There was also the private property acquired from conquered territories and shared by the kings among the rural plebeians. This latter type of property had its origins in a voluntary gesture by the state and may be regarded as part of the public lands sector. There were the royal possessions, the lands destined for temple use, and finally those public lands that were (as is later stated explicitly) the subject of *occupatio* by the private sector, a move that favoured the wealthy.

King Tullius Hostilius, in turn, distributed *viritim* to the poor citizens the vast and fertile royal lands that Romulus had reserved for himself and which were also enjoyed by Numa. In the past these lands had, in addition, served to meet cult expenses and would thus seem to have been identified with sacred lands. By the action of Tullius Hostilius the poor would no longer have been constrained to work as menials on the property of others (λατρεύοντας ἐν τοῖς ἀλλοτρίοις: III.1.4–5). The social category referred to in this passage is a matter of dispute. In all probability we are still concerned with the poor rural grouping rather than the client class (III.1.4: τὸ θητικὸν τοῦ δήμου καὶ ἄπορον οἰκεῖον). The king also expanded the city, extending

38. J. Martinez-Pinna Nieto, "La reforma de Numa y la formación de Roma," *Gerión* 3 (1985) 97–124.

the walled area to the Caelian to provide housing space for the needy,[39] a provision not neglected by other kings.

All the subsequent agrarian development took place on public lands that were the fruits of victory. King Ancus Marcius distributed the conquered territories (Cicero *De re publica* II.33). Servius Tullius, in his policy oration in IV.9, proposed a series of popular measures, one of which was the distribution of public lands among those who had, in fact, conquered them by force of arms. These lands were previously in the hands of unscrupulous citizens who had obtained them through favouritism (χάριτι) or who had acquired them when impoverished freemen were forced to work the lands of others rather than their own (IV.9.8). The overall tone of the passage and the subsequent promise to make ἴσην καὶ κοινὴν τὴν πολιτείαν (IV.9.9) reflect arguments and themes typical of the Gracchan era and are included in the "popular" representation of King Servius. The other references to the fulfillment of this agrarian programme (IV.10.3, 11.2, 13.1)[40] should be understood in this light. The distribution of public land to the more needy citizens is, in any event, a preliminary step in the timocratic system created by the king for the census classes and the *centuriae*. It was a move that he had earnestly desired, and he had known how to interpret the tradition toward this end.[41] He stabilized social and economic inequality

39. In order to move there the inhabitants of Alba Longa: III.31.3 (another distribution of public land τοῖς θητεύουσιν of the Albans); Livy I.30.1 and 33.2; Cic. *Rep.* II.33.

40. A. Magdelain, "Remarques sur la société romaine archaique," *REL* 49 (1971) 107, supposes that θητεύουσιν hints at the client-serfs of the patricians, now transformed into free citizens endowed with private property.

41. Dionys. IV.16–18, 19–21. In "Studi su Dionigi da Alicarnasso. II," 107–9 and 114 I attempted to demonstrate the juxtaposition of two diverging tendencies in Dionysius that aimed at evaluating the Servian system either in popular terms, that is, as a surmounting of the nobility's arrangements, or in the aristocratic/oligarchic sense as an accommodation of the preeminence of the wealthy classes. In "Esercito e fiscalità a Roma in età repubblicana," in *Armées et fiscalité dans le monde antique* (Paris, 1977), 13–17, I maintained that the theoretical ideologizing of the system of *centuriatio* in Cicero's *De re*

within the civic body. In this way he rationalized the social system that had been introduced by Romulus, operating it with greater success. One can readily understand how the Italian philosopher G. B. Vico could take the Servian timocratic system for agrarian legislation.[42]

V

Before continuing with the examination of Dionysius's text dealing with the land problems of archaic Rome, some thought must be given to the background to this analysis. The effort being made here (not of itself new) is to interpret what Dionysius tells us concerning Roman agrarian history from the earliest era in terms of the historiographical context and the historic developments in which his account has its share. It seems fundamentally unmethodical in this instance (and for other problems of the same era) to disturb his narrative, which has its own unity (however self-contradictory) and is, moreover, envisaged as unitary, in order to extract particular elements from it for entirely different ends. As a specific prerequisite for the understanding of Dionysius's design in the *History,* comparisons with other evi-

---

publica and in Dionysius must originate in a reassessment of the constitutional history of archaic Rome, which occurred between 80 and 50 B.C. This reassessment was linked to thinking on the constitution of Romulus with which it went hand in glove. The period following the Social War and the first Civil War, a period of great institutional change, saw the greatest application of this thinking on the historical foundations of the state (something that had not occurred in the age of the Gracchi). The ancient constitutional framework was seen as an organic complex, the next best thing to a full-scale model for the exigencies of the contemporary political scene. Such ideas would have been unthinkable during the Triumvirate or the reign of Augustus.

42. *La scienza nuova,* 1744 ed. (Bari, 1974), sections 107, 108, 604, 613, 640, 653, 654, 772, 989, 1065. A. Momigliano, "Roman 'Bestioni' and Roman 'Eroi' in Vico's Scienza Nuova," *H&T* 5 (1966) 3–23, now in Momigliano, *Terzo contributo alla storia degli studi classici e del mondo antico* (Rome, 1966), 1:171–72, and "La nuova storia romana di G. B. Vico," *RSI* 77 (1965) 773–90, now in Momigliano, *Sesto contributo alla storia degli studi classici e del mondo antico* (Rome 1980), 1:205–6.

dence in the tradition are made only where they can serve to clarify the ideas of the Greek historian. On the other hand, these pages are in no way an attempted history of the development of agrarian property or the methods of land use at Rome. They simply make an effort to understand how an ancient tradition pictured and described this history in the clear realization that it was a key aspect in the secular development of Rome. Having said that, we may proceed by indicating briefly and comparing with the ancient tradition the positions taken, in their interpretation of these problems, by G. B. Niebuhr and Th. Mommsen.

To Niebuhr[43] belongs the credit for definitively distinguishing the private ownership of land from the occupation of the *ager publicus*. He showed that Roman agrarian law referred to the use of the *ager publicus* and did not impinge on private property until the civil wars of the first century B.C. Such distinctions had been absent from earlier treatments, and the lacuna had led to a total misunderstanding of the agrarian problem at Rome in authors from Machiavelli to A. Ferguson. As we know, Chr. G. Heyne provides an exception to this statement, specifically in his famous essay "Leges Agrariae pestiferae et execrabiles" (1793),[44]

43. *Römische Geschichte,* 3d ed. (1832), 2:146ff., 694ff. (= ed. Isler [1873], 2:121ff., 535ff.), where is partially presented in revised form the essay on the Roman *agrimensores,* which in the first edition was a separate appendix (now in *Kleine Historische und Philologische Schriften* 1:81ff.): see A. Heuss, *Barthold Georg Niebuhrs wissenschaftliche Anfänge, AAWG,* 3d ser., 114 (1981) 153ff., 189ff.

44. *Opuscula Academica* (Göttingen, 1796), 4:350–73. In truth, at least two other works should be mentioned on this subject. L'Abbé de Vertot, *Histoire des révolutions arrivées dans le gouvernement de la république romaine* (Amsterdam, 1759), follows ancient tradition and attributes the fresh land acquisitions of the state to military conquest, some of the territory being apportioned as communal land. This latter was annexed, with varying degrees of legality, by the wealthy: 1:169–72. Despite some confusion he realizes that both the Lex Licinia and that of Gracchus refer to public land: 1:482–84 and 2:35ff., *vide* Heuss, 250–51; M. Raskolnikoff, "Caius Gracchus ou la révolution introuvable," in *Demokratia et Aristokratia,* ed. C. Nicolet (Paris, 1983), 127–30. G. M. Butel-Dumont, *Récherches historiques et critiques sur l'administration publique et privée des terres chez les Romains* (Paris, 1779),

which was written in response to proposals for the redistribution of land ownership circulating at the time of the French Revolution. It has been well demonstrated how comparisons with existing situations in certain areas of India, which came to Niebuhr's attention during his youthful sojourn in Scotland,[45] aided the historian in understanding the hereditary occupation of public domains by the patrician orders (and hence the rich) to the detriment of the lower classes.

When Niebuhr makes his reconstruction of archaic Roman society in the pre-Servian and Servian periods, he bases his work on a contrast between city and country that is undoubtedly part of the tradition as we have it.[46] It is also present in Dionysius and particularly so in his treatment of Servius Tullius. In addition, Niebuhr had in mind the conditions prevalent in medieval and renaissance cities, with their opposition between the nobility, who had switched to living in the city, and the peasant population. In the pre-Servian period, Rome had been organized into four civic areas, while the peasants were organized into *pagi*.[47] Niebuhr's point of departure acknowledges an already existing "state." The patricians are dominant in the city and have the royal patrimony (public domains) at their disposal, and it is they who supply their clients with shares of two *jugera* of land (Festus p. 288 Lindsay) in addition to the use of com-

chapters 2–4, also interprets the matter in this light. (I am very grateful to Prof. J. L. Ferrary for having checked this information for me in the Bibliothèque Nationale in Paris.)

45. Momigliano, *New Paths of Classicism*, 3–15.

46. *Römische Geschichte*, 3d ed., 1 : 339 ff., 446 ff. (= ed. Isler, 1 : 251 ff., 330 ff.).

47. On the four *regiones:* Dionys. IV.14; Livy I.43.13; the *pagi* were organized by Numa Pompilius: Dionys. II.76.1; Plut. *Numa* 16.6: Gabba, "The Collegia of Numa: Problems of Method and Political Ideas," *JRS* 74 (1984) 81–86. The countryside was divided into *pagi* by King Servius: Dionys. IV.15 (the passage is not clear: Gabba, "Studi su Dionigi da Alicarnasso. II," 104–5; Schröder, fr. 23, with commentary p. 188 ff.); and Varro *De vita pop. Rom.* fr. 8 Riposati.

monage. Ownership is thus a patrician institution.[48] Subsequently conquered enemy territories would be distributed to the plebeians, and plebeian ownership came about with the rustic tribes, who thus had a place of residence and point of entry to citizenship. Only later would the patricians and their clients be inscribed in the same way as the rustic tribes. Niebuhr had to explain, however, why the old rural tribes bore the nomenclature of patrician *gentes*. According to him, the tribal name was not directly linked to the patrician *gens*, but instead both groups derived their common name from an indigenous divinity. For Niebuhr, the *gens* is an artificial creation of the state, and its descent from an original common ancestor cannot be traced. The rural tribes, therefore, are not to be connected genetically to the *gentes*, and the plebeians are a group distinct from the clients. It must be admitted that there is some basis for Niebuhr's theory of the rural tribes being reserved for the plebeians, and, as we have noted above, supporting passages may be found in Varro and Dionysius. Nonetheless, one should note that Varro's division of the peasants (*extra urbem*) into *pagi* is not, in Niebuhr's view, the same as the creation of rural tribes.[49] (He views the latter as territorially distinct from the *pagi*.) The person seen to transform these patrician land concessions into actual ownership was Servius Tullius, with his agrarian reforms (Dionysius IV.9.8 and 13.1). This occurred prior to the creation of the rural tribes.[50]

48. On the origins of the clients Niebuhr propounded different interpretations: *Römische Geschichte*, 3d ed., 1:358 ff., 649 (= ed. Isler, 1:265 ff., 481 ff.).

49. According to Beloch, *Römische Geschichte bis zum Beginn der Punischen Kriege* (Berlin, 1926), 334, the tribes should have received their names from the *pagi* and these in turn from the most prominent *gentes* living within them; his evidence is the *tribus Lemonia: Festus Pauli excerpta* p. 102, 20 Lindsay.

50. Magdelain, "Remarques sur la société romaine archaique," holds that the clients were freemen and not citizens, living in the country and working

Niebuhr's reconstruction is based on the theory of the *gentes* as a creation of the state. Since, however, the names of the tribes seem strongly to favour arguments for a connection with the patricians, he is forced to deny any direct link between the rural tribes and the *gentes*.

Mommsen's stance is very different and is primarily grounded in the pre-civic period of Roman history. In *Römische Geschichte* 1:182−84 he develops the theory that land, in the earliest times, was cultivated in common by separate groups of nobles. The most ancient form of the client system arose from the concession of land use by the *gens* (1:189), and therefore the client system predates private land acquisition. Mommsen implicitly regards the *gens* as a pre-civic grouping; indeed, his theory of land takeover by the nobles is based on this premise. In essence Mommsen founds his ideas on three arguments. First, the name of the oldest rural tribe is undoubtedly the same as that of certain great and noble patrician groupings (*Röm. Gesch.* 1:35−36, *Römische Forschungen* 1:105−7: the names of the *curiae*, which we know seem to be derived instead from place names). Mommsen, basing his argument on the passages quoted from Varro and Dionysius, holds (*Röm. Gesch.* 1:35) that the rural tribes owed their names and their ancient habitats to an even older division of the primitive *ager romanus* into *pagi;* the *pagi* would have derived their names from the patrician groups, and the names would then have been handed on to the tribes. The tribes are understood as groups or unions of families, with a shared portion of land that was cultivated in common right up to the later periods of Roman history. A clas-

---

the land for the patricians; the plebeians were free peasants living in the city. Servian and subsequent legislation gave the clients ownership of the land they worked and access to citizenship. When this happened is not stated with any certainty. According to Magdelain, some of the rural tribes were later than the laws of the Twelve Tables. The names of the rural tribes may in certain cases have been derived from local place names.

sic example was provided by the *gens Claudia,* which, perhaps as early as the monarchic era, settled on the river Aniene.

To this fundamental argument Mommsen adjoined his second, based on the tradition of the *heredium.* Both in *Röm. Gesch.* 1 : 183–84 and in the classic treatment in *Römisches Staatsrecht* 3 : 22–27, the Romulean distribution of two *jugera* in inheritable property[51] is understood as the first step in the development of private ownership of the land, though initially limited to the area of the house site and the surrounding garden. Since a family could not live on such a small holding, the *heredium* must needs be on the basis that the arable land, which was not yet subject to individual ownership, belonged to the *gens.* Mommsen is well aware (*Staatsrecht* 3 : 25 n. 1) that the traditional *bina jugera* distribution is never recorded by historiographical texts, and that his interpretation is a result of the study and combination of a variety of data. For example, the idea of the acquisition and exploitation of the land by the nobles finds support in information on the equal division of allotments among the *curiae,* which is found in Dionysius. Mommsen is convinced that the division of arable land occurred before the Servian constitution. He interprets the information in the annalists on the monarchic distributions as indicative of the move to progressively greater private ownership (*Staatsrecht* 3 : 25 n. 1).

We have already seen, and not for the last time, how the annalistic tradition offers an unexpected, often anachronistic perspective on all these problems, though it is in itself coherent, conscious, and unified and must be recognized as such. Mommsen's third argument is of a legal nature and quite impressive. He holds that the procedure of *mancipatio* (*Röm. Gesch.* 1 : 183) is the oldest means of property acquisition. It was valid only for movable goods; the *mancipatio* would thus

51. In the Twelve Tables *heredium* means *hortus:* Pliny *NH* XIX.50; Festus *Pauli excerpta* p. 91 Lindsay.

reflect a phase in history when the individual's patrimony consisted of livestock (*pecunia*) and slaves (*familia*).[52] Separate and individual land ownership was a later phenomenon that came about in the first monarchic period. As may be readily understood, Mommsen's theory is linked to important cultural factors that cannot be gone into here. The greatest point of contrast between Mommsen and the annalistic tradition occurs where the ancient tradition asserts private ownership of land from the very foundation of the state.

VI

The sources followed by Dionysius are based on the definite idea that the subsequent development of large-scale ownership occurred on the *ager publicus,* where the private occupancy by the patricians and other wealthy classes expanded over the years to the detriment of the plebeians and the poorer classes. The problem thus centred on the *ager publicus,* and the political

52. For the famous theory of P. Bonfante that viewed the *res mancipi* as social wealth centred on the *gens,* see Bonfante, *Res mancipi e nec mancipi* (Rome, 1888–89), republished with corrections in Bonfante, *Scritti giuridici vari,* vol. 2 (Torino, 1918); cf. Momigliano, *New Paths of Classicism,* 24–28. See also Bonfante, *Corso di diritto romano,* vol. 2, *La proprietà* (Rome, 1926; reprint, Milan, 1966), pt. 1, 201–15. In the light of Mommsen's theory, it is worth recalling the position taken by F. De Martino, *Storia della costituzione romana,* 2d ed. (Naples, 1972–74), 1:8 ff., who shows how the problem of the origin of the *gens* is directly connected to that of the original system of land appropriation. De Martino accepts the idea that the *gens* was an ancient offshoot from a greater mass and that this grouping preceded the emergence of the national, ethnic state. From the tribe of nobles held together by the notion of some common ancestry there came about the development of the *gens* with its own lands in the *pagus* and its own leader. Following a more primitive phase without inequalities, there was a further development, where the change is in fact represented by the client system. This view presupposes an original form of collective land appropriation, specifically by the nobility; thus the early system of land ownership had no individual basis. For De Martino (27) the legendary tradition on Romulus and Numa also conceals real events, nothing less than the origin of private ownership of the land. See also De Martino, "Clienti e condizioni materiali in Roma arcaica," in *Miscellanea di studi classici in onore di Eugenio Manni* (Rome, 1979), 2:681–705.

struggle revolved, for the most part, about it. The first effort at an agrarian law in the republican era was made by the consul Spurius Cassius, and it centred on the discussion of the best method (that is, the most convenient for society and the state) of exploiting the public domains. The political situation appears to have been complicated by the presence of allies among the possible assignees, which may perhaps be a reference to the Gracchan period.[53]

In reality, all the agrarian laws or law proposals that the tradition assigns to the fifth century B.C. follow a typical pattern, substantially based on the different social and economic conditions of the second century B.C., which in turn exacerbated the land problem and resulted in laws for *modo agrorum* and other agrarian measures.[54] The Roman people of the fifth century are seen as a proletariat struggling to gain possession of the means of production (the exploitation of the public domains) even though political feuding, which underlined profound social differences within the group itself, occurred. The clear anachronisms in the account of these events make it difficult to appreciate the reality of these unique situations. The internal logic of the narrative is no guarantee of an authentic and reliable tradition; it is, rather, an aspect of a well-prepared political and historiographical reassessment, which pictures and reconstructs the political conflict in terms of the decisive liberation of 367 B.C. Legitimate doubt may be aroused by the appearance of the same basic motif of a patrician *occupatio* of the *ager publicus* in the first republican period, especially when the means involved are typical of the post-Hannibalic period. Among other things we know that, as more and more land was conquered, there followed *viritim* distributions of land among the plebeians and

53. Gabba, "Studi su Dionigi d'Alicarnasso. III. La proposta di legge agraria di Spurio Cassio," *Athenaeum* n.s. 42 (1964) 29–41.

54. Gabba, "Per un'interpretazione storica della centuriazione romana," *Athenaeum* n.s. 63 (1985) 268–70.

sometimes even among the allies. We may therefore be a little hesitant in accepting the idea of a continuous plebeian pressure for land in the fifth century B.C. In any event, whatever the general economic conditions at Rome in that era, we are dealing with an entirely different situation from that of the third, and even more so from that of the second century B.C. That period was characterized by widespread private occupation of the public domains, which the state sought to restrict while attempting to regain land for itself. The problem of plebeian land agitation at the end of the fifth century B.C. and the beginning of the fourth century B.C., as well as the controversies over military booty, ought to be seen in relation to the altered nature of the Roman army's interventions in the workings of Roman society.[55]

I would now like to summarize certain key points. In the tradition followed by Dionysius, the agrarian problem undoubtedly has a central importance from the very beginning of the city's existence. It is seen in all its social and political implications. It is an economic problem that gains great emphasis in ancient historical texts, and it is characteristic of Rome. The historic problem of land in Greece, from Solon to the third century B.C. reforms of the Spartan kings, does not occupy a central position in the histories. In Rome, however, even a mediocre historian like Velleius Paterculus in the age of Tiberius could explain the phenomenon of Roman expansion in Italy as a development linked to Roman colonization and the granting of citizenship, that is to say, in terms of land use and its political implications.[56]

This view of Roman history undoubtedly has a nucleus of truth to it. It is connected with the awareness of a noteworthy

55. The best analysis in F. Serrao, ed., *Leggi e società nella repubblica romana*, vol. 1 (Naples, 1981), on which see F. Dal Cason, "La tradizione annalistica sulle più antiche leggi agrarie: riflessioni e proposte," *Athenaeum* n.s. 63 (1985) 174–84.

56. Gabba, "Italia e Roma nella Storia di Velleio Patercolo," *CS* 1 (1962) 1–9, now in Gabba, *Esercito e società nella tarda repubblica romana* (Florence, 1973), 347–60.

uniformity in Roman and Italian agrarian systems. In this same light we must understand the works of Roman authors when dealing with agricultural problems. The communal lands are the fundamental element, a reality that persisted over a long period in the Roman and Italian sector. The exploitation of common lands, which were the fruits of military conquest, was a social and economic factor present in varying degrees in the Romano-Italian history from the earliest times to the second century B.C. This is connected with the existence and survival of the small peasant holding, as well as with the process that brought about vast private properties.

In the area of historiography, the political and social events surrounding the agrarian problem are a definite prelude to the history of Tiberius Gracchus's tribunate of 133 B.C. The brief history of the *ager publicus,* which we read in Plutarch and Appian as an explanatory introduction to the proposals for agrarian law by the Gracchi (also found systematically in the *agrimensores*), is perfectly at one with the history of the agrarian problem for the monarchic and republican periods that we find in the historiography of the annalists.[57] The comparison is obvious, because it was the tribunates of the Gracchi that supplied the pattern on which the earliest events were modelled, but the historical realities of the land problem could not be denied.

57. Plut. *Gracchi* 8.1–5; App. *BCiv.* I.27–34; Hyg. *De cond. agr.* 115, 15 ff. Lachmann = 78, 18 ff. Thulin. Plutarch and Appian consider the history of the *ager publicus* gained by conquest in terms of land use. They pay particular attention to the most advanced phase of this historical process, when large concerns were being set up on the *ager publicus* by the wealthy. In Appian from I.28 on, as well as in Plutarch, reference is made to a time that is certainly later than the Hannibalic War, and I personally doubt whether the information they supply can be credited or applied to the fifth century. (See also Momigliano, *New Paths of Classicism,* 5–6.) There are differences between Plutarch and Appian that, however, even from my point of view, seem relatively simple to reconcile: G. Tibiletti, "Il possesso dell'*ager publicus* e le norme *de modo agrorum* sino ai Gracchi," *Athenaeum* n.s. 26 (1948) 206–9. Cf. Gabba, "Storia e politica nei gromatici," in *Akten des Gromatiker-Symposions Wolfenbüttel* (Göttingen, 1988).

Naturally, our sources strongly reflect the conservative ideologies of the first century B.C. This observation is further confirmed by the fact that it acknowledges an awareness, reflected in the period's historiography, of the seriousness of the social and political problems as well as their roots. These problems had retained their impact even in the Augustan era and in the imperial context. Along with his other contributions, Dionysius has given us this chapter of Roman history.

CHAPTER SIX

The Political Meaning of Dionysius's History

I

The preface to Dionysius's work covers the first eight chapters of Book I. Formally, it corresponds to the traditional technical principles that had been elaborated for proems of this genre. These were designed to remind one of the advantages of the historical narrative. They gave depth to the author's personality, his cultural background, and his aims, while showing the chosen subject to be worthy of historical treatment. Freely adapting this general scheme, Dionysius delineated the fundamental purpose of his work and described his approach to the understanding and writing of history.

How carefully he prepared for this task is clearly shown by his wide reading of Greek history, his knowledge of Latin, and his direct tapping of Roman historiography. Another factor lay in the opportunity he had to gain information by word of mouth from educated Romans.[1] His was a novel undertaking insofar as no overall history of ancient Rome had as yet been written in Greek. Dionysius makes this clear by a reasoned review of his Greek predecessors and those Roman historians who had written in Greek.[2]

1. I.7.1–3.
2. I.6.1–2.

Moreover, Dionysius refuses to consider the writing of history as mere rhetorical ostentation or an excuse for self-display. Nor does he neglect form and content. As I have already shown in Chapter 3, he clearly indicates the literary character of his work and its intended audience. Dionysius states that his work is designed to fill a gap in historiography and to rescue from oblivion the memory and glory of great figures from the past. This latter aim recalls the work of Herodotus, but Dionysius interestingly adds that the memory of the past should also serve as spur to the present and future descendants of these illustrious men, so that they may not be unworthy of their ancestry.[3] It is an initial discreet hint at the decadence of at least part of the Roman ruling class. We know how insistently this theme recurs in the preface to Livy's work. Livy held that the entire body politic was already in the grip of a moral crisis that compromised the very survival of the state.

Dionysius repeats that the goal of his work lies in the search for truth and right. Far removed though his work may be from any intention to flatter, he nonetheless cannot deny his own favourable attitude toward the city that both welcomed him and supported him culturally.[4] Be that as it may, his own impartiality, as opposed to the bias of many other historians, is reasserted.

In demonstrating the novelty of this particular historical work Dionysius is soon seen to adopt a decisive political stance. The works of some historians had contained strongly anti-Roman sentiments. These had been written with polemic intent and were slavishly ingratiating to barbarian kings, who detested Roman supremacy. In alluding to them Dionysius seems to point to Mithridatic historiography and the work of Metrodorus of Scepsis in particular.[5]

3. I.6.3–4.
4. I.6.5.
5. I.4.3: Jacoby, *FGrHist* II C 224; Bowersock, *Augustus and the Greek World,* 108, 131 n.5; Fuchs, *Der geistige Widerstand,* 41 and 44; J. M.

This hostility to Rome was, however, still alive in the historian's own age, the period of Augustus's reign, manifesting itself as a psychological attitude. It was an hostility based on preconceptions and ill-founded emotions whose roots were to be sought in an ignorance of early Roman history, which was due, in turn, to the absence of a competent Greek history of the city's origins. Dionysius views the Greek world within the context of the Roman empire and surely deals with an attitude that must have been widespread among the Greek upper classes. The political function and cultural significance of Dionysius's teaching, which I have endeavoured to describe in the previous chapters, becomes clearer when viewed from this perspective.

We know that in the Augustan age this anti-Roman attitude found expression in a polemical extolling of Alexander's personality and the greatness of his achievements. Sometimes the Parthian empire was exalted at Rome's expense. Livy, in the famous excursus of Book IX of his work, refuted this tendency, which probably had the historian Timagenes as its champion.[6]

Roman history is viewed by Dionysius within a universal framework, that is to say, a history of the supremacy of successive cities and nations. Following a theory that appears to have Greek rather than Oriental origins, universal history was understood as a succession of more or less worldwide hegemonies. Supremacy, restricted of course in time and space, had passed from the Assyrians to the Medians, Persians, and Macedonians in turn. From the beginning of the second century B.C., Roman expansion was already considered in the light of a new world hegemony taking the place of Macedonian domination. This theory was combined with a cyclic conception of history, and

---

Alonso-Núñez, "L'opposizione contro l'imperialismo romano e contro il principato nella storiografia del tempo di Augusto," *RSA* 12 (1982) 131–41.

6. Livy IX.16.19–19.17; P. Treves, *Il mito di Alessandro e la Roma di Augusto* (Milan, 1953); Bowersock, *Augustus and the Greek World,* 108–10; Fuchs, *Der geistige Widerstand,* 13–14, 40–42.

thereby assumed and indeed forecast the obvious consequence that Roman hegemony would also be replaced, sooner or later, by another power, which would, conceivably, come from Asia.[7]

According to his theory of a biological evolution of history, Polybius implicitly foretold the decline of Roman supremacy in Book VI of his work.[8] The theory of successive worldwide hegemonies is revived by Dionysius, but with a more positive emphasis, for he strengthens his case by stressing the breadth and duration of the Roman empire as a proof of its superiority and a guarantee of its future expansion.[9] With even greater justification Appian, in the preface to his *History of Rome,* expounded on this theory at some length a century and a half later.[10] More important again is the fact that Flavius Josephus, the Jewish histo-

7. I.2.1−4. The Greek origin of the theory of the Four Empires is defended by A. Momigliano, "Daniele e la teoria greca della successione degli imperi," *RAL* 35 (1980) 157−62, now in Momigliano, *La storiografia greca* (Torino, 1982), 293−301, and "The Origins of Universal History," *ASNP*, 3d ser., 12 (1982) 533−60, now in Momigliano, *Settimo contributo alla storia degli studi classici e del mondo antico* (Rome, 1984), 77−103. On the oriental ascendancy D. Flusser, "The Four Empires in the Fourth Sibyl and in the Book of Daniel," *IOS* 2 (1972) 148−75. D. Mendels, "The Five Empires. A Note on a Propagandistic Topos," *AJPh* 102 (1981) 330−37, maintains that the Greek theme entered Rome only in the second half of the first century B.C.; F. Fabbrini, *Traslatio imperii. L'impero universale da Ciro ad Augusto* (Rome, 1983), 251 ff.; Gruen, 1:328−29; F. Gasco la Calle, "La Teoria de los cuatros imperios. Reiteración y adaptación ideológica. I. Romanos y griegos," *Habis* 12 (1981) 179−96.

8. Polyb. VI.57; F. W. Walbank, "The Idea of Decline in Polybios," in *Niedergang. Studien zu einen geschichtlichen Thema,* ed. R. Kossellek and P. Widmer (Stuttgart, 1980), 41−51.

9. I.3.3−5 (there are no longer any to contend with Rome for universal dominion, nor dispute her right to rule over them); J. M. Alonso-Núñez, "Die Abfolge der Weltreiche bei Polybios und Dionysios von Halikarnassos," *Historia* 32 (1983) 411−26.

10. App. *Praef.* 29−48, clearly under the influence of Dionysius: G. Kaibel, "Dionysios von Halikarnassos und die Sophistik," *Hermes* 20 (1885) 497−513; Gabba, *Appiano e la storia delle guerre civili* (Florence, 1956), 95, and "Storici greci dell'impero romano da Augusto ai Severi," *RSI* 71 (1959) 374−76; J. M. Alonso-Núñez, "Appian and the World Empires," *Athenaeum* n.s. 62 (1984) 640−44.

rian, shared these views, as his history of the Jewish war, written in the seventies of the first century A.D., shows. Mingling ideas derived from Polybius with eschatological views found in the Book of Daniel, Josephus conceded that Tyche, following the will of God, had allowed world hegemony to shift to the Roman sphere, and any resistance to God's will would be fruitless.[11]

In addition, the history of Greece had, from Ephorus on, been viewed in the light of the hegemony of individual cities such as Athens, Sparta, or Thebes. Any comparison between the small Greek cities and the great city of imperial Rome was obviously unthinkable, but this did not rule out a comparison with the original small city of Rome, the more so since it had, in fact, been a Greek city, as Dionysius will demonstrate.[12] In his other works, he confirms that the hegemony of Rome cannot be compared to those of Athens and Sparta on the basis of their respective political and military capacities, and even less when one considers the progressive growth of Roman dominion, understood as an historical process that was both necessary and ineluctable. Whenever comparisons are made during the course of his work, for instance between the exclusive attitudes of Athens and Sparta and Roman magnanimity in granting the privilege of citizenship, or again when he admires the extension of the Roman censor's authority even into the life of the private individual, the comparison is always to Rome's advantage. This also applies in the fields of civic and political virtue.[13]

11. Gabba, "L'impero romano nel discorso di Agrippa II (Ioseph. B.I. II 345–401)," *RSA* 6–7 (1967–77) 189–94.

12. I.3.1–2.

13. I.3.1–5, II.17.1–4. This passage, clearly influenced by the work of Polybius, rejects the accusation that Rome owed her empire to a whim of Fortune. A comparison with Athens serves to indicate the extent of Veii as well as the size of the Roman city, defined by the Servian walls (II.54.3, IV.13.5, IX.68.5). The promised description of the size and beauty of Rome would have been found in the lost section of the work (possibly after the section on the burning of the city by the Gauls). Cf. XIV.6, XX.13.2.

II

Athens, as I have already shown, had always been seen as the birthplace of civilization even by such writers as Lucretius and Cicero. On the other hand others, such as Sallust and afterward Livy, asserted that Athens had been overpraised because of its *magna ingenia*. Polybius, in turn, while comparing Rome and the Greek cities, had passed over Athens, regarding it as unimportant from a military point of view.[14] In Dionysius's opinion the process of Rome's hellenization culminated with its taking Athens's place as world leader in culture and morals. The motives behind the anti-Roman polemics had been constant for at least two centuries.[15] These had seen the Romans as barbarians, whose status was clearly demonstrated by their origins as a gathering of homeless vagabonds, brigands, and ex-slaves. It is also worth noting that Polybius did not quite know how to categorize the Romans and therefore decided to create an intermediate group between Greeks and barbarians.[16] It was, moreover, held that the Romans had attained hegemony not through virtue or reverence for the gods, but as an unjustified favour of Fortune to a most undeserving people. Some indeed added that the blessings of the Greeks had been bestowed on the basest of the barbarians.

It is well known that the Romans had always, even in official documents, underlined the support they had received from the gods in return for their piety.[17] In the poetess Melinno's hymn

14. Polyb. I.2.1–6; J.-L. Ferrary, "L'empire de Rome et les hégémonies des cités grecques chez Polybe," *BCH* 100 (1976) 283–89.

15. I.4.1–3.

16. H. H. Schmitt, "Hellenen, Römer und Barbaren. Eine Studie zu Polybios," *Wissenschaftliche Beilage zum Jahresbericht 1957–58 des Humanistischen Gymnasiums Aschaffenburg*.

17. *SIG* 601 (193 B.C.); Gabba, "Aspetti culturali dell'imperialismo romano," 58 and n.23.

to Rome, probably written in the first half of the second century B.C., the Roman hegemony is described as indestructible precisely because conferred by Fate.[18]

Dionysius's historiographical work was specifically devoted to refuting all of these arguments and accusations, which he held to be rooted in prejudice, misunderstandings, and ignorance. His reasoning is based on the existence of a universal natural law that time cannot destroy. Under this law the strongest (κρείττονες) will always rule over their inferiors to their own advantage.[19] I share the opinion that this theory had already been applied to Rome and its hegemony in the second half of the second century B.C.[20] That period had been particularly difficult for the friends of Rome. In the aftermath of the destruction of Carthage and Corinth in 146 B.C., Roman hegemony had changed into open despotism (as had previously occurred, though on a smaller scale, with the Athenian and Spartan hegemonies).[21] This theory had later been revived, probably by Posidonius, and became canonical.[22]

18. Diehl, _Anthologia lyrica graeca_ 2:315–16; C. M. Bowra, "Melinno's Hymn to Rome," _JRS_ 47 (1957) 21–28; H. Bengtson, "Das Imperium Romanum in griechischer Sicht," _Gymnasium_ 71 (1964) 153–54, now in Bengtson, _Kleine Schriften zur Alten Geschichte_ (Munich, 1974), 552–54; Gabba, "Storiografia greca e imperialismo romano," 635–36; Gruen, 1:337 with n. 105 (after 168 and maybe after 146 B.C.).

19. I.5.2–3; according to Gruen, 1:351–52 (and n. 187), this rationalized view of the Roman empire should not be prior to the Augustan age.

20. Gabba, "Storiografia greca e imperialismo romano," 639–40; "Per un'interpretazione politica del de officiis," 120–22, 133–35; this interpretation is linked to the evaluation of Carneades' speeches at Rome in 155 B.C. and the assessment of the political and cultural activities of Panaetius. Gruen, 1:341–42, takes a negative line on both problems from a viewpoint that excessively reduces the extent of Greek interest in Roman affairs in the second century B.C. Doubts are also voiced by Momigliano, _Alien Wisdom. The Limits of Hellenization_ (Cambridge, 1975), 31.

21. Polyb. XXXVI.9.5–8; Diod. XXXII.2 and 4 (Polybius is probably the source: M. Gelzer, _Kleine Schriften_ [Wiesbaden, 1963], 2:64–66; Walbank, _Polybius_ 178–81).

22. This interpretation of the political and historiographical thinking of Posidonius about Rome may, with reason, be deduced from an examination

The theory denying the emigration of Aeneas and the Trojans, held by the Greek historians and antiquarians of the second century B.C., served to refute the thesis of a Trojan origin for the Romans. The theory of a Trojan origin was widespread and had been exploited politically (though Polybius seems to make no mention of it). The denial of any connection between the founding of Rome and essential episodes of Greek history gave credence to the miserable obscurity of Rome's origins and underlined its inherent unworthiness to assume world dominion.[23]

Dionysius, however, maintained and stressed the original Greek character of the Romans in the face of their presumed barbarity. He upheld the validity of the institutions and customs that had helped them to acquire world hegemony. We have already seen his efforts to prove the Greek character of the Roman ethnos. It is worth repeating that Dionysius outdoes Livy when dealing with the tradition of *asylum,* established under Romulus to welcome foreign fugitives, by denying that it was open to any other than free men.

He answered the grave accusation that Rome came about from a gathering of homeless vagabonds (I.6.2) by depicting Rome as a Greek colony, that is to say, a proper city. This argument was of fundamental importance and in Greek eyes entailed a founder and a lawgiver, in Rome's case Romulus. Only in this way could a precise dating of the city's foundation be sought

---

of the latter's judgment cum justification of the servile relationship of the Margianites to the Heracleites; Jacoby, *FGrHist* 87 F 8 = F 147 Theiler. The latter finds confirmation in F 448 Theiler (Sen. *Ep.* 90.4: "naturae est enim potioribus deteriora submittere"); see Theiler's remarks in *Posidonios. Die Fragmente* (Berlin, 1982), 2:385, and also J. Malitz, *Die Historien des Posidonios* (Munich, 1983), 141–42. In general cf. the famous essay by W. Capelle, "Griechische Ethik und römischer Imperialismus," *Klio* 25 (1932) 86–113, as well as Desideri, "L'interpretazione dell'impero romano in Posidonio." More cautious is H. Strasbürger, "Posidonios on the Problem of the Roman Empire," *JRS* 55 (1965) 40–53; unconvinced are Momigliano, *Alien Wisdom* 32, and Gruen, 1:351–54.

23. Gabba, "Sulla valorizzazione politica," 84–101.

and eventually indicated. Between the years 144 and 119 B.C.,
at a time when Roman dominion was firmly established in
both Greece and the Greek east, the well-known *Chronicle* of
Apollodorus of Athens was published in four books. This work,
along with that of Eratosthenes, was of fundamental importance
to the study and history of Greek chronography. Apollodorus
did not mention the foundation of Rome. This omission was deliberate, since the author could not have been unaware of the
historical writings of the Sicilian Timaeus and his suggested
chronology for Rome's early history. Apollodorus, furthermore,
neglected the entire history of Rome before the Second Punic
War.[24] The ideological implications of such omissions were important. Dionysius reacted by devoting two very long chapters
of Book I (I.74–75) to a review of those Greek and Roman
sources that had suggested differing dates for the city's foundation. He was thus able to prove three different foundations of
the city, fixing their chronology, though only the latest of the
three was historically verifiable.

The problems of chronology in Roman affairs and the parallels to be found in Greek history were of such importance to
Dionysius that he had previously devoted a specific scientific
work to it, his no longer extant Περὶ χρόνων.[25] This small work
must have consisted of a theoretical examination of the chronological criteria used by Eratosthenes, followed by a series of syn-
chronic parallels between the Roman and Greek systems of the
regal and republican periods, as well as a calculation of the individual reigns of the Roman kings. This work formed the basis
for the chronology followed in his *History of Archaic Rome.*

24. F. Jacoby, *Apollodoros Chronik; eine Sammlung der Fragmente* (Berlin,
1902), 26–28; *FGrHist* II B 723; Gabba, "Sulla valorizzazione politica," 91
and n. 19; contra, S. Mazzarino, *Il pensiero storico classico*, vol. 2, pt. 1,
354–55.
25. I.74.2–4, 75; Clem. Al. *Strom.* I.102; Jacoby, *FGrHist* 251; II B
826–27.

The comparison of Roman data (and thereby the evolution of Roman history) with Greek history naturally had ideological and cultural implications. There was no desire to vaunt a Roman priority over Greece, as happened, for instance, in the tabulation of Hebraic, Oriental, and Greek chronology. Placing Rome in relation to the basic system of Greek chronology was a form of historical legitimization, a comparison of parallel stages of civilization.

The anti-Roman polemic became even more pointed when it dealt with the origins of the patriciate or ruling class of Rome.[26] It was difficult to account for the origin of the term *patres*. One interpretation, hostile to Rome and also found in Plutarch, maintained that the term did not originate from nobility of birth or from any feeling of respect, but simply because only a handful of the original Romans could point with any certainty to their fathers among the mass of fugitives and slaves.[27] Because of this there could be no possible comparison between the patricians and the Greek Eupatridai. Such an attack on the patriciate of Rome's regal age probably served to denigrate the origins of the Roman Senate and ruling class. This was a reaction to the tendency found as early as the second century B.C. in Polybius, for example, and in the biographies of Plutarch, to cite outstanding Roman personalities (Marcellus, Scipio Africanus, Flamininus, Aemilius Paulus, and Scipio Aemilianus, for instance) as paradigms of noble behaviour and high morality.

26. The matter is dealt with in II.8.3−4 à propos of the Romulean constitution. Dionysius notes that the polemic was fuelled by those who taunted Rome with the humble background of her founders. These then are Greek accusations as distinct from the internal Roman quarrels that may be discerned in Livy X.8.10 (the speech of P. Decius Mus in support of the admission of plebeians to the priesthood: "en unquam fando audistis patricios primo esse factos non de coelo demissos, sed qui patrem ciere possunt, id est nihil ultra quam ingenuos?"). Cf. Cic. *Rep.* II.14, 23, 50; Livy I.8.7; Plut. *Quaest. rom.* 58.

27. Plut. *Rom.* 13.2−7.

The movement implying divinity for the Senate as well as the city of Rome may indeed have originated at about this time, given that the Senate (if the famous passage in I Maccabees 8 [28] is any indication) must have been held in high esteem by all who were friendly to Rome. Rome's right to world hegemony was legitimized primarily by an argument based on the moral superiority of the Roman people as witnessed from the earliest times by examples of civic and military virtue, of which no other Greek or barbarian city could boast. [29]

Their respect for the gods ($\varepsilon\dot{v}\sigma\acute{\varepsilon}\beta\varepsilon\iota\alpha$), which gave rise to their benevolence ($\varepsilon\ddot{v}vo\iota\alpha$), was accompanied by a sense of moderation ($\sigma\omega\phi\rho\sigma\sigma\acute{v}v\eta$) and justice ($\delta\iota\kappa\alpha\iota\sigma\sigma\acute{v}v\eta$). From these came harmony ($\dot{o}\mu\acute{o}vo\iota\alpha$) in their own social and political relations. Happiness ($\varepsilon\dot{v}\delta\alpha\iota\mu\sigma v\acute{\iota}\alpha$) was measured by worthy actions. All these virtues found their practical application through the exercise of martial valour ($\gamma\varepsilon v v\alpha\iota\acute{o}\tau\eta s$). They also correspond to the great ideals in the political life of the Greek cities that Isocrates had emphasized and which Dionysius now discovered in the politics of Roman history.

The presence of these virtues throughout Roman history supplements the validity of the ethnic principle, which would not of itself provide a sufficient guarantee of Rome's superiority over the Greek cities. Such virtues are not innate to the human soul, nor is their presence and development in society a matter of chance. According to Dionysius these virtues and the citizens who practice them are the product of wisely established political institutions and government. [30]

28. See Polyb. XXX.18. According to G. Forni, "'Ιερὰ ε θεὸς σύγκλητος. Un capitolo dimenticato nella storia del senato romano," *MAL*, 8th ser., 5 (1953), fasc. 3, the deification of the Roman Senate could go back to the second or first century B.C.; Gabba, "Posidonio, Marcello e la Sicilia," in ΑΠΑΡΧΑΙ: *Nuove ricerche e studi sulla Magna Grecia e la Sicilia antica in onore di P. E. Arias* (Pisa, 1982), 2:611–14.

29. I.5.2–3; the mention is developed at length at II.18.1.

30. II.18.1; the opposite idea is found in Sall. *Cat.* IX.1: "ius bonumque apud eos [the Romans] non legibus magis quam natura valebat." Dionysius

III

This emphasis on political institutions highlights the great importance of the Roman constitution, which was another reason for Roman superiority. Its origins may be traced back to the political and social system set up by the very founder of the city, its first lawgiver, and it had endured, in essence, over the centuries. This idea, of course, was not essentially new. Polybius had previously, in the sixth book of his *Histories*, explained the efficacy of the Roman political system and expounded on its superiority to the Hellenistic monarchies. Polybius was concerned with the practical operation of Roman institutions. He admired their flexibility as well as the complementary and precise coordination of the various components that made up the body politic. Polybius felt that he had discovered, in the workings of the Roman constitution, the best concrete application of the theory of a mixed constitution. Dionysius's approach is certainly different and, in a way, more complex. In the first place, the monarchic regime was seen as the interaction of monarchy and aristocracy fighting one against the other, with the aristocracy finally pre-

cannot be said to contradict himself when, in his praise of Coriolanus (VIII.60.1), he remarks that the virtues of the hero are derived not so much from the implementation of the laws as from an innate disposition. The virtues of Coriolanus were, however, accompanied by a rigidity of character, a severity of behaviour, and a desire to apply the laws with excessively harsh consistency, to such an extent that he became alienated from his fellow citizens. Virtue, according to the Aristotelian model, should look to the mean, not the extreme (Arist. *Eth. Nic.* II.6.8–13, V.5.17–19). The man who acts in this way will get scant recognition while alive, but, if the soul does survive death, those who fell foul of Fortune while practicing virtue will always be remembered by the living. Such indeed was the fate of this pious and just hero, whose memory was still celebrated and praised after 500 years (ᾄδεται καὶ ὑμνεῖται, VIII.62.3); as R. Reitzenstein indicated ("Philologische Kleinigkeiten," *Hermes* 48 [1913] 268–72), the passage has nothing to do with hymns as such and therefore has no justifiable connection with the discussion of Rome's oldest poetic tradition: A. Momigliano, "Perizonius, Niebuhr, and the Character of Early Roman Tradition," in Momigliano, *Secondo contributo alla storia degli studi classici* (Rome, 1960), 81–82.

vailing. A system generally recognized as the best and wisest form of government thus came into being.

The political struggle that took place in the republican period was viewed as a plebeian attempt, under the leadership of demagogues (the tribunes), to wrest power and supremacy from the aristocracy or "best" elements. This was unfortunately the case with Caius Gracchus, who is identified as the destroyer of τὴν τοῦ πολιτεύματος ἁρμονίαν after 630 years, more or less, of harmony. Longevity and continuity were seen as an obvious guarantee of the worth of the political system.[31]

These concepts are also found in a speech in Book VIII of Dionysius's work, placed, significantly, in the mouth of Coriolanus.[32] According to these ideas the plebeian attack is repelled by the oligarchs not from any desire to enslave the people of Rome but rather in order to preserve the liberty of the entire citizen body and to entrust the best people of the state with the management of public affairs. The destruction of the best is always the object of a tyranny arising from the masses. This notion undoubtedly reflects Dionysius's own political ideas, and to confirm this one need only recall the social motivation behind his attack on contemporary Asian eloquence.

31. In II.2.3 Dionysius seems to want to postpone an explanation of the outbreak of civil war at Rome in the time of Caius Gracchus to a more appropriate occasion. Since the facts of the matter fell outside the scope of his historical framework, I think Dionysius had in mind his concluding arguments on the long narration concerning the first stasis (VII.66). The chronology centred on Caius Gracchus glosses over the revolutionary tribunate of Tiberius Gracchus in 133 (Cicero does otherwise in *De re publica* II.31, but his work is centred on the year 129 B.C.), and instead concentrates on the idea expressed by Varro in *De vita pop. rom.* fr. 114 Riposati (Gracchus "bicipitem civitatem fecit discordiarum civilium fontem"), which saw the rupture between the Senate and knights over the matter of the judicial laws as a decisive juncture in the political struggle (C. Nicolet, "Varron et la politique de Caius Gracchus," *Historia* 28 [1979] 276–300). The idea that internal political conflicts prior to the era of the Gracchi had always been resolved without bloodshed is also present in the initial chapters of Appian, *BCiv.* I.1–8, where the episode of Coriolanus is duly recalled: Appian probably drew on Dionysius.

32. VIII.5–8 (a speech delivered before the Volscian assembly).

No less significant is the fact that this depiction of oligarchic government is founded on the aristocratic notion of concord (ὁμόνοια), which admits a subordinate popular participation in political life. This concept was still active in Greek political thought and practice during the fourth century B.C.[33] As far as Rome was concerned it found its first and best theorist in Menenius Agrippa, whose apologue, Dionysius notes, was quoted in all the Roman histories; mention of it coincidentally allows our author to introduce a long programmatic speech.[34] Of course, an organic conception of the state and society as analogous to the human body presupposes the political leadership of the Senate. In Agrippa's words, the ignorant masses will never cease to need prudent leadership, while the Senate, which has the capacity for leadership, will always require a submissive multitude.[35]

In other words, Dionysius maintains that the Roman people, as a social organization and political framework elaborated by Romulus, had functioned in line with the best ethical and civic principles of the Greeks themselves. These principles, which were to be found in outstanding personalities and mirrored in the whole population, had guaranteed the persistent continuity of those structures and in doing so had enabled Rome to expand its territories, maintain its capacity for assimilation, and eventually rationalize the political system itself. This was no nostalgic bow to the value of *mores maiorum*, for here the *mores* rep-

---

33. A. Momigliano, "Camillus and Concord," *CQ* 36 (1942) 111–20, now in Momigliano, *Secondo contributo alla storia degli studi classici* (Rome, 1960), 89–104: he rejects the thesis of W. Nestle ("Die Fabel des Menenius Agrippa," *Klio* 21 [1927] 350–60), which held that the penetration of the Greek notion of ὁμόνοια dated only to the first century B.C., with the episode of Menenius, whereas it must appertain to the first half of the fourth century B.C. The reference to 494 B.C. can perhaps be explained by the institution of the plebeian tribunate: L. Bertelli, "L'apologo di Menenio Agrippa: incunabolo della 'Homonoia' a Roma?" *Index* 3 (1972) 224–34.

34. VI.83–86: Menenius's speech in the historical tradition: 83.2.

35. VI.85.1.

resent Greek virtues; they are in fact ethical principles or, to put it another way, ideal pressures working upon history itself. These found their ultimate expression in the politics of Rome. Leaving aside the many crises encountered, these were the very principles that had permitted fresh advances in the classicistic renaissance in the historian's own lifetime. Livian pessimism, which had confined its admiration to the aristocratic models in the era of the Samnite and Hannibalic wars (IX.16.19; XXI.1.2), was thus superseded.

This line of interpretation also differs from that of Cicero, who had described the democratic and socioeconomic growth of Rome in his *De re publica*. As Dionysius saw it, Rome, through its history and its support of the elite, offered certain guarantees to the world. These guarantees applied on a civic and moral plane and were still a force in Dionysius's lifetime. He felt, indeed, that they could still be fully recovered by a cultural movement in which he saw himself as a participant.

He applied these notions to the area of foreign policy and gave a particular sense of immediacy to the notion of *concordia*. In a speech attributed to Servius Tullius on the occasion of a proposal to build a Latin federal sanctuary to Diana at Rome, the king gives voice to the theory that concord between states can only be realized under the leadership of the most powerful among them. Such leadership was natural, given the size of the chief city, Rome, and the favours bestowed upon it by the gods in granting it preeminence. Concord of this type (ὁμοφροσύνη) is also a source of strength for the weaker states.[36]

The aristocratic ideal of concord subsequently leads Dionysius to reflect on the republican constitution of Rome, which he regards as a mixed constitution.[37] Lord Acton, in his essay

36. IV.26.1–2.
37. The Romulean constitution (ὁ κόσμος τῆς πολιτείας) seemed to Dionysius, on the whole, better ordered (αὐταρκέστατον) under the constraints of war and peace: II.7.2. The distribution of powers and prerogatives defined

"The History of Freedom in Antiquity," has already asserted that "the point on which the ancients were most nearly unanimous is the right of the people to govern, and their inability to govern alone. To meet this difficulty, to give to the popular element a full share without a monopoly of power, they adopted very generally the theory of a mixed Constitution. They differed from our notion of the same thing, because modern Constitutions have been a device for limiting monarchy; with them they were invented to curb democracy."[38]

The theory behind a mixed constitution when applied to Rome also served both to justify and to legitimize the superiority of the aristocratic or better elements. This outlook was already evident in Polybius and in Cicero's *De re publica*. It receives even greater emphasis throughout the work of Dionysius; particularly noteworthy is the great speech of M'. Valerius Maximus, brother of Valerius Publicola. This important speech has as its central theme the concept of *concordia*, with the participation of every social element in the management of the state.[39] It is probably the single most complete theoretical programme for the mixed constitution as applied to the Roman republic. In it the judicial powers of the *comitia* represent the principal role of the people within the system. These powers are seen as an essential defence against any potential malfeasance by a single eminent citizen (such as occurred in the case of Coriolanus). The main threat to the organic oligarchical system lies in the support of individual power by a combination of the

---

it as a mixed constitution: II.14. G. J. D. Aalders, *Die Theorie der gemischten Verfassung im Altertum* (Amsterdam, 1968), 117 ff.

38. J. E. Acton, "The History of Freedom in Antiquity" (1877), reprinted in Acton, *Essays on Freedom and Power* (1957), 71.

39. VII.54–56; Gabba, "Dionigi e la dittatura a Roma," 222–24. On the man himself see H. Volkmann, *PW* s.v. "Valerius (243)." The intervention of Manius Valerius takes place during the first plebeian sedition of 494 B.C., and in one variant of the tradition his action supersedes the role of Menenius Agrippa.

masses and a senatorial faction. More or less the same theory
was expounded by Cicero in his *De officiis*. He was influenced
by his own experiences during the civil wars and the dictatorship of Caesar.[40] The theory of a mixed constitution was therefore open to interpretation, even to distortion. Such distortions
were seen by Polybius as a necessary part of the cyclic permuta-
tion of every political system. A remedy against the process of
decay was suggested by Dionysius. The Senate, he held, should
appoint a dictator with constituent powers, for a period of six
months, whose express duty was a reform of customs and laws
and the nomination of trustworthy magistrates. Once this was
accomplished the constitutional system would again begin to
operate normally. This suggestion is certainly a curious one.
Both the annalistic tradition and Dionysius mention a Roman
dictator "seditionis sedandae causa," in order to suppress a
sedition, but in the speech of Valerius mentioned above a constituent dictatorship is proposed. Again, according to a famous
passage in the *Somnium Scipionis* in Cicero's *De re publica*
(VI.12), it seems that someone proposed the appointment of
Scipio Aemilianus as dictator during the difficult internal situation of 129 B.C. In the case of Manius Valerius's proposal, the
dictatorship envisaged naturally took into account the rule of
Sulla (82 B.C.) and reflects a strictly oligarchic vision of Roman
politics.

The problem becomes more complex because we must ask
what was entailed by a proposal to relaunch the model of a
mixed constitution in the Augustan age, despite the fact that the
model was presented in the context of an archaic history. Polybius's reflections on the matter were prompted by his investigation into the reasons for Rome's emergence. The theoretical
aspects, while not neglected by the historian, are clearly an ap-
pendage, in some way not quite related to the thrust of his po-

40. Gabba, "Per un'interpretazione politica del de officiis," 125–29.

litical reasoning. Cicero's aim in the *De re publica,* written in
54–51 B.C., was to show the historical development of the Roman state, which, through wise adjustments and increased political acquisitions, had eventually attained its finest stage after
the Decemvirate, achieving a balance of the different political
powers in what amounted to a true mixed constitution. Cicero
himself, however, in his final and more involved political statement, the *De officiis* (composed in the last months of 44 B.C.),
had practically put aside the theoretical ideal of the mixed constitution. He insisted on the necessity of a direct and conscious
political commitment by the citizens of the new Roman and Italian middle classes.[41]

Dionysius is the last ancient authority to advance, at least implicitly, the model of a mixed constitution. The historical and
political thinkers of the imperial age tried to understand and define the position of imperial power within the Roman state.
They formulated a variety of interpretations in order to characterize such power as the optimum system of government, even
representing it as the most perfect form of democracy.[42] Tacitus
also mentions the theory of a mixed constitution in a well-
known passage of the *Annals,* only to dismiss it immediately as
unfeasible or at best a temporary state of affairs. We cannot be
sure whether Tacitus's statement echoes contemporary discussion of the question or, as Sir Ronald Syme maintains, merely
reflects his own anti-Ciceronian position.[43] It seems quite clear

41. Gabba, "Per un'interpretazione politica del de officiis," 117–41.
42. Aalders, 120 ff.; Gabba, "The Historians and Augustus," 67–75.
43. *Ann.* IV.33.1. The passage of Tacitus should be considered in context:
M. A. Giua, "Storiografia e regimi politici in Tacito, *Annales* IV 32–33,"
Athenaeum n.s. 63 (1985) 5–27, and for our own passage pp. 16–17 in particular. For possible contemporary discussion: Aalders, 123; R. Syme, *Ten
Studies on Tacitus* (Oxford, 1970), 119 ff. (on the possibility of hostile references to Cicero); cf. C. Wirszubski, *Libertas as a Political Idea at Rome during
the Late Republic and Early Principate* (Cambridge, 1950), 162. In the summary of Arius Didymus's peripatetic ethic (Stobaeus II.150–51 Wachsmuth)
the mixed constitution is naturally touched upon and recognized as the best

to me that the theory of a mixed constitution was revived and praised by Dionysius because it restated and reaffirmed, on a theoretical level, the indispensable historical function of the upper classes in the political life of the nation even under a monarchical regime. The contemporary value of the theory lay in its oligarchic character, for it once again stressed the right of the best to rule, by contrast with the uncultivated lower classes or, indeed, the emperor.

IV

Despite the fact that in Cicero's view the mixed constitution was the result of a long historical process,[44] the theory of *concordia* on which it was based, and hence its political and historiographical application in the work of both Cicero and Polybius, was by its very nature static, since it served to describe and interpret the state as an organic, self-contained structure. The practical operation of this concept in the continuous development and adaptation of the Roman civic body is not quite clear. Dionysius succeeds, to a certain extent, in overcoming this difficulty because he places his interpretation of the Roman political system, as a mixed constitution, in tandem with the ongoing exploitation of assimilation on a political level. This is perhaps the high point of Dionysius's historiography. For Dionysius the outstanding characteristic of Roman history, still active in his own age, lay in this very element of assimilation, which allowed the Romans to advance beyond their ethnic origins.

In a mixed constitution where the oligarchic component prevailed, an increase in the civic body could be allowed if the upper classes were fundamentally concordant. In this case the

---

form, but it does not follow that Didymus, who was Augustus's teacher, was also a proponent of the theory (thus J. M. Alonso-Núñez, "Il supposto trattato di Plutarco sulle forme di governo," *A&R* 30 [1985] 34).

44. The remark in Momigliano, "Camillus and Concord."

policy of assimilation is the logical development and complement of a mixed constitution. The most important assimilation
had always occurred at the upper level of Roman society. This
had been the case since the selection of Numa Pompilius and
Servius Tullius as kings, as well as with the admission of Atta
Clausus, the Sabine, into the patriciate.[45] This capacity for assimilation had always been the basis of Rome's historical merit
and of her true superiority to the narrow-mindedly exclusive
Greek cities. Thus in the author's own day the Greek upper
classes could, as previously, be absorbed into the political life of
the imperial state, on account of their cultural and moral background. This view was not widely accepted, and Plutarch, for
one, rejected it. At the beginning of the third century A.D., however, in Book LII of his *Roman History*, Cassius Dio, the historian and senator from Bithynia, historicized the views of Aelius
Aristides in a speech put into the mouth of Maecenas, in which
he theorized on the participation in government of the best
people chosen from throughout the empire.[46] In the view of
Dionysius the moral basis for assimilation was grounded on the
ethical principles elaborated by the Greeks in the fourth century B.C. and was embodied in the history of Rome. A return to
the classics, he held, could lead to a revival of these principles.

This problem was confronted by Dionysius in the long debate
between Tullius Hostilius, king of Rome, and the Alban dictator
Mettius Fufetius on the occasion of the vicissitudes that eventually led to the destruction of Alba Longa and the transfer of its
inhabitants to Rome. The Alban dictator contended that the
preservation of an original ethnic character, entailing the right
to rule, was the best guarantee of virtue. The Roman king, on
the other hand, replied that admission of foreign elements to the

45. Cf. Livy IV.3–4.
46. LII.14–15 and 19. Gabba, "Sulla Storia romana di Cassio Dione,"
RSI 67 (1955) 322, and *The Historians and Augustus,* 70–75.

civic body was no sign of corruption; nobility of birth must be supplemented with merit so that those in government are always the best, and they must be backed and supported in their decisions by the people. Tullius also laid stress on the emulation necessary between old and new citizens, with political differences being viewed as a constructive factor.[47]

Naturally, Dionysius was well aware of the limitations inherent in the principle of assimilation. An expansion beyond the ethnic base must not lead to a total denial of that base. In Book IV he advances a very strong polemic against the indiscriminate admission of slaves to Roman citizenship. Such an approach, Dionysius feels, would undermine the dignity that the city must maintain to be worthy of its hegemonic status. He lists the various ways in which these later manumissions came about and differentiates between these and the original reason for the introduction of this custom, at a time when the slave was usually a defeated but loyal enemy.[48] The policy of assimilation had had the consequence of constantly increasing the military capacity of Rome, and this was an obvious reason for Roman superiority over the Greek cities. This comment clearly smacks of Polybius and must be taken in conjunction with Dionysius's admiring remarks on Italy's great economic wealth and self-sufficiency. The rhetoric and patriotic motive behind the *laudes Italiae* are transformed into a political reflection and become another justification for Roman hegemony.

If this account accurately reflects the political position taken by Dionysius in his work (as the evidence seems to indicate) then two questions cannot be avoided: (a) How can the paradigmatic value of Rome's early history be reconciled with its re-

47. III.9–11; Walbank, "Nationality as a Factor in Roman History," *HSPh* 76 (1972) 145–68, now in Walbank, *Selected Papers* (Cambridge, 1985), 57–76.

48. IV.22–24; Gabba, review of *Ancient Slavery and Modern Ideology*, by M. I. Finley, 279.

cent history of civil wars? (b) What was the status of Dionysius's historical thinking in the atmosphere of the Augustan age?

Dionysius was fully aware that the Rome of ancient history, with its austerity and illustrious personalities, had since undergone a phase of moral and political decline. Dionysius naturally omits the typical conception found in much historiography of the second and first centuries B.C., which linked the internal crisis of the Roman state with imperial expansion. We have already seen that the origins of internal feuding and the collapse of *concordia* are dated to the tribunates of Caius Gracchus. This dating had been accepted by tradition. Dionysius states that the excessive power of the tribunes could destroy the state and could ultimately lead only to civil war—even the resort to dictatorship gave way to tyranny under Sulla. The violent destruction of private rights to land ownership with the advent of the triumvirate indicated the extent of contemporary alienation from the principles laid down by Numa Pompilius.[49] The comments we find in Book V are even harsher. The generals of old, Dionysius maintains, were loyal and faithful to the state, far removed from any dereliction of duty and presumption of personal power, whereas few contemporary generals had been able to resist the temptation to abuse their power. Of particular relevance here is the comparison made with Cincinnatus and his contemporaries in Book X. The modern Romans bore no resemblance to their illustrious predecessors, but practiced the opposite in every case, while only a handful maintained the dignity of the commonwealth and preserved the image of their an-

---

49. II.74.5. Here are the other principal references and allusions to contemporary Roman history: I.6.4 (decline in the descendants of Rome's great men); II.11.3 (Caius Gracchus); II.6.4 (Crassus's spurning of divine warnings and his ruin); V.77.4–6 (dictatorship of Sulla); VIII.80.1–3 (the Sullan Civil War, proscriptions, and measures taken by Caesar); X.35.2 (the tribunate's responsibility and role in the collapse of the political order). See also the following note.

cestors.[50] Corruption is not, however, seen as being universal or extending to the entire ruling class. In the preface to his essay *On the Ancient Orators* Dionysius had great praise for the integrity and wisdom of Rome's leading men. In this light a certain degree of contradiction is undeniable.

Certain episodes in the civil wars of the first century B.C. are hinted at, but the naming of political personalities after Sulla and Crassus is avoided. Caesar, Pompey, Antony, and Octavian, as well as Cicero, are never mentioned. This difficult aspect of Dionysius's thought may be explained by arguing that the historian, when recalling the cultural and moral world of the fourth century B.C. and using the Rome of before the Punic wars as a model, was obliged to skip over the period of revolution, an age of political and moral decline. In contrast to Sallust and Livy, but in agreement with Posidonius, Dionysius had both hope and confidence in the regeneration of the Roman state. His readers could not but have noticed that in extolling the nonviolent political life of the ancients, he not only contrasted the Greek cities with Rome to the latter's advantage in terms of moral superiority, but he also openly reproached Rome for her most recent history, while offering an example for the future.

His silence on Augustus, much as his silence on Livy, no doubt has significant overtones.[51] Apart from this silence we have no further hints that Dionysius may have opposed the *princeps* who had restored order and peace.[52] Nonetheless the laudatory

50. V.60.2; X.17.6. The motif is frequent in the historiography on the civil wars.

51. Augustus is mentioned in I.7.2 to date the arrival of Dionysius at Rome at the end of the civil wars (30 B.C.), and in I.70.4 where Dionysius recalls the lineage of the *gens Iulia,* tracing it back to Iulus, son of Aeneas, and his priesthood, an office still enjoyed by his descendants in the historian's time (an allusion to Caesar and Augustus as *pontifex maximus?*). Dionysius proposes to write elsewhere of his family, the greatest and most illustrious at Rome. It is impossible to say where this excursus may have been inserted in the lost section of his work.

52. Hill, "Dionysius of Halicarnassus and the Origins of Rome."

allusions to Augustus that some scholars have tried to detect in Dionysius's work seem to me nonexistent.[53] Livy and his works are never cited, but the preface to Dionysius's history contains many possible references to Livy's work, all, in one way or another, polemical. Remote as he was from Livy's pessimism, the Greek historian viewed and judged imperial Rome from the perspective of Greek universalism, which was distinct from the Roman and Italian views of Augustus and Livy. Dionysius wrote of Rome's archaic period, but he was intent on imperial Rome. He was more concerned with the new historical reality, its cultural presuppositions, and its political and social functions than with the form of its government or the dominant ideology expounded by the *princeps*.

V

Dionysius's work was certainly read and studied by Greek readers in the first two centuries of the empire. I have already attempted to show how the author of the *Ineditum Vaticanum,* implicitly criticizing Dionysius's *History,* cast doubt upon the civilized, learned, and hence anachronistic depiction of archaic Rome and in particular the reign of Romulus. Much of the antiquarian and ethnographic material employed by Strabo in his description of the Sabine territory and Latium (V.3), which betrays a Varronian ascendancy, could derive from Dionysius's *History.*

Plutarch cited Dionysius directly and was largely dependent on his work while writing the lives of Romulus, Numa, Coriolanus, Publicola, Camillus, and also, in all probability, of Pyrrhus.[54]

53. Martin, "La propagande augustéenne" and "Héracles en Italie"; I. E. M. Edlund, "Dionysios of Halicarnassos: Liberty and Democracy in Rome," *CB* 53 (1976) 27–31.

54. B. Scardigli, *Die Römerbiographien Plutarchs* (Munich, 1979), has usefully compiled all the bibliographical references as well as the various modern critical stances. For Coriolanus see also D. A. Russell, "Plutarch's Life of Coriolanus," *JRS* 53 (1963) 21–28; for Pyrrhus: E. Bickerman, "Apocryphal

But, as I have tried to demonstrate, Plutarch could not share the commitment to the Roman empire that Dionysius had openly advocated in his historical work and literary activity. Indeed, Plutarch wrote against the direct participation of the Greek upper classes in the political life of the empire.

The difference between Plutarch's attitude and Dionysius's political commitment is, in my opinion, well illustrated by two points. First, Plutarch, while closely following Dionysius's work and exploiting it, does not accept any of the numerous speeches that Dionysius inserted for the purpose of voicing his own political and ideological viewpoints. These speeches, in view of their length, could not easily be inserted into a biographical schema. In addition, Plutarch's preface to the lives of Theseus and Romulus completely denies the historicity of Romulus and the value of the historical traditions relating to the king. He thus refutes the political exploitation of the reign, which had been one of the principal pillars of Dionysius's interpretation of Roman history.[55]

Appian of Alexandria, on the other hand, openly adhered to Dionysius's political principles when writing his own work.[56]

The relationship between Dionysius's *History* and the *Antiquitates Iudaicae* of Flavius Josephus is more complex, naturally, and has little to do with the historical content of the two works. It is quite obvious that Dionysius's historical work must have provided Josephus with a structural model for his own. Both works have similar titles ('Ρωμαϊκὴ 'Αρχαιολογία, 'Ιουδαϊκὴ 'Αρχαιολογία) and each has twenty books. If there are any apparent points of contact between the preface of Josephus (*A.I.*

Correspondence of Pyrrhus," *CPh* 42 (1947) 137–46. In *Publ.* 9.10–11 Plutarch hints, without a direct quotation, at the literary polemics of Dionysius V.17 about the Roman priority in delivering funeral speeches.

55. Plut. *Thes.* I.1–5.

56. Gabba, *Appiano e la storia delle guerre civili*, 95–96. Dionysius was exploited also by Eusebius of Caesarea, *Praep. evang.* II.8: Gabba, "Dionigi, Varrone, e la religione senza miti," 857.

I.1–4) and that of Dionysius, these are a matter of coincidence, being confined to the usual declarations of intent common to all historians. Josephus proclaims the antiquity and veracity of the Hebraic tradition, which from its very beginnings displayed its historicity in the person of Moses, in sharp contrast to the free and often fabulous nature of other nations' elaborations concerning the human or divine. He is thinking of the Greeks in particular. This idea would later be reaffirmed by Josephus in a specific work of his, *Contra Apionem,* which deals with a traditional aspect of the polemic between the Greek and Hebraic cultures on history and chronology: there is no reference to Dionysius. Instead Josephus asserts that historical judgment should be measured in terms of observance of the laws and conformity to the will of God. The historian makes an explicit comparison between Moses and the type of legislator who attributed shameful faults to the gods through the invention of myth, thus providing a ready excuse for wrongdoers. These ideas recall Dionysius's reflections on the reign of Romulus and his opposition to the acceptance of Greek myth.[57] Other points of comparison in matters of style and historiographical technique (the use of counterpoised orations, for instance) are in fact common to every piece of historiography written according to the established canons and do not indicate or indeed prove any closer similarity between their works.[58]

I suspect that the exemplary value of Dionysius's work for Josephus is to be sought on a deeper level than surface technique and arrangement. In writing his *Antiquitates Iudaicae,* Josephus aimed primarily at an audience among the Greek-educated upper classes of the Jewish diaspora. In the wake of the tragedy

57. Above, pp. 119–122.
58. H. Thackeray, *Josephus. The Man and the Historian* (New York, 1929), 56–58, and *Josephus,* Loeb Classical Library, vol. 4 (London, 1930), ix; H. W. Attridge, *The Interpretation of Biblical History in the Antiquitates Iudaicae of Flavius Josephus* (Missoula, 1976), 43–57; T. Rajak, *Josephus. The Historian and His Society* (London, 1983), 9, 48, 89.

of 70 A.D. his goal was the reaffirmation, through a complete and exemplary review of Jewish history, of the Jewish culture, its continuity, and the Hebrew nation's capacity for survival. He paid particular attention to the possibility of an accommodation of the Jewish ethnos within the framework of Roman dominion.[59] In this way Josephus readapted to a less favourable historical context a perspective previously elaborated, in happier times, by Nicolaus of Damascus and in particular by Philo of Alexandria. This view held the Roman empire to be the unique historical framework that both consented to and guaranteed the free cohabitation of a diversity of traditions and cultures.[60] In a certain sense this universalist vision of the Roman empire resembled that of Dionysius. For although Dionysius gave the decisive role to the high values and influence of Greece (Rome being part and parcel of this nexus), he did present the possibility, demonstrated by the very example of Roman history, of a direct assimilation of elites, along with experiments in the cohabitation of different ethnic groups. If Dionysius's insights lie at the base of Cassius Dio's and Aelius Aristides' theories on an ecumenical empire, so too Josephus's ideas on an association of the Jews within the empire may be seen in the same perspective.

The *History of Archaic Rome* of Dionysius thus reflects an incisive interpretation of the political role of Greek influence over Rome. This interpretation would see events in the development of the Roman empire as widespread and positive consequences of such influences. Dionysius knowingly sought to justify the legitimacy of Rome's assumed direction of this unitary historical process, which posited the great ethical principles of classical Greece, mediated by the Roman political experience, as the basis for civic cohabitation in the Mediterranean world.

59. L. Troiani, "I lettori delle *Antiquitates Iudaicae* di Giuseppe: prospettive e problemi," *Athenaeum* n.s. 64 (1986) 343–53.

60. Gabba, *The Historians and Augustus,* 61–64. Noteworthy in Josephus, *A.I.* XVI.31 ff. Nicolaus's speech: L. Troiani, "Un nuovo studio su Giuseppe," *Athenaeum* n.s. 63 (1985) 192.

Bibliography

Aalders, G. J. D. *Die Theorie der gemischten Verfassung im Altertum.* Amsterdam, 1968.

Abel, K. H. "Die kulturelle Mission des Panaitios." *A&A* 17 (1971) 119–43.

Acton, J. E. "The History of Freedom in Antiquity." 1877. Reprinted in J. E. Acton, *Essays on Freedom and Power,* 1957.

Alföldi, A. *Early Rome and the Latins.* Ann Arbor, 1965.

Alonso-Núñez, J. M. "Die Abfolge der Weltreiche bei Polybios und Dionysios von Halikarnassos." *Historia* 32 (1983) 411–26.

———. "Appian and the World Empires." *Athenaeum* n.s. 62 (1984) 640–44.

———. "L'opposizione contro l'imperialismo romano e contro il principato nella storiografia del tempo di Augusto." *RSA* 12 (1982) 131–41.

———. "Il supposto trattato di Plutarco sulle forme di governo." *A&R* 30 (1985) 32–36.

Ambaglio, D. *L'opera storiografica di Ellanico di Lesbo.* Ricerche di storiografia antica, 2. Pisa, 1980.

Ampolo, C. "La storiografia su Roma arcaica e i documenti." In *Tria corda. Scritti in onore di Arnaldo Momigliano,* edited by E. Gabba, 9–26. Como, 1983.

Anderson, W. S. *Pompey, His Friends, and the Literature of the First Century B.C.* University of California Publications in Classical Philology 19, no. 1. Berkeley, 1963.

Andrén, A. "Dionysius of Halicarnassus on Roman Monuments." In *Hommages à Leon Herrmann*, 88–104. Brussels, 1960.

Arnim, H. von. "*Ineditum Vaticanum.*" *Hermes* 27 (1892) 118–30.

Asheri, D. "La declamazione 261 di Quintiliano." In *Studi in onore di Edoardo Volterra*, vol. 1, 309–21. Milan, 1971.

——. *Fra ellenismo e iranismo. Studi sulla società e cultura di Xanthos in età achemenide.* Bologna, 1983.

Attridge, H. W. *The Interpretation of Biblical History in the Antiquitates Iudaicae of Flavius Josephus.* Missoula, 1976.

Aujac, G., ed. and tr. *Denys d'Halicarnasse. Opuscules rhétoriques.* Vol. 1. Paris, 1978.

——. *Strabon, Géographie.* Paris, 1966–.

Badian, E. "A Phantom Marriage Law." *Philologus* 129 (1985) 82–89.

Baldry, H. C. "The Idea of the Unity of Mankind." In *Grecs et barbares,* 169–95. Fondation Hardt, Entretiens 8. Geneva, 1962.

Balsdon, J. P. V. D. "Dionysius on Romulus." *JRS* 61 (1971) 18–27.

Bause, J. "Περὶ ὕψους Kapitel 44." *RhM* n.s. 123 (1980) 258–66.

Bayet, J. *La religion romaine: histoire politique et psychologique.* Paris, 1976.

Beaufort, Louis de. *Dissertation sur l'incertitude des cinqs premiers siècles de l'histoire romaine.* 1738. New ed. by A. Blot. 2 vols. in 1. Paris, 1866.

Becker, W. G. *Platons Gesetze und das griechische Familienrecht.* Munich, 1932.

Beloch, J. *Römische Geschichte bis zum Beginn der Punischen Kriege.* Berlin, 1926.

——. "Der Verfall der antiken Kultur." *HZ* 48 (1900) 1–38.

Bengtson, H. "Das Imperium Romanum in griechischer Sicht." *Gymnasium* 71 (1964) 150–66. Reprinted in H. Bengtson, *Kleine Schriften zur Alten Geschichte.* Munich, 1974.

Bertelli, L. "L'apologo di Menenio Agrippa: incunabolo della 'Homonoia' a Roma?" *Index* 3 (1972) 224–34.

Bickerman, E. "Apocryphal Correspondence of Pyrrhus." *CPh* 42 (1947) 137–46.

——. "La chaîne de la tradition pharisienne." *RBi* 59 (1952) 44–54. Reprinted in E. Bickerman, *Studies in Jewish and Christian History,* vol. 2, 256–69. Arbeiten zur Geschichte des Antiken Judentums und des Urchristentums, vol. 9, pt. 2. Leiden, 1980.

———. "Origines Gentium." *CPh* 47 (1952) 65–81. Reprinted in E. Bickerman, *Religions and Politics in the Hellenistic and Roman Periods*, 399–417. Como, 1985.

———. "Une question d'authenticité: Les privilèges juifs." *AIPhO* 13 (1953) 11–34. Reprinted in E. Bickerman, *Studies in Jewish and Christian History*, vol. 2, 24–43. Arbeiten zur Geschichte des Antiken Judentums und des Urchristentums, vol. 9, pt. 2. Leiden, 1980.

———. "Some Reflections on Early Roman History." *RFIC* 97 (1969) 393–408. Reprinted in E. Bickerman, *Religions and Politics in the Hellenistic and Roman Periods*, 525–40. Como, 1985.

Bleicken, J. "Der Preis des Aelius Aristides auf das römische Weltreich." *NAWG* (1966) no. 7, 225–77.

Bluhme, F., K. Lachmann, and A. Rudorff, eds. *Die Schriften der Römischen Feldmesser*. 2 vols. 1848–52. Reprint. Hildesheim, 1967.

Bonamente, G. "La storiografia di Teopompo fra classicità e ellenismo." *AIIS* 4 (1973–75) 9–86.

Bonfante, P. *Corso di diritto romano*. Vol. 2, *La proprietà*. Rome, 1926. Reprint. Milan, 1966.

———. *Res mancipi e nec mancipi*. Rome, 1888–89. Republished with corrections in P. Bonfante, *Scritti giuridici vari*, vol. 2, 1–326. Torino, 1918.

Bonner, S. F. *The Literary Treatises of Dionysius of Halicarnassus: A Study in the Development of Critical Method*. Cambridge, 1939. Reprint. Amsterdam, 1969.

Bowersock, G. W. *Augustus and the Greek World*. Oxford, 1965.

———. "Historical Problems in Late Republican and Augustan Classicism." In *Le classicisme à Rome aux I^{ers} siècles avant et après J.-C.*, 57–75. Fondation Hardt, Entretiens 25. Geneva, 1979.

Bowie, E. L. "Greeks and Their Past in the Second Sophistic." *P&P* 46 (1970) 3–41. Reprinted in *Studies in Ancient Society*, edited by M. I. Finley, 166–209. London, 1974.

Bowra, C. M. "Melinno's Hymn to Rome." *JRS* 47 (1957) 21–28.

Boyancé, P. "Les implications philosophiques des recherches de Varron sur la réligion romaine." In *Atti del congresso internazionale di studi varroniani, Rieti, settembre 1974*, vol. 1, 137–61. Rieti, 1976.

———. "Sur la théologie de Varron." *REA* 57 (1955) 57–84. Reprinted in P. Boyancé, *Etudes sur la réligion romaine,* 253–82. Rome, 1972.

Braccesi, L. *Epigrafia e storiografia.* Naples, 1981.

Briquel, D. "L'autochtonie des étrusques chez Denys d'Halicarnasse." *REL* 61 (1983) 65–86.

————. *Les pélasges en Italie. Recherches sur l'histoire de la légende.* Rome, 1984.

Broughton, T. R. S. "Roman Asia." In *An Economic Survey of Ancient Rome,* edited by Tenney Frank, vol. 4, 499–916. Baltimore, 1938.

Brown, T. S. *Timaeus of Tauromenium.* University of California Publications in History, 55. Berkeley, 1958.

Brunt, P. A. "Cicero and Historiography." In *Miscellanea di studi classici in onore di Eugenio Manni,* vol. 1, 311–40. Rome, 1980.

Brzoska, J. "Damas (4)." *PW* 4 (1901) cols. 2034–35.

Buckler, W. H. "Augustus, Zeus Patroos." *RPh* 9 (1935) 182–86.

Bürchner, L. "Halikarnassos." *PW* 7 (1912) cols. 2253–64.

Burck, E. *Die Erzählungskunst des T. Livius.* 1934. Reprint. Berlin, 1964.

Burkert, W. "Caesar and Romulus-Quirinus." *Historia* 11 (1962) 356–76.

Butel-Dumont, G. M. *Recherches historiques et critiques sur l'administration publique et privée des terres chez les Romains.* Paris, 1779.

Cagnazzi, S. "Politica e retorica nel preambolo del Περὶ τῶν ἀρχαίων ῥητόρων di Dionigi di Alicarnasso." *RFIC* 109 (1981) 52–59.

Calabi, F. "Sulla proprietà della terra in Aristotele." *RSF* 32 (1977) 195–203.

Camassa, G. *L'occhio e il metallo. Un mitologema greco a Roma?* Genoa, 1983.

Cantarelli, F., tr. and ed. *Dionisio di Alicarnasso. Storia di Roma arcaica (Le antichità romane).* Milan, 1984.

Capelle, W. "Griechische Ethik und römischer Imperialismus." *Klio* 25 (1932) 86–113.

Capogrossi Colognesi, L. "La figura dell'heredium nella storiografia di fine 800." *BIDR* 85 (1982) 41–75.

————. *La terra in Roma antica. Forme di proprietà e rapporti produttivi.* Vol. 1. Rome, 1981.

Cardauns, B. "Varro und die römische Religion." *ANRW* II.16.1 (1978) 80–103.

————, ed. M. *Terentius Varro. Antiquitates rerum divinarum.* 2 vols. Mainz, 1976.

Cary, E., ed. and tr. *The Roman Antiquities of Dionysius of Halicarnassus.* 7 vols. Loeb Classical Library. Cambridge, Mass., 1937–50.

Castagnoli, F., ed. *Lavinium.* Vol. 2. Rome, 1973.

Cavallaro, M. A. "Dicearco, l'*Ineditum Vaticanum* e la crisi della cultura siceliota." *Helikon* 11–12 (1971–72) 213–28.

————. "Dionisio, Cecilio de Kalē Aktē e l'*Ineditum Vaticanum.*" *Helikon* 13–14 (1973–74) 118–40.

Coarelli, F. *Il foro romano.* Vol. 1, *Periodo arcaico.* Rome, 1983.

Colonna, G. "Tarquinio Prisco e il tempio di Giove Capitolino." *PP* 36 (1981) 41–59.

————. "Virgilio, Cortona e la leggenda etrusca di Dardano." *ArchClass* 32 (1980) 1–15.

Cornell, T. "Alcune riflessioni sulla formazione della tradizione storiografica su Roma arcaica." In *Roma arcaica e le recenti scoperte archeologiche: giornate di studio in onore di Ugo Coli.* Milan, 1980.

————. "Etruscan Historiography." *ASNP,* 3d ser., 6 (1976) 411–39.

Costa, E. *Cicerone giureconsulto.* 2d ed. 2 vols. Bologna, 1927.

Crawford, M. H. "Greek Intellectuals and the Roman Aristocracy in the First Century B.C." In *Imperialism in the Ancient World,* edited by P. D. A. Garnsey and C. R. Whittaker, 193–207. Cambridge, 1978.

Crossett, J. M. and J. A. Arieti. *The Dating of Longinus.* Studia Classica, 3. Department of Classics, Pennsylvania State University. University Park, 1975.

Dal Cason, F. "La tradizione annalistica sulle più antiche leggi agrarie: riflessioni e proposte." *Athenaeum* n.s. 63 (1985) 174–84.

De Martino, F. "Clienti e condizioni materiali in Roma arcaica." In *Miscellanea di studi classici in onore di Eugenio Manni,* vol. 2, 681–705. Rome, 1979.

————. "Intorno all'origine della schiavitù a Roma." *Labeo* 20 (1974) 163–93. Reprinted in F. De Martino, *Diritto e società nell'antica Roma,* 130–61. Rome, 1979.

————. *Storia della costituzione romana.* 2d ed. Naples, 1972–74.

De Sanctis, G. Review of *Grandezza e decadenza di Roma,* by G. Ferrero. *BFC* 8 (1901–2) 274–79. Reprinted in G. De Sanctis, *Scritti minori,* vol. 6, pt. 1, 37–42. Storia e letteratura, 125. Rome, 1972.

————. Review of *Studies on Scipio Africanus*, by R. M. Haywood. *RFIC* n.s. 14 (1936) 189–203. Reprinted in G. de Sanctis, *Scritti minori*, vol. 6, pt. 1, 506–24. Storia e letteratura, 125. Rome, 1972.

De Vivo, A. *Tacito e Claudio: Storia e codificazione letteraria*. Naples, 1980.

Deininger, J. *Der politische Widerstand gegen Rom in Griechenland. 217–86 v. Chr.* Berlin, 1971.

Della Corte, F. "L'idea della preistoria in Varrone." In *Atti del congresso internazionale di studi varroniani, Rieti, settembre 1974*, vol. 1, 111–36. Rieti, 1976.

Desideri, P. *Dione di Prusa, un intellettuale greco nell'impero romano*. Messina, 1978.

————. "L'interpretazione dell'impero romano in Posidonio." *RIL* 106 (1972) 481–93.

————. "Posidonio e la guerra Mitridatica." *Athenaeum* n.s. 51 (1973) 3–62.

Develin, R. "Pompeius Trogus and Philippic History." *SS* 8 (1985) 110–15.

Diehl, E., ed. *Anthologia lyrica graeca*. 3d ed. 3 vols. Leipzig, 1949.

Dihle, A. "Der Beginn des Attizismus." *A&A* 23 (1977) 162–77.

D'Ippolito, F. "Le XII tavole; il testo e la politica." In *Storia di Roma*, edited by A. Momigliano and A. Schiavone, vol. 1, 397–413. Torino, 1988.

Dörrie, H. "Die Wertung der Barbaren im Urteil der Griechen." In *Antike und Universalgeschichte. Festschrift Hans Erich Stier*, edited by R. Stiehl and G. Lehmann, 146–75. Münster, 1972.

Drachmann, A. B. *Diodors Römische Annalen bis 302 a. Chr. samt dem Ineditum Vaticanum*. Bonn, 1912.

Ducos, M. *L'influence grecque sur la loi des douze tables*. Paris, 1978.

Dumézil, G. *La réligion romaine archaïque*. Paris, 1966.

Düring, I. *Aristotle in the Ancient Biographical Tradition*. Göteborg, 1957.

Edlund, I. E. M. "Dionysios of Halicarnassos: Liberty and Democracy in Rome." *CB* 53 (1976) 27–31.

Egermann, F. "Die Proömien zu den Werken des Sallust." *SAWW* 214 (1932), 3d. abh.

Erdmann, W. *Die Ehe im Alten Griechenland*. Munich, 1934.

Evans, E. C. *The Cults of the Sabine Territory*. Papers and Monographs of the American Academy in Rome, 11. Rome, 1939.

Fabbrini, F. *Traslatio imperii. L'impero universale da Ciro ad Augusto.* Rome, 1983.

Fabre, G. *Libertus. Recherches sur les rapports patron-affranchi à la fin de la république.* Rome, 1981.

Ferenczy, E. "Clientela e schiavitù nella repubblica romana primitiva." *Index* 8 (1978–79) 167–72.

———. "Le legge delle XII tavole e le codificazioni greche." In *Sodalitas: Scritti in onore di Antonio Guarino,* vol. 4, 2001–12.

———. "Römische Gesandtschaft im Perikleischen Athen." *Oikumene* 4 (1983) 37–41.

Ferrara, G. "Commenti al dopoguerra aziaco." *La Cultura* 8 (1970) 22–39.

Ferrario, M. "Ricerche intorno al Trattato del sublime." *RIL* 106 (1972) 765–843.

Ferrary, J.-L. "L'archéologie du *de re publica* (2, 2, 4–37, 63): Cicéron entre Polybe et Platon." *JRS* 74 (1984) 87–98.

———. "L'empire de Rome et les hégémonies des cités grecques chez Polybe." *BCH* 100 (1976) 283–89.

Ferrero, G. *Grandezza e decadenza di Roma.* 5 vols. Milan, 1902–7.

———. *The Greatness and Decline of Rome.* Translated by A. E. Zimmern and H. J. Chaytor. 5 vols. New York, 1908.

Ferrero Raditza, L. "Augustus' Legislation Concerning Marriage, Procreation, Love Affairs and Adultery." *ANRW* II.13 (1980) 278–339.

Finley, M. I. "L'héritage d'Isocrate." In M. I. Finley, *Mythe, mémoire, histoire,* 175–207. Paris, 1981.

Flashar, H. "Die klassizistische Theorie der Mimesis." In *Le classicisme à Rome aux I^{ers} siècles avant et après J.-C.,* 79–97. Fondation Hardt, Entretiens 25. Geneva, 1979.

Flusser, D. "The Four Empires in the Fourth Sibyl and in the Book of Daniel." *IOS* 2 (1972) 148–75.

Fontenelle, B. "De l'origine des fables." In B. Fontenelle, *Oeuvres,* vol. 3, 160–75. Amsterdam, 1764.

Forni, G. "Ἱερὰ ε θεὸς σύγκλητος. Un capitolo dimenticato nella storia del senato romano." *MAL,* 8th ser., 5 (1953) fasc. 3, 49–168.

Forte, B. *Rome and the Romans as the Greeks Saw Them.* Papers and Monographs of the American Academy in Rome, 24. Rome, 1972.

Fraccaro, P. "Livio e Roma." 1942. Reprinted in P. Fraccaro, *Opuscula,* vol. 1, 81–102. Pavia, 1956.

————. "I processi degli Scipioni." 1911. Reprinted in P. Fraccaro, *Opuscula*, vol. 1, 263–392. Pavia, 1956.

————. *Studi varroniani. De gente populi romani*. Padua, 1907.

Freeman, E. A. *The Chief Periods of European History*. London, 1886.

Fritz, K. von. "The Historian Theopompus: His Political Convictions and His Conception of Historiography." *AHR* 46 (1941) 765–87.

Fuchs, H. "Der Friede als Gefahr." *HSPh* 63 (1958) 363–85.

————. *Der geistige Widerstand gegen Rom in der antiken Welt*. Berlin, 1938.

Gabba, E. *Appiano e la storia delle guerre civili*. Florence, 1956.

————. "Aspetti culturali dell'imperialismo romano." *Athenaeum* n.s. 55 (1977) 49–74.

————. "Il 'Brutus' di Accio." *Dioniso* 53 (1969) 377–83.

————. "The Collegia of Numa: Problems of Method and Political Ideas." *JRS* 74 (1984) 81–86.

————. "Considerazioni sulla tradizione letteraria sulle origini della repubblica." In *Les origines de la république romaine*, 135–69. Fondation Hardt, Entretiens 13. Geneva, 1967.

————. "Dionigi d'Alicarnasso sul processo di Spurio Cassio." In *La storia del diritto nel quadro delle scienze storiche. Atti del 1. congresso internazionale della società italiana di storia del diritto*, 143–53. Firenze, 1966.

————. "Dionigi e la dittatura a Roma." In *Tria corda. Scritti in onore di Arnaldo Momigliano*, edited by E. Gabba, 215–28. Como, 1983.

————. "Dionigi, Varrone e la religione senza miti." *RSI* 96 (1984) 855–70.

————. "Un documento censorio in Dionigi d'Alicarnasso I 74.5." In *Synteleia Vincenzo Arangio-Ruiz*, 486–93. Naples, 1964.

————. "Eduard Schwartz e la storiografia greca." *ASNP*, 3d ser., 9 (1979) 1033–49.

————. "Esercito e fiscalità a Roma in età repubblicana." In *Armées et fiscalité dans le monde antique*, 13–17. Centre national de la recherche scientifique, colloques nationaux, no. 936. Paris, 1977.

————. "The Historians and Augustus." In *Caesar Augustus. Seven Aspects*, edited by F. Millar and E. Segal, 61–88. Oxford, 1984.

————. "L'impero romano nel discorso di Agrippa II (Ioseph. B.I. II 345–401)." *RSA* 6–7 (1976–77) 189–94.

————. "Italia e Roma nella storia di Velleio Patercolo." *CS* 1 (1962) 1–9. Reprinted in E. Gabba, *Esercito e società nella tarda repubblica romana,* 347–60. Florence, 1973.

————. "Il latino come dialetto greco." In *Miscellanea di studi alessandrini in memoria di A. Rostagni,* 188–94. Torino, 1963.

————. "Literature." In *Sources for Ancient History,* edited by M. H. Crawford, 1–79. Cambridge, 1983.

————. "Mirsilo di Metimna, Dionigi e i Tirreni." *RAL,* 8th ser., 30 (1975) 35–49.

————. "Per la tradizione dell'heredium romuleo." *RIL* 112 (1978) 250–58.

————. "Per un'interpretazione politica del de officiis di Cicerone." *RAL,* 8th ser., 34 (1979) 117–41.

————. "Per un'interpretazione storica della centuriazione romana." *Athenaeum* n.s. 63 (1985) 265–84.

————. "Political and Cultural Aspects of the Classicistic Revival in the Augustan Age." *ClAnt* 1 (1982) 43–65.

————. "Posidonio, Marcello e la Sicilia." In *AΠAPXAI: Nuove ricerche e studi sulla Magna Grecia e la Sicilia antica in onore di P. E. Arias,* vol. 2, 611–14. Pisa, 1982.

————. "Il problema dell' 'unitá' dell'Italia Romana." In *La cultura italica,* edited by E. Campanile, 11–27. Pisa, 1978.

————. "Riflessioni antiche e moderne sulle attività commerciali a Roma nei secoli II e I a.C." *MAAR* 36 (1980) 91–102.

————. "Scienza e potere nel mondo ellenistico." In *La Scienza Ellenistica,* edited by G. Giannantoni and M. Vegetti. Naples, 1985.

————. "La 'Storia di Roma arcaica' di Dionigi d'Alicarnasso." *ANRW* II.30.1 (1982) 799–816.

————. "Storia e politica nei gromatici." In *Akten des Gromatiker-Symposions Wolfenbüttel.* Göttingen, 1988.

————. "Storici greci dell'impero romano da Augusto ai Severi." *RSI* 71 (1959) 361–81.

————. "Storiografia greca e imperialismo romano (III–I sec. a.C.)." *RSI* 86 (1974) 625–42.

————. "Studi su Dionigi da Alicarnasso. I. La costituzione di Romolo." *Athenaeum* n.s. 38 (1960) 175–225.

————. "Studi su Dionigi da Alicarnasso. II. Il regno di Servio Tullio." *Athenaeum* n.s. 39 (1961) 98–121.

————. "Studi su Dionigi d'Alicarnasso. III. La proposta di legge agraria di Spurio Cassio." *Athenaeum* n.s. 42 (1964) 29–41.

————. "Sulla Storia romana di Cassio Dione." *RSI* 67 (1955) 289–333.

————. "Sulla valorizzazione politica della leggenda delle origini troiane di Roma fra III e II secolo a.C." In *I canali della propaganda nel mondo antico,* edited by M. Sordi, 84–101. Contributi dell'istituto di storia antica, 4. Milan, 1976.

————. "True History and False History in Classical Antiquity." *JRS* 71 (1981) 50–62.

————. Review of *Ancient Slavery and Modern Ideology,* by M. I. Finley. *Athenaeum* n.s. 60 (1982) 276–81.

————. Review of *Tacito e Claudio,* by Arturo De Vivo. *Athenaeum* n.s. 59 (1981) 245–46.

————. Review of *The Hellenistic World and the Coming of Rome,* by E. S. Gruen. *Athenaeum* n.s. 65 (1987) 205–10.

Garlan, Y. *Les ésclaves en Grèce ancienne.* Paris, 1982.

Gasco la Calle, F. "La teoria de los cuatros imperios. Reiteración y adaptación ideológica. I. Romanos y griegos." *Habis* 12 (1981) 179–96.

Gauger, J.-D. "Der Rom-Hymnos der Melinno (Anth. Lyr. II² 6, 209f.) und die Vorstellung von der 'Ewigkeit' Roms." *Chiron* 14 (1984) 267–99.

Gautier, P. "'Generosité' romaine et 'avarice' grecque: sur l'octroi du droit de cité." In *Mélanges d'histoire ancienne offerts a W. Seston,* 207–15. Paris, 1974.

Geiger, J. "Plutarch's Parallel Lives: The Choice of Heroes." *Hermes* 109 (1981) 85–104.

Gelzer, M. *Kleine Schriften.* 3 vols. Wiesbaden, 1963.

Gelzer, T. "Klassizismus, Attizismus und Asianismus." In *Le classicisme à Rome aux Iᵉʳˢ siècles avant et après J.-C.,* 1–41. Fondation Hardt, Entretiens 25. Geneva, 1979.

Giua, M. A. "Storiografia e regimi politici in Tacito, *Annales* IV 32–33." *Athenaeum* n.s. 63 (1985) 5–27.

————. "La valutazione della monarchia a Roma in età repubblicana." *SCO* 16 (1967) 308–29.

Goold, G. P. "A Greek Professional Circle at Rome." *TAPhA* 92 (1961) 168–92.

Gozzoli, S. "Polibio e Dionigi d'Alicarnasso." *SCO* 25 (1976) 149–76.

———. "Una teoria antica sull'origine della storiografia greca." *SCO* 19–20 (1970–71) 158–211.

Griffiths, J. G. *Plutarch's De Iside et Osiride*. Cambridge, 1970.

Grilli, A. "La posizione di Aristotele Epicuro e Posidonio nei confronti della storia della civiltà." *RIL* 86 (1953) 1–44.

Gros, P. "Vie et mort de l'art hellénistique selon Vitruve et Pline." *REL* 56 (1978) 289–313.

Grube, G. M. A. "Dionysius of Halicarnassus on Thucydides." *Phoenix* 4 (1950) 95–110.

———. *The Greek and Roman Critics*. Toronto, 1968.

Gruen, E. S. *The Hellenistic World and the Coming of Rome*. 2 vols. Berkeley, 1984.

Habicht, C. "Die augusteische Zeit und das Erste Jahrhundert nach Christi Geburt." In *Le culte des souverains dans l'empire romain*, 41–88. Fondation Hardt, Entretiens 19. Geneva, 1973.

———. "Epigraphische Zeugnisse zur Geschichte Thessaliens unter der Makedonischen Herrschaft." In *APXAIA MAKEΔONIA (Ancient Macedonia: Papers Read at the First International Symposium Held in Thessaloniki, 26–29 August 1968)*, edited by B. Laourdas and C. Makaronas, 265–79. Thessaloniki, 1970.

———. "New Evidence on the Province of Asia." *JRS* 65 (1975) 64–91.

———. *Pausanias' Guide to Ancient Greece*. Berkeley, 1985.

———. "Zur Personenkunde des Griechisch-Römischen Altertums." *BASP* 21 (1984) 69–75.

Hahn, I. "The Plebeians and Clan Society." *Oikumene* 1 (1976) 47–75.

Hengel, M. *Jews, Greeks and the Barbarians*. Philadelphia, 1980.

Henry, R., ed. and tr. *Photius, Bibliothèque*. 8 vols. Paris, 1959–77.

Hermon, E. "Réflections sur la propriété à l'époque royale." *MEFRA* 90 (1978) 7–31.

Heurgon, J. "Les penestes étrusques chez Denys d'Halicarnasse (IX 5, 4)." *Latomus* 18 (1959) 712–23.

Heuss, A. *Barthold Georg Niebuhrs wissenschaftliche Anfänge*. *AAWG*, 3d ser., 114. Göttingen, 1981.

Heyne, C. G. "Leges agrariae pestiferae et execrabiles." 1793. Reprinted in C. G. Heyne, *Opuscula academica*, vol. 4, 350–73. Göttingen, 1796.

Hill, H. "Dionysius of Halicarnassus and the Origins of Rome." *JRS* 51 (1961) 88–94.

Hornblower, S. *Mausolus.* Oxford, 1982.

Horsfall, N. "Varro and Caesar: Three Chronological Problems." *BICS* 19 (1972) 120–28.

Hurst, A. "Un critique grec dans la Rome d'Auguste: Denys d'Halicarnasse." *ANRW* II.30.1 (1982) 839–65.

Isnardi Parente, M., ed. and tr. *Frammenti: Senocrate, Ermodoro.* Naples, 1982.

Jacoby, C., ed. *Dionysi Halicarnasensis Antiquitates romanae.* 4 vols. Leipzig, 1885–1905. *Supplementum et indices.* Leipzig, 1925.

Jacoby, F. *Apollodoros Chronik; eine Sammlung der Fragmente.* Philologische Untersuchungen, 16. Berlin, 1902.

Joly, R. *Le thème philosophique des genres de vie dans l'antiquité classique.* Brussels, 1956.

Jones, A. M. H. *Athenian Democracy.* Oxford, 1957.

Jones, C. P. "Diotrephes of Antioch." *Chiron* 13 (1983) 369–80.

———. *Plutarch and Rome.* Oxford, 1971.

Kaibel, G. "Dionysios von Halikarnassos und die Sophistik." *Hermes* 20 (1885) 497–513.

Kennedy, G. *The Art of Persuasion in Greece.* Princeton, 1963.

———. *The Art of Rhetoric in the Roman World, 300 B.C.–A.D. 300.* Princeton, 1972.

———. *Classical Rhetoric and Its Christian and Secular Tradition from Ancient to Modern Times.* Chapel Hill, 1980.

Kienast, D. "Der Heilige Senat. Senatskult und kaiserliches Senat." *Chiron* 15 (1985) 253–83.

Koch, C. *Der römische Juppiter.* Frankfurt am Main, 1937.

Lachmann, K. *See* Bluhme, F., K. Lachmann, and A. Rudorff, eds.

Lange, J. "Beiträge zur Caesar-Kritik." *JCP* 41 (1895) 737–63, 799–832.

Lasserre, F. "Prose grecque classicisante." In *Le classicisme à Rome aux I^ers siècles avant et après J.-C.,* 135–63. Fondation Hardt, Entretiens 25. Geneva, 1979.

Latte, K. *Römische Religionsgeschichte.* Munich, 1970.

———. "Ueber eine Eigentümlichkeit der italischen Gottesvorstellung." *ARW* 24 (1926) 244–58.

Laumonier, A. *Les cultes indigènes en Carie.* Paris, 1958.

Le Bonniec, H. *Le culte de Cérès à Rome. Des origines à la fin de la république.* Paris, 1958.

Leo, F. "Die Staatsrechtlichen Exkurse in Tacitus' Annalen." 1896. Reprinted in F. Leo, *Ausgewählte Kleine Schriften,* vol. 2, 298–317. Rome, 1960.

Letta, C. "L' 'Italia dei *mores romani*' nelle *Origines* di Catone." *Athenaeum* n.s. 62 (1984) 1–30, 416–39.

Lieberg, G. "Die theologia tripertita in Forschung und Bezeugung." *ANRW* I.4 (1973) 63–115.

———. "Varros Theologie im Urteil Augustins." In *Studi classici in onore di Quintino Cataudella,* vol. 3, 185–201. Catania, 1972.

Lindsay, W. *Sexti Pompei Festi De verborum significatu quae supersunt cum Pauli epitome.* Leipzig, 1913.

Luce, T. J. "Design and Structure in Livy: 5, 32–55." *TAPhA* 102 (1971) 265–303.

———. *Livy. The Composition of His History.* Princeton, 1977.

Luck, G. "Die Schrift vom Erhabenen und ihr Verfasser." *Arctos* 5 (1967) 97–113.

MacMullen, R. *Enemies of the Roman Order.* Cambridge, Mass., 1966.

Maddoli, G. "Contatti antichi del mondo latino col mondo greco." In *Alle origini del latino,* edited by E. Vineis, 43–64. Pisa, 1981.

———. "Il rito degli Argei e le origini del culto di Hera a Roma." *PP* 26 (1971) 153–66.

Magdelain, A. "Remarques sur la société romaine archaique." *REL* 49 (1971) 103–27.

Magie, D. *Roman Rule in Asia Minor.* 2 vols. Princeton, 1950.

Malitz, J. *Die Historien des Posidonios.* Munich, 1983.

Marenghi, G., ed. and tr. *Dionisio di Alicarnasso: Dinarco.* Milan, 1970.

Marin, D. "Dionisio di Alicarnasso e il latino." In *Hommages à Marcel Renard,* 595–607. Brussels, 1969.

———. "L'opposizione sotto Augusto e la datazione del 'Saggio sul sublime.'" In *Studi in onore di Aristide Calderini e Roberto Paribeni,* vol. 1, 157–85. Milan, 1957.

Martin, P. M. "Denys d'Halicarnasse et l'autochtonie des étrusques." In *Colloque histoire et historiographie Clio,* edited by R. Chevallier, 47–59. Caesarodunum, 15 bis. Paris, 1980.

———. "Héraklès en Italie d'après Denys d'Halicarnasse (*A.R.*, I, 34–44)." *Athenaeum* n.s. 50 (1972) 252–75.

———. *L'idée de royauté à Rome.* Vol. 1, *De la Rome royale au consensus républicain.* Clermont-Ferrand, 1982.

———. "La propagande augustéenne dans les Antiquités romaines de Denys d'Halicarnasse (livre I)." *REL* 49 (1971) 162–79.

Martinez-Pinna Nieto, J. "La reforma de Numa y la formación de Roma." *Gerión* 3 (1985) 97–124.

Mastrocinque, A. *La Caria e la Ionia meridionale in epoca ellenistica (323–188 B.C.).* Rome, 1979.

Mazzarino, S. *Il pensiero storico classico.* 2 vols. in 3. Bari, 1966.

Mendels, D. "The Five Empires. A Note on a Propagandistic Topos." *AJPh* 102 (1981) 330–37.

Mirsch, P. "De M. Terenti Varronis Antiquitatum rerum humanarum libris XXV." *Leipziger Studien zur Classischen Philologie* 5 (1882) 1–144.

Momigliano, A. *Alien Wisdom, The Limits of Hellenization.* Cambridge, 1975.

———. "Atene nel III secolo a.C. e la scoperta di Roma nelle Storie di Timeo di Tauromenio." *RSI* 71 (1959) 529–56. Reprinted as "Athens in the Third Century B.C. and the Discovery of Rome in the Histories of Timaeus of Tauromenium" in A. Momigliano, *Essays in Ancient and Modern Historiography,* 37–66. Middletown, Conn., 1977.

———. "Camillus and Concord." *CQ* 36 (1942) 111–20. Reprinted in A. Momigliano, *Secondo contributo alla storia degli studi classici,* 89–104. Storia e letteratura, 77. Rome, 1960.

———. "Daniele e la teoria greca della successione degli imperi." *RAL* 35 (1980) 157–62. Reprinted in A. Momigliano, *La storiografia greca,* 293–301. Torino, 1982.

———. "L'Europa come concetto politico presso Isocrate e gli isocratei." *RFIC* n.s. 11 (1933) 477–87. Reprinted in A. Momigliano, *Terzo contributo alla storia degli studi classici e del mondo antico,* vol. 1, 489–97. Storia e letteratura, 108. Rome, 1966.

———. "How to Reconcile Greeks and Trojans." *MAWA* n.s. 45 (1982) no. 9, 231–54.

———. "Livio, Plutarco e Giustino su virtù e fortuna dei Romani." *Athenaeum* n.s. 12 (1934) 45–56. Reprinted in A. Momigliano,

Terzo contributo alla storia degli studi classici e del mondo antico, vol. 1, 499–511. Storia e letteratura, 108. Rome, 1966.

———. *New Paths of Classicism in the Nineteenth Century*. Middletown, Conn., 1982.

———. "La nuova storia romana di G. B. Vico." *RSI* 77 (1965) 773–90. Reprinted in A. Momigliano, *Sesto contributo alla storia degli studi classici e del mondo antico*, vol. 1, 191–210. Storia e letteratura, 149. Rome, 1980.

———. "The Origins of Universal History." *ASNP*, 3d ser., 12 (1982) 533–60. Reprinted in A. Momigliano, *Settimo contributo alla storia degli studi classici e del mondo antico*, 77–103. Storia e letteratura, 161. Rome, 1984.

———. "Perizonius, Niebuhr, and the Character of Early Roman Tradition." *JRS* 47 (1957) 104–14. Reprinted in A. Momigliano, *Secondo contributo alla storia degli studi classici*, 69–87. Storia e letteratura, 77. Rome, 1960.

———. "Roman 'Bestioni' and Roman 'Eroi' in Vico's Scienza Nuova." *H&T* 5 (1966) 3–23. Reprinted in A. Momigliano, *Terzo contributo alla storia degli studi classici e del mondo antico*, vol. 1, 153–77. Storia e letteratura, 108. Rome, 1966.

———. "Teopompo." *RFIC* 59 (1931) 230–42, 335–53. Reprinted in A. Momigliano, *La storiografia greca*, 174–203. Torino, 1982.

———. *Tra storia e storicismo*. Pisa, 1985.

Mommsen, T. *Die römische Chronologie bis auf Caesar*. 2d ed. 1859. Reprint. Osnabruck, 1981.

———. *Römische Forschungen*. 2 vols. 1864–79. Reprint. Hildesheim, 1962.

———. *Römische Geschichte*. 9th ed. 4 vols. Berlin, 1903–4.

———. *Römisches Staatsrecht*. 3d ed. 1887–88. Reprint. Graz, 1952.

Münzer, F. "Domitius (23)." *PW* 5 (1905) cols. 1328–31.

Musti, D. "Etruschi e greci nella rappresentazione dionisiana delle origini di Roma." In *Gli etruschi e Roma: Atti dell'incontro di studio in onore di Massimo Pallottino, Roma, 11–13 dicembre 1979*. Rome, 1981.

———. *Tendenze nella storiografia romana e greca su Roma arcaica. Studi su Livio e Dionigi d'Alicarnasso*. Rome, 1970.

Nestle, W. "Die Fabel des Menenius Agrippa." *Klio* 21 (1927) 350–60.

Nicolet, C. "Le De re publica et la dictature de Scipion." *REL* 42 (1964) 212–30.

———. "L'idéologie du système centuriate et l'influence de la philosophie politique grecque." In *La filosofia greca e il diritto romano: Colloquio italo-francese, Roma, 14–17 aprile 1973*, vol. 1, 111–37. Rome, 1976–77.

———. "Varron et la politique de Caius Gracchus." *Historia* 28 (1979) 276–300.

Niebuhr, B. *Kleine historische und philologische Schriften.* 2 vols. 1828–43. Reprint. Osnabruck, 1969.

———. *Römische Geschichte.* 3d ed. 3 vols. Berlin, 1832.

———. *Römische Geschichte.* Edited by M. Isler. 3 vols. Berlin, 1873–74.

Noè, E. "Ricerche su Dionigi d'Alicarnasso: la prima stasis a Roma e l'episodio di Coriolano." In *Ricerche di storiografia greca di età romana*, 21–116. Ricerche di storiografia antica, 1. Pisa, 1979.

Ogilvie, R. M. *A Commentary on Livy, Books 1–5.* Oxford, 1965.

Oliver, J. H. *The Athenian Expounders of the Sacred and Ancestral Law.* Baltimore, 1950.

Pais, E. "Dionigi d'Alicarnasso e la legge Aelia Sentia." *RAAN* n.s. 18 (1904) 191–99.

———. *Storia di Roma dalle origini all'inizio delle guerre puniche.* 3d ed. 5 vols. Rome 1926–28.

Palm, J. *Rom, Römertum und Imperium in der griechischen Literatur der Kaiserzeit.* Lund, 1959.

Palmer, R. E. A. *The Archaic Community of the Romans.* Cambridge, 1970.

Pavano, G. "Sulla cronologia degli scritti retorici di Dionisio d'Alicarnasso." *AAPal*, 4th ser., vol. 3, pt. 2 (1942) 211–363.

Peppe, L. *Studi sull'esecuzione personale.* Vol. 1, *Debiti e debitori nei primi due secoli della repubblica romana.* Milan, 1981.

Peremans, W. "Egyptiens et étrangers dans l'Egypte ptolémaïque." In *Grecs et barbares*, 123–55. Fondation Hardt, Entretiens 8. Geneva, 1962.

Perrelli, L. "Epicuro e la dottrina di Crizia sull'origine della religione." *RFIC* 33 (1955) 29–56.

Peruzzi, E. *Myceneans in Early Latium.* Rome, 1980.

Peter, H. *Historicorum romanorum reliquiae.* Vol. 1, 2d ed., 1914. Vol. 2, 1906. Leipzig.

Pinto, M. "Aspetti dell'atticismo nell'autore del Sublime." *A&R* 20 (1975) 60–71.

Pittaluga, G. *Terminus. I segni del confine nella religione romana.* Rome, 1974.

Pöhlmann, R. von. *Geschichte der sozialen Fragen und des Sozialismus in der antiken Welt.* 2 vols. 2d ed. Munich, 1912. 3d ed. Munich, 1925.

Poma, G. "Schiavi e schiavitù in Dionigi di Alicarnasso." *RSA* 11 (1981) 69–101.

————. *Tra legislatori e tiranni. Problemi storici e storiografici sull'età delle XII tavole.* Bologna, 1984.

Price, S. R. F. *Rituals and Power. The Roman Imperial Cult in Asia Minor.* Cambridge, 1984.

Pritchett, W. K. *Dionysius of Halicarnassus on Thucydides.* Berkeley, 1975.

Radermacher, L. "Dionysokles." *PW* 5 (1905) col. 1007.

————. "Hybreas (1)." *PW* 9 (1914) cols. 29–31.

Rajak, T. *Josephus. The Historian and His Society.* London, 1983.

Raskolnikoff, M. "Caius Gracchus ou la révolution introuvable." In *Demokratia et aristokratia,* edited by C. Nicolet, 127–30. Paris, 1983.

Rawson, E. *Intellectual Life in the Late Roman Republic.* London, 1985.

————. "The Interpretation of Cicero's 'De legibus.'" *ANRW* I.4 (1973) 334–56.

Reardon, B. P. *Courants littéraires grecs des IIe et IIIe siècles après J.-C.* Paris, 1971.

Reitzenstein, R. "Philologische Kleinigkeiten." *Hermes* 48 (1913) 268–72.

Renoirte, T. *Les "Conseils politiques" de Plutarque: Une lettre ouverte aux grecs a l'époque de Trajan.* Louvain, 1951.

Riccobono, S. *Leges.* Vol. 1 of *Fontes iuris romani anteiustiniani,* edited by S. Riccobono, J. Baviera, C. Ferrini, J. Furlani, and V. Arangio-Ruiz. 2d ed. Florence, 1940–43.

Richard, J.-C. "Ennemis ou alliés? Les troyens et les aborigines dans les Origines de Caton." *Hommages à Robert Schilling,* 403–12. Paris, 1983.

————. "Recherches sur l'interprétation populaire de la figure du roi Servius Tullius." *RPh* 61 (1987) 205–25.

————. "Varro, l'Origo gentis romanae et les aborigènes." *RPh* 57 (1983) 29–37.

Richter, W. "Einige Rekonstruktions- und Quellenprobleme in Cicero *De Re Publica*." *RFIC* 97 (1969) 55–81.

Riposati, B. M. *Terenti Varronis De vita populi romani*. 2d ed. Milan, 1972.

Rizzo, F. P. "Mitridate contro Roma tra messianesimo e messaggio di liberazione." In *Tra Grecia e Roma: Temi antichi e metodologie moderne*. Biblioteca internazionale di cultura, 3. Rome, 1980.

Roberts, W. Rhys. "The Literary Circle of Dionysius of Halicarnassus." *CR* 14 (1900) 439–42.

Rohde, E. "Die Asianische Rhetorik und die zweite Sophistic." *RhM* 41 (1886) 170–90.

Romilly, J. de. *Histoire et raison chez Thucydide*. Paris, 1956.

Rose, V. *Aristotelis qui ferebantur librorum fragmenta*. Leipzig, 1886. Reprint. Stuttgart, 1967.

Rostagni, A., ed. and tr. *Del sublime*. Milan, 1947.

Rostovtzeff, M. *The Social and Economic History of the Hellenistic World*. 3 vols. Oxford, 1941.

Russell, D. A. "Plutarch's Life of Coriolanus." *JRS* 53 (1963) 21–28.

————, ed. *'Longinus' On the Sublime*. Oxford, 1964.

Sacks, K. *Polybius on the Writing of History*. University of California Classical Studies, 24. Berkeley, 1981.

————. "Rhetoric and Speeches in Hellenistic Historiography." *Athenaeum* n.s. 64 (1986) 383–95.

Scardigli, B. *Die Römerbiographien Plutarchs*. Munich, 1979.

Schepens, G. "The Bipartite and Tripartite Divisions of History in Polybius (XII 25e & 27)." *AncSoc* 5 (1974) 277–87.

Schiavone, A. *Nascita della giurisprudenza*. Bari, 1976.

Schmitt, H. H. "Hellenen, Römer und Barbaren. Eine Studie zu Polybios." *Wissenschaftliche Beilage zum Jahresbericht 1957–1958 des Humanistischen Gymnasiums Aschaffenburg*.

Schröder, W. A. M. *Porcius Cato. Das Erste Buch der Origines, Ausgabe und Erklärung der Fragmente*. Meisenheim am Glan, 1971.

Schultze, C. "Dionysius of Halicarnassus and His Audience." In *Past Perspective. Studies in Greek and Roman Historical Writing*, edited by I. S. Noxon, J. D. S. Smart, and A. J. Woodman, 121–41. Cambridge, 1986.

Schwartz, E. "Dionysios von Halikarnassos." *PW* 5 (1905) cols.

934–61. Reprinted in E. Schwartz, *Griechische Geschichtschreiber*, 319–60. Leipzig, 1957.

Schwenn, F. *Die Menschenopfer bei den Griechen und Römern*. Giessen, 1915. Reprint. Berlin, 1966.

Segal, C. P. "Ὕψος and the Problem of Cultural Decline in the *De Sublimitate*." *HSPh* 64 (1959) 121–46.

Serrao, F., ed. *Legge e società nella repubblica romana*. Vol. 1. Naples, 1981.

Spanheim, E., ed. *Iuliani imp. opera quae supersunt omnia; et S. Cyrilli, Alexandriae archiepiscopi, contra impium Iulianum libri decem*. Leipzig, 1696.

Stadter, P. A. *Arrian of Nicomedia*. Chapel Hill, 1980.

Stein, A. *Römische Inschriften in der antiken Literatur*. Prague, 1931.

Stephans, D. *Critias. Life and Literary Remains*. Cincinnati, 1939.

Stewart, A. *Attika: Studies in Athenian Sculpture of the Hellenistic Age*. London, 1979.

Strasbürger, H. "Posidonios on the Problem of the Roman Empire." *JRS* 55 (1965) 40–53.

Swinnen, W. "Herakleitos of Halikarnassos, an Alexandrian Poet and Diplomat?" *AncSoc* 1 (1970) 39–52.

Syme, R. "Livy and Augustus." *HSPh* 64 (1959) 27–87. Reprinted in R. Syme, *Roman Papers*, vol. 1, 400–54. Oxford, 1979.

———. *Ten Studies on Tacitus*. Oxford, 1970.

———. Review of *Der Römische Juppiter*, by C. Koch. *JRS* 29 (1939) 108–10.

Täubler, E. *Untersuchungen zur Geschichte des Decemvirats und der Zwölftafeln*. Berlin, 1921.

Taylor, L. R. "Aniconic Worship among the Early Romans." In *Classical Studies in Honor of John C. Rolfe*, 305–14. Philadelphia, 1931.

———. "Varro's *De Gente Populi Romani*." *CP* 29 (1934) 221–29.

Thackeray, H. *Josephus. The Man and the Historian*. New York, 1929.

———, ed. and tr. *Josephus*. Vol. 4. Loeb Classical Library. London, 1930.

Theiler, W. *Posidonios. Die Fragmente*. 2 vols. Berlin, 1982.

Thuillier, J.-P. "Denys d'Halicarnasse et les jeux romains (Antiquités romaines VII 72–73)." *MEFRA* 87 (1975) 563–81.

Thulin, C. *Corpus agrimensorum romanorum*. 1913. Reprint. Stuttgart, 1971.

Tibiletti, G. "Il possesso dell'*ager publicus* e le norme *de modo*

agrorum sino ai Gracchi (cap. I–III)." *Athenaeum* n.s. 26 (1948)
173–236.
Timpe, D. "Die Germanische Agrarverfassung nach den Berichten
Caesars und Tacitus'." In *Untersuchungen zur eisenzeitlichen und
frühmittelalterlichen Flur in Mitteleuropa und ihrer Nutzung,* edited
by H. Beck, D. Denecke, and H. Jankuhn, vol. 1, 11–40. *AAWG,*
3d ser., 115. Göttingen, 1979.
Tondo, S. "Ermodoro e Eraclito." *SIFC* 49 (1977) 37–67.
Torelli, M. *Elogia tarquiniensia.* Florence, 1975.
———. "Senatori etruschi della tarda repubblica e dell'impero."
DArch 3 (1969) 285–363.
Tränkle, H. "Der Anfang des römischen Freistaats in der Darstellung
des Livius." *Hermes* 93 (1965) 311–37.
Treves, P. *Il mito di Alessandro e la Roma di Augusto.* Milan, 1953.
Troiani, L. "Contributo alla problematica dei rapporti fra storiografia
greca e storiografia vicino-orientale." *Athenaeum* n.s. 61 (1983)
427–38.
———. "I lettori delle *Antiquitates iudaicae* di Giuseppe: prospettive
e problemi." *Athenaeum* n.s. 64 (1986) 343–53.
———. "Un nuovo studio su Giuseppe." *Athenaeum* n.s. 63 (1985)
184–95.
Untersteiner, M. "Dionisio di Alicarnasso fondatore della critica
pseudepigrafica." *AFC* 7 (1959) 72–93.
———. *Senofane: Testimonianze e frammenti.* Florence, 1956.
Usener, H. and L. Radermacher, eds. *Dionysii Halicarnasei opuscula.*
2 vols. 1899–1929. Reprint. Stuttgart, 1965.
Usher, S. *Dionysius of Halicarnassus, the Critical Essays.* 2 vols. Loeb
Classical Library. Cambridge, Mass., 1974.
Vahlen, J. *Ennianae poesis reliquiae.* 2d ed. Leipzig, 1903.
Van Der Vliet, E. C. L. "L'ethnographie de Strabon: idéologie et tra-
dition." In *Strabone. Contributi allo studio della personalità e
dell'opera,* edited by F. Prontera, vol. 1, 27–86. Perugia, 1984.
Verdin, H. "La fonction de l'histoire selon Denys d'Halicarnasse."
AncSoc 5 (1974) 289–307.
Vertot, l'Abbé de. *Histoire des révolutions arrivées dans le gouverne-
ment de la république romaine.* Nouvelle édition. Amsterdam, 1759.
Veyne, P. *Les grecs ont-ils cru à leur mythes?* Paris, 1983.
———. *Le pain et le cirque.* Paris, 1976.
Vico, G. *La scienza nuova.* 1744. Reprint. Bari, 1974.

Villers, R. "Le mariage envisagé comme institution d'état dans le droit classique de Rome." *ANRW* II.14 (1982) 285–301.

Volkmann, H. "Valerius (243)." *PW* 8A (1955) cols. 116–20.

Volterra, E. "La graduum agnationis vetustissima descriptio segnalata da Cujas." *MAL*, 8th ser., 22 (1978) fasc. 1, 1–109.

Wachsmuth, C., and O. Hense, eds. *Ioannis Stobaei Anthologium.* 5 vols. Berlin, 1884–1912.

Walbank, F. W. *A Historical Commentary on Polybius.* 3 vols. Oxford, 1957–59.

———. "The Idea of Decline in Polybios." In *Niedergang. Studien zu einen geschichtlichen Thema,* edited by R. Kossellek and P. Widmer, 41–51. Stuttgart, 1980.

———. "Nationality as a Factor in Roman History." *HSPh* 76 (1972) 145–68. Reprinted in F. W. Walbank, *Selected Papers,* 57–76. Cambridge, 1985.

———. *Polybius.* Berkeley, 1972.

———. *Speeches in Greek Historians.* Third Myres Memorial Lecture. Oxford, 1965. Reprinted in F. W. Walbank, *Selected Papers,* 242–61. Cambridge, 1985.

Walser, G. *Caesar und die Germanen.* Wiesbaden, 1956.

Watson, A. "Roman Private Law and the Leges Regiae." *JRS* 62 (1972) 100–105.

———. *Rome of the XII Tables. Persons and Property.* Princeton, 1975.

Wehrli, C. "Les gynéconomes." *MH* 19 (1962) 33–38.

Wehrli, F. *Die Schule des Aristoteles: Texte und Kommentar.* 2d ed. Basel, 1967.

Weinstock, S. "Penates." *PW* 19 (1937) cols. 417–57.

Williams, G. *Change and Decline: Roman Literature in the Early Empire.* Berkeley, 1978.

Wirszubski, C. *Libertas as a Political Idea at Rome During the Late Republic and Early Principate.* Cambridge, 1950.

Wiseman, T. P. *Clio's Cosmetics.* Leicester, 1979.

———. "Practice and Theory in Roman Historiography." *History* 66 (1981) 375–93.

Wissowa, G. *Religion und Kultus der Römer.* 2d ed. Munich, 1912.

———. "Römische Sagen." 1888. Reprinted in G. Wissowa, *Gesammelte Abhandlungen zur römischen Religions- und Stadtgeschichte.* Munich, 1904. Reprint. New York, 1975.

————. "Die Ueberlieferung über die röm. Penaten." 1886. Reprinted in G. Wissowa, *Gesammelte Abhandlungen zur römischen Religions- und Stadtgeschichte*. Munich, 1904. Reprint. New York, 1975.

Wooten, C. "The Speeches in Polybius. An Insight into the Nature of Hellenistic Oratory." *AJPh* 95 (1974) 235–51.

General Index

Aborigines, 104, 107–8, 113–15, 116
Accius, Lucius, 164
Achaia, 114
Actium, Battle of, 2
Acton, Lord, 204–5
Aelii Tuberones (family), 43
Aelius Aristides, 216
Aelius Tubero, Q., 30–31
Aeneas, 12, 15, 116–17, 197; Etruscan traditions concerning, 14; Greek character of, 109; shrine of, 139
Ager publicus, 180, 185–86, 188; private occupation of, 187
Agrarian law, 179–89; in republican period, 186
Agrimensores, 188
Agroikoi (in Athenian society), 167
Aisumnetai (rulers), 141–42, 145
Alba, kings of, 109
Alba Longa, destruction of, 209
Alcibiades, 57
Alexander the Great: acceptance of barbarians by, 51–52; death of, 35; destruction of Halicarnassus by, 2n; Eratosthenes on, 51–52; idealization of, 56; personality of, 57, 192; in Strabo, 49
Alexandrian age, post-, 28, 29, 57
Alphabet, Greek, 108, 138–39
Ancus Marcius, 156, 165–66; land reforms of, 178
Annalists, 74, 87, 143; Dionysius's use of, 96

Annalists, Roman, 10, 20–22, 83–84; Dionysius's attitude toward, 97; on Etruscans, 111n
Anthropomorphism, 132, 133
Antonine empire, 8
Antonius, M., 38
Apollodorus of Athens, 198
Appian of Alexandria, 2n, 58–59; on philosophers, 37; on supremacy of Rome, 193; use of Dionysius by, 214
Arcadians, 15, 107–8, 137–38
Archaeology, 133, 135, 136n; in Dionysius, 153–54, 165; importance of Dionysius to, 139
Aristocracy, Roman, 4, 24, 83, 161, 164; and Augustus, 42; Cicero on, 204; corruption of, 33, 191, 211–12; and monarchy, 201. *See also* Patrician class
Aristodemus of Cumae, 85
Aristotle, 51, 62; on conduct of women, 149; and ideal state, 168–72; knowledge of Rome, 13
Aristoxenus, 13
Arrian, view of Greek culture, 57
Asianism (in rhetoric), 24–27, 32, 35–36, 38; climax of, 30; growth of, 28
Assyrians, 192
Asylum, institution of, 103, 197
Athens: class structure of, 167; defeat of by Sparta, 81; idealization of, 34–35, 56, 68, 195; political experience of,

Index Locorum